20'th Annual Tcl Association Tcl/Tk Conference Proceedings

New Orleans, LA

September 23-26, 2013

TclA Publications

TCL Association Publications

Proceedings of the 20'th Annual Tcl/Tk Conference
ISBN: 978-0-578-13517-5

Cover art by Darryl Downie

Special thanks to Dawson Cowals for designing the Tcl Association logo.
For graphic design or web development consulting please visit him on the web at
http://www.dawsoncowals.com/

TclA Publications

Table Of Contents

Tcl 2013
New Orleans, LA
September 23-27, 2013

Session I
Wednesday September 25, 2013

10:45am-12:15

SML

A simpler and shorter representation of XML data inspired by Tcl

Jean-François Larvoire,
9 Chemin des Gandins, 38660 Saint Hilaire du Touvet, France
jf.larvoire@free.fr

2013-09-24

Abstract

XML is now the most popular standard for representing structured data as text.

Yet, despite all its successes, XML has failed one of its original design goals: Being easy to read and edit by human beings.

To address this problem, many others have proposed alternatives to XML. Some are indeed better, being both simple and more powerful. Yet I think they're missing the point. The benefits of having united the industry under a common data exchange standard far out weight the weaknesses of XML itself. It would be pointless to propose any alternative incompatible with XML now.

This paper proposes instead a Simplified representation of XML data (SML for short), inspired by the Tcl syntax, that is strictly equivalent to XML. But SML data files are smaller, and much easier to work with by mere humans.

A Tcl script called sml is available for converting files back and forth between the XML and SML formats.

The original idea was to use this script for converting XML files into this SML format; read them or edit them using a plain text editor; and convert them back to XML.

But other unexpected benefits came out of this Simplified XML representation:

- SML files are noticeably smaller than XML files. Using this format directly for storage or data transfer protocols would save space or network bandwidth.

- Using SML for data serialization is easier to work with than with XML, while future-proofing the compatibility with tools that know only of XML. Actually the SML format is so readable that I started using it as the native output format of all the management tools I wrote that output structured data... Some of which later got reused as XML input to other tools having no knowledge about SML.

- SML is a nice format for reviewing small file system trees contents, for example the Linux /proc/fs trees.

Introduction

We increasingly have to deal with XML files.

I started thinking about alternative views into XML files because of a personal itch: I needed to repeatedly tweak a complex XML configuration file for a Linux Heartbeat cluster in the lab. No DTDs available. No specialized XML editors installed on that machine. Editing the file using a plain text editor was painful every time.

Why had it to be so? XML is a text format that was supposed to be designed for easy manual edition by humans. And XML proponents actually list this feature as an advantage of XML. Yet XML tags are so verbose that it is a pain to manually review and edit anything but trivial XML files. The numerous XML editors available are a relief, but do not resolve the fundamental problem of XML verbosity when it comes to simply reading the file. (Actually I think their very existence is proof that XML has a problem!)

In the absence of a solution, I avoided using XML for my own projects as much as I could, and kept looking at alternatives, in the hope that one of them would eventually ...

Alternatives to XML

Many other people have complained about XML unfriendly syntax too, and many have proposed alternatives. Simply search "XML alternatives" of the Web and you'll find plenty!
(One of which was actually called SML too! No resemblance to this one).

A few important ones are:

- ASN.1 XER (XML Encoding Rules) [2]
  Pro: Powerful (more that XML). XER documents compatible with XML document model.
  Con: An adaptation of ASN.1 compatible with ASN.1 text format, but not with XML text format. i.e. conversion back to XML cannot yield identical files.
- JSON JavaScript Object Notation [3]
  Pro: Powerful (more that XML) and simple. Easy to use, with I/O libraries available for most languages. The most popular of the alternatives now, by far.
  Con: Completely incompatible with XML.
- Google Protocol Buffers [8]
  Pro: Simple syntax. Compiler for generating compact and fast binary encodings for wire transfers.
  Con: Even Google seems to prefer JSON for end-user APIs.

Some others have also attempted to "fix" XML by keeping only a subset of XML, for example by abandoning attributes (Ex: Simple XML [12]). Although this does make the tree structure simpler, this definitely does not make the document more readable. Even the W3C has made a proposal to simplify their own baby, also called Simple XML [11], although it does not go as far as the previous ones.

And in all cases backwards compatibility is lost.

Finally, there were even a few proposals made on the tcl.tk wiki:

- Xmlgen [13]
  Only designed to make it simple to generate XML, not as an alternative.
- TDL [14]
  Very similar to SML in many respects.
  Pro: Closer to the Tcl syntax than what I propose, and easier to parse as pure Tcl.
  Con: Not binary compatible; Less human friendly syntax for text, cdata, comments, etc.

Alternative views of XML

At the same time, I was writing Tcl scripts for managing Lustre file systems on that cluster. The instances of my scripts on every node were exchanging increasingly big Tcl structures (As strings, embedded in network packets), for synchronizing their action. And I kept finding this both convenient, and easy to program and debug. (ie. Review the structures exchanged when something goes wrong!)

And then I began to think that the two problems were linked: XML is nothing more than a textual presentation of a structured tree of data. A Tcl program or a Tcl data structure is also a textual presentation of a structured tree of data. And the essence of XML is not its <tagged><blocks>, but rather its logical structure with a tree of elements, attributes, and content blocks with other embedded elements inside. In other words its DOM (Document Object Model).

All programs written in C, Java, Tcl, PHP, etc, share a common simple syntax for representing program trees {based on {nested blocks} surrounded by parentheses}, which is much easier to read by humans than the <tagged><blocks> used by XML</blocks></tagged>. The Tcl language has the simplest syntax of them all, with a grammar with just a dozen rules. This makes it particularly easy to read and parse. And its one-instruction-per-line standard is a natural match to all modern XML files with one element per line.

Instead of reinventing a new data structure presentation language, it should be possible to convert XML into an equivalent Tcl-like format, while preserving all the elements, attributes, and data structures.

This defined a new problem: Find a text format inspired by Tcl, which is simpler than XML, yet is strictly equivalent to it. Equivalent in the mathematical sense that any XML file can be converted to that simpler format, then back into XML with no change whatsoever.

Non-goals: We do not try to generate a valid Tcl list of lists.

The SML Solution

Keep the XML data tree model with elements made of a tag, optional attributes, and an optional data block, but use a simpler text representation based on the syntax of C-style languages.

The basic idea is that XML and SML elements correspond to each other like this:

- XML elements: <tag attribute="value" ...>contents</tag>
- SML elements: tag attribute="value" ... {contents}

But the devil lies in the details, and it took a while to find a set of rules that would cover all XML syntax cases, allow fully reversible conversions, optimize the readability of real-world files, and remain reasonably simple. After experimenting with a number of alternatives, I arrived at the set of rules defined further down, which give good results on real-world documents. Example extracted from a Google Earth file:

XML (from a Google Earth .kml file)

```
<?xml version="1.0" encoding="UTF-8"?>
<kml>
  <Folder>
    <name>Take off zones in the Alps</name>
    <open>1</open>
    <Folder>
      <name>Drome</name>
      <visibility>0</visibility>
      <Placemark>
        <description>Take off</description>
        <name>Mont Rachas</name>
        <LookAt>
          <longitude>5.0116666667</longitude>
          <latitude>44.8355</latitude>
          <range>4000</range>
          <tilt>45</tilt>
          <heading>0</heading>
        </LookAt>
      </Placemark>
    </Folder>
  </Folder>
</kml>
```

SML (generated by the sml script)

```
?xml version="1.0" encoding="UTF-8"
kml {
  Folder {
    name "Take off zones in the Alps"
    open 1
    Folder {
      name Drome
      visibility 0
      Placemark {
        description "Take off"
        name "Mont Rachas"
        LookAt {
          longitude 5.0116666667
          latitude 44.8355
          range 4000
          tilt 45
          heading 0
        }
      }
    }
  }
}
```

The difference in readability should be immediately obvious!

SML Syntax rules

Elements

- Elements normally end at the end of the line.
- They continue on the next line if there's a trailing '\'.
- They also continue if there's an unmatched "quotes" or {curly braces} block.
- Multiple elements on the same line must be separated by a ';'.

Attributes

- The syntax for attributes is the same as for XML. Including the rules for using quotes and escape chars. (And so is different from Tcl's string quoting rules.)
- There must be at least one space between the last attribute and the beginning of the content data.

Content data

- The content data are normally inside a {curly braces} block.
- The content text is between "quotes". Escape '\' and '"' with a '\'.
- If there are no further child elements embedded in contents (i.e. it's only text), the braces can be omitted.
- Furthermore, if the text does not contain blanks, '"', '=', ';', '#', '{', '}', '<', '>', nor a trailing '\', the quotes around the text can be omitted too.
  (ie. If the text cannot be confused with an attribute or a comment or any kind of SML markup.)

Other types of markup

All use the same rules as the elements for juxtaposition and continuation.

- This is a **?Processing instruction** . (The final '?' in XML is removed in SML.)
- This is a **!Declaration** . (Ex: a !doctype definition)
- This is a **#-- Comment block, ending with two dashes --** .
- Simplified case for a **# One-line comment** .
- This is a **<[[Cdata section]]>** .
  An optional new line, immediately following the opening <[[, is discarded if present.

Heuristics for XML<->SML conversion

- Spaces/tabs/new lines are preserved.

- The sml program adds one space after the end of the element definition (ie. after the last attribute and optional trailing spaces inside the element head), before the beginning of the data block.
  This considerably improves the readability of the sml output.
  Then it removes it when converting SML back to XML.
  An SML file is invalid without that space anyway.
- Empty data blocks (i.e. Blocks containing just spaces) encoding: Use {} for multiline blocks, and "" for single-line ones.
- Unquoted attribute values are accepted, in an attempt to be compatible with HTML-style attributes, which do occur in poorly-written XML files.

Syntax rules discussion

Except fo XHTML, real world XML files usually contain a hierarchy of outer elements, with 0 or more inner elements, but no text. Then the terminal elements (the inner-most elements) contain just text.

- *SML elements normally end at the end of the line.*
  A natural match for most modern XML files, which usually have one XML terminal element per line.
- *They continue on the next line if there's a trailing '\'.*
  Same rule as for Tcl, and many other programming languages.
- *They also continue if there's an unmatched "quotes" or {curly braces} block.*
  This is a major advantage of the Tcl syntax, allowing to minimize the syntactic glue characters.
- *Multiple elements on the same line must be separated by a ';'.*
  Again, the same as Tcl.
- *The syntax for attributes is the same as for XML:* name="value"
  XML attribute name ::= (Letter | '_' | ':') (Letter | Digit | '.' | '-' | '_' | ':' | CombiningChar | Extender)*
  XML attribute value ::= ('"' ([^<&"] | Reference)* '"') | ("'" ([^<&'] | Reference)* "'")
  Use references like & , < , > , ' , " to quote the special characters in values.
  I considered using Tcl's quoting rules instead. But this made the conversion program more complex, and did not make the SML more readable. (Actually it made it less readable, making it more difficult to read long lists of attributes.)
  Most real-world attribute values will look exactly the same as the equivalent Tcl string anyway.
  => I'm open to changing this rule for compatibility with Tcl quoting.
  Also TDL [14] proposes an interesting alternative: Write attributes are Tcl functions options with a dash: -name value
  Pro: Easier to parse as a Tcl list.
  Con: Less intuitive to people who don't know Tcl.
  Con: Makes it more difficult to deal with HTML-like attributes that have no value.
- *The content data are normally inside a {curly braces} block. Braces in the content text must be escaped by a '\'.*
  Same as Tcl {blocks}. Works well for XML outer elements containing inner elements.
- *If there are no further child elements embedded in contents (i.e. only text), a "quotes" block should be used instead. In that case, braces in the text need not be escaped, but the '\' and '"' should be instead.*
  Works well with terminal elements containing just text.
- *The quotes around text can be omitted if the text does not contain blanks, '"', '=', ';', '#', '{', '}', '<', '>', nor a trailing '\', and if there are no other elements at the same tree depth. (ie. It cannot be confused with an attribute or a comment or any kind of SML markup.)*
  Maximizes readability by removing all extra characters around simple values.

Possible alternative: In the cases where text and elements are mixed at the same tree depth (rare, except in XHTML), use a pseudo element tag like !text or just @ (But not #text which would look like a comment) to flag it. This would allow extending the SML syntax to support element names with spaces. See the "show script" chapter below for a useful application of that.

- *This is a* ?Processing instruction .
  This is a !Declaration . (Ex: A !doctype definition)
  Both are treated like XML empty elements, with a name beginning with an '?' or a '!'.
  All contents are preserved, except for the final ?> and > respectively.
  Add a '\' at the end of lines if the element continues on the following lines.

- *Simplified case for a* # One-line comment .
  Same as for Tcl, and many other scripting languages.

- *This is a* #-- Comment block -- .
  I considered using existing syntaxes, like <# Multiline comment #> in PowerShell. But this was barely more concise, and this created problems to deal with the -- sequence in SML (not valid in an XML comment), or the #> sequence in XML (not valid in an SML comment in that case)
  In fine, the simplest was to stick to the -- delimiters like in XML.

- *This is a* <[[CDATA section]]>
  Like for comment blocks, sticking to the XML termination sequence proved to be the easiest option. Any other type of delimiter would have required complex escaping rules, for the case that delimiter appears in the CDATA itself. The possibility of having adjacent CDATA sections would have made these rules even more complex.
  By symmetry, I used `<[[` for the opening sequence.
  Note that the CDATA `]]>` end markers cannot be confused with the `]]>` end markers at the end of some complex !declarations, because those ones become `]]` after the final '>' is removed in SML.

  An optional new line, immediately following the opening <[[, is discarded.
  This makes it easy to view multiple lines of CDATA. The first line will begin on the first column, like all the others.
  Gotcha: That additional new line <u>must</u> be inserted if the CDATA begins with an initial new line. Else the initial new line would be lost during the conversion back to XML.

  Possible alternative: I experimented with simpler alternatives in other programs.
  One is the indented block, used in the "show" program described further down:
```
Preceding content{
  This is a sample CDATA with an XML <tag>
}Following content
```
  Here, the rule is that all CDATA block contents are indented by two more spaces than the previous line.
  The first '}' at the same indentation as the opening '{' sign marks the end the CDATA.
  The CDATA begins after the new line following the opening '{' (So this new line is not optional here), and ends before the final new line before the closing '}'.
  Pro: More lightweight syntax, more in the spirit of Tcl.
  Pro: Looks better in deep trees, as multi-line CDATA blocks are indented like the rest.
  Con: Adds numerous spaces, and makes the CDATA block weight more in bytes.
  Con: Made the sml conversion program more complex and slower.

  Variation on the same theme: Particular case of a CDATA section that makes up the whole content of an element:
  Instead of encoding this content block with double parenthesis `{{\n  CDATA\n}}`, it'd be written `={\n  CDATA\n}`

The sml script

A working proof of concept program, called sml.tcl, is available at URL:
http://jf.larvoire.free.fr/progs/sml.tcl

It works in any system with a Tcl interpreter. (Standard in Linux. A free version for Windows is available at http://www.activestate.com/activetcl)

I've tested it on a number of sample XML files from various sources, totaling about 1 MB.

It is able to convert them all to SML, then back into XML, with the final XML files binary equal to the originals.

A simple glance at the contents of the SML files will show, as in the example above, that the "useful" information is much easier to find. The eye is not distracted anymore by the noise of useless end tags and brackets.

Current Status

The proof of concept is written in Tcl, and works fine on my sample files. I've been using it regularly for several years.

The file has about 3000 lines of code, half of which are an independent debugging library.

The only issue is performance: It converts about 10 KB/s of data on a 2 GHz machine. Rewriting it in C and optimizing the lowest I/O routines should be able to increase performance by several orders of magnitude.

Actually the best bet would be to start with an XML parsing library, and modify it to parse or generate either XML or SML. This should be easy since the only difference is the tree representation, not the DOM.

I've not attempted to use Tcl's own XML parsing libraries, like TclDOM or tDOM, mostly for lack of time, and because the performance on small to medium XML files is adequate for me. Also I'm a bit concerned about the way spaces are handled by these libraries. They must be preserved and provided to the caller for reversibility. But maybe they are already?

Known limitations:

- The converted files use the local operating system line endings (a combination of \r and \n). So if the initial XML file was encoded with line endings for another operating system, converting it to SML then back will not be binary equal to the initial file. But it will still be logically equal, as the XML spec states that all line endings are equivalent to \n.
- As of 2013-09-22, complex !doctype declarations with locally defined !elements are not supported.

Sml files size

An interesting side benefit of the conversion is that the total size of the converted files is 12% smaller than the original XML files. Among big files, that reduction goes from 4% for a file with lots of large CDATA elements, to 17% for a file with deeply nested elements.

Even after zipping the two full sets of samples, the SML files archive is 2% smaller than the XML files archive. Not much I admit, but this may help Microsoft alleviate the new Office documents bloat. ☺

As for XML compression, many dedicated compressors are available (Ex [4], [5]). Obviously they give better results than SML. But just as obviously the compressed files are unreadable by humans!

Reductions are much better on xml documents using name spaces. For example on the sample SOAP envelope from the SOAP 1.2 specification, the gain is 30%. Transporting SOAP messages in their SML form instead of

The show script

This script allows displaying a file tree as experimental SML.

Available at URL: http://jf.larvoire.free.fr/progs/show.tcl

The principle is that each file or directory is an SML element. Directories contain inner elements that represent files and subdirectories. File contents are displayed as text if possible, else are dumped in hexadecimal.

It also has options for generating several alternative experimental SML formats, which have helped convince me which was the most readable solution.

The show script has two major modes of operation:

- A simplified mode, which is not fully SML-compatible, but produces the shortest output, easiest to read. (This is the default mode of operation)
- A strict mode, which produces a fully SML-compatible output, at the cost of a heavier output.

The simple file system representation

- The tag name is the file or directory name. (This is what is not XML compatible. XML requires tag names to begin by a letter and contain only alphanumeric characters plus '–' and '_'. Names containing spaces, or SML markup characters like a '#' in the first place, must be "quoted"... Which the sml script would consider as the beginning of text content, not an element.)
- Directory names end with a '/'.
- The file size, date/time, owner, etc, are SML attributes, not shown by default.
- Files contents are shown indented. (By default, only the first 10 lines are shown.)
- Text files are shown as they are, except for the indent.
  Binary files are shown as an hexadecimal dump.

Example under Linux:

```
[root@xena1 ~]# /k/Tools/show.tcl /proc/fs/cifs
/proc/fs/cifs/ {
  cifsFYI 0
  DebugData {
    Display Internal CIFS Data Structures for Debugging
    ---------------------------------------------------
    CIFS Version 1.68
    Active VFS Requests: 0
    Servers:
    1) Name: 10.16.131.25  Domain: LAB Uses: 1 OS: Windows Server 2008 R2
Enterprise 7601 Service Pack 1
        NOS: Windows Server 2008 R2 Enterprise 6.1      Capability: 0x1e3fc
        SMB session status: 1  TCP status: 1
        Local Users To Server: 1 SecMode: 0x3 Req On Wire: 0
        Shares:
  } ...
  LinuxExtensionsEnabled 1
  LookupCacheEnabled 1
  MultiuserMount 0
  OplockEnabled 1
```

```
    SecurityFlags 0x7
    Stats {
      Resources in use
      CIFS Session: 2
      Share (unique mount targets): 2
      SMB Request/Response Buffer: 2 Pool size: 6
      SMB Small Req/Resp Buffer: 2 Pool size: 30
      Operations (MIDs): 0

      9 session 1 share reconnects
      Total vfs operations: 1252680 maximum at one time: 2

    } ...
    traceSMB 0
  }
[root@xenal ~]#
```

The strict file system representation

- The tag name is the object type (Ex: "file" or "directory" or "symlink", etc.)
- The name is an SML attribute called name. (Ex: file name="SML specification.pdf")
- All other file properties, like date/time, modes, owner, access control lists, etc, are SML attributes.

This one is fully SML and XML compatible. And the textual output can be (in theory) used to recreate the complete file system.

The spath script

This script does not exist, but this chapter is a thought experiment that gives some insight on the power of the SML concept:

I had made another script called xpath.tcl, which makes it easy to use XPATH to view the contents of XML files, or extract data from them. This script does nothing fancy. All it does is to pretend the XML file represents a file system, and allow accessing its contents using Unix-style commands like cat or ls. XML elements are considered as directories, and attributes as files. The content data for a terminal element is considered as an unnamed file. Examples:

```
xpath sites.kml ls /kml/Folder/Folder
```

lists all inner elements as directories, and attributes as files.

```
xpath sites.kml cat /kml/Folder/Folder/name
```

Displays attribute values, or the text content for elements. Here it outputs “Drome”.

The idea here is to write an spath.tcl script that does the same for SML data instead of XML.

Supporting all features of XPATH would be difficult, as xpath.tcl uses Tcl’s TclDOM package to do the real work. But in the short term, it’s possible to get the same functionality using a one-line shell script:

`sml | xpath %*` (Or $* for Unix)

1) This example shows the power of having a data format that is equivalent to XML.

2) Notice how this works nicely with the output of the show script described in the previous chapter:

captures the contents of a real file system, where files are normally displayed with the `cat path` command. Then spath.bat allows extracting the contents of individual files from that sml file using `--cat path`. The `path` is the same. Gotcha: Unfortunately this does not work with file names that are not XML tag compliant, for example if they contain spaces, or begin with a digit, etc. A possible addition to XML 2.0 maybe? ☺

Exporting Tcl data

The SML data format would be a natural format for exporting any kind of Tcl data:
- SML looks a lot like Tcl itself. (Particularly when not using attributes.)
- In simple cases (without attributes), SML can usually be parsed by the Tcl interpreter directly as Tcl lists of lists.
- You get for free the compatibility with any outside tool that only supports XML.

Side note about Tcl name spaces

The convergence of XML element trees, file system trees, and variable name spaces, leads me to think that the natural syntax for name spaces should be /namespace/subspace/variable, not ::namespace::subspace::variable.

SML management libraries

An SML parsing library?

I never had to write one…

- In simple cases (often) SML just looks like tcl lists, which the tcl interpreter can digest directly.

- In complex cases (rarely), it was too easy to use the sml script to generate XML, then the TclDOM package to parse it. So I never took the time to write a full-fledged parsing library.

Of course, ~~for the sake of the art~~ for performance reasons, it would be nice to write one in C or C++, using APIs similar to XML parsing libs.

An SML generation library?

I never had needs that required a full-fledged library like what TclDOM or tDOM allows to do for XML.

For my simple needs, I usually generated the output recursively, with the terminal elements first, then a call to a very simple IndentString routine to indent a block, which becomes the content block of an outer element, etc. This works well enough for small output files. For bigger ones, with deep element indentation levels, this will not scale well, as the inner elements have to be indented over and over again.

Curiously the best SML generation routines I have are written in PowerShell. These routines use yet another file system paradigm variation, with enclosing elements thought of as directories, and terminal elements thought of as files. Also they can generate either XML or SML at the flip of a global (shame on me) switch:

Put-Dir dirname [attributes] [script_block]	Begins an element, and opens an indented block. If the script block is present, its output will be indented in the content block, then that block will be closed immediately afterwards.
Put-EndDir dirname	Closes a content block. (Not necessary when using a script block with Put-Dir.)

<table>
<tr><td></td><td>The dirname argument is only necessary for generating XML, and even then I could get rid of it with a little more work, by recording names in a stack.</td></tr>
<tr><td>Put-Value name value [attributes] [options]</td><td>Ouputs a terminal element. Options include:<table><tr><td>-nameWidth N</td><td>Force the width of the element name. Allows aligning several name/value pairs, making them easier to read.</td></tr></table></td></tr>
</table>

Rewriting these routines in Tcl would be easy. (In part due to the similarity of Tcl and PowerShell for passing script blocks as arguments.) In PowerShell, the attributes are passed in a hashtable. In Tcl they'd be in a dictionary.

Next Steps

- Let people experiment with the tools, and give feedback about the syntax, and the possible alternatives. Is there any error or inconsistency that remains, preventing full XML compatibility in some case?
- If interest grows, work with interested people to freeze a standard, and create a simple SML generation and parsing library.
- If interest grows even further, work with the TclDOM and tDOM developers to see if this could be added to their libraries as an alternative XML encoding format, for both input and output.
- Any project which stores data as XML files, even zipped like in MS Office, would save space and increase ease of use by using the SML format instead.
- The savings potential is even better in XML-based network protocols, such as SOAP. Adapting existing XML-based protocols to use SML instead would be very easy, and increase bandwidth considerably. Creating new ad-hoc SML-based protocols would be easy too, and packet analysis would be much easier!
- Any new project which does not know what data format to use, could get an easy-to-use format by adopting this SML format, while ensuring compatibility with XML-compatible-only tools, should the need arise.

References

[1] XML specification: http://www.w3.org/TR/xml/

[2] ASN.1 XER (XML Encoding Rules): http://asn1.elibel.tm.fr/xml/xer.htm
http://www.itu.int/ITU-T/studygroups/com17/languages/X.693-0112.pdf

[3] JSON JavaScript Object Notation: http://www.crockford.com/JSON/

[4] Open Mobile Alliance WBXML (Wireless Binary XML Encoding) Specification
http://www.openmobilealliance.org/tech/affiliates/wap/wap-192-wbxml-20010725-a.pdf

[5] Compressing XML with Multiplexed Hierarchical PPM Models
http://xmlppm.sourceforge.net/paper/paper.html

[6] A list of XML

[7] XML compression bibliography: http://xmlppm.sourceforge.net/paper/node9.html

[8] Google Protocol Buffers: https://code.google.com/p/protobuf/
http://google-opensource.blogspot.fr/2008/07/protocol-buffers-googles-data.html

[9] XML discussions on Tcl's wiki: http://wiki.tcl.tk/1740

[10] TDL proposal on Tcl's wiki: http://wiki.tcl.tk/25681

[11] Simple XML: http://www.w3.org/XML/simple-XML.html

[12] Simple XML (unrelated to the previous one): http://en.wikipedia.org/wiki/Simple_XML

[13] Xmlgen presentation on Tcl's wiki: http://wiki.tcl.tk/5976?redir=3210

[14] TDL proposal on Tcl's wiki: http://wiki.tcl.tk/25681

Web(-like) Protocols for the Internet of Things

Dr. Emmanuel Frécon
ICE - Interactive Collaborative Environments Laboratory
SICS Swedish ICT
emmanuel@sics.se

Abstract

This paper describes the motivation for and implementation of two Web-oriented protocols for the Internet of Things. While building upon the ubiquity and flexibility of the Web, WebSockets and STOMP minimise headers to the benefit of payload, thus adapting to the scarce resources available in IPv6 mesh networks. The websocket library provides a high-level interface to open client connections and further exchange data, along with the building blocks necessary to upgrade incoming connections to a WebSocket in servers. The STOMP library offers a near-complete implementation of the latest STOMP specification, together with a simple broker for integration in existing applications.

1. Introduction

The Internet of Things promises a near future where domestic and work environments, but also cities and factories, are augmented with sensors and actuators that all are Internet entities. The deployment of IPv6 together with mesh networks is key to this evolution by enabling each sensor or actuator to be accessed from any Internet enabled application or user, thus from almost anywhere. Given the widespread deployment of Web technologies, extending their reach to sensors and actuators would facilitate their integration in the fabric of our lives.

Being "everywhere" imposes a number of technological and economical constraints on sensor networks, leading to few radio, storage and computing resources available at each sensor. In particular, keeping protocol-relevant state to ensure the reliability of TCP imposes challenges to mesh networks since transmitting a packet reliably will require the resources of several sensors in the mesh. In addition, radio constraints impose small packet sizes, leaving little space to application data and protocol headers.

This paper describes the implementation of two Web(-like) protocols: WebSockets [1] and STOMP [2], targeting their integration in applications based on IPv6 mesh networks [3]. While being based on TCP, both protocols exhibit features making them suitable for low-level communication within a whole application deployment: from tiny sensors to users, via cloud services. WebSockets is merely a way to upgrade a regular Web connection to a lightweight and symmetrical communication channel, making possible data flows in both directions between the server and client. Within a WebSocket connection, individual packets are led by small binary headers. STOMP is also a bidirectional protocol, but with textual headers following rules similar to regular HTTP, and kept to a minimum.

2. Motivation

Most currently available sensor networks technologies use solutions for the "last mile" that are unlike the remaining of the Internet. Z-Wave[1], ZigBee[2], BTLE (bluetooth low energy)[3], EnOcean[4] are a few examples of these standardised radio and network technologies that have reached penetration in consumer and industrial applications. Being different from the transport protocols over which the Internet is built requires that information flowing from and to the sensors and actuators needs to be translated within bridges connected to both incompatible "worlds". This transition adds complexity to application development and deployment while introducing possible points of failure. There exists a number of middleware platforms [4] [5] [6] that attempt to hide the variety of sensor and actuator technologies. However, using these also introduces some complexity or at least programming and architectural models that are not always suitable for the final application at hand [7].

The motivation for this work is to experiment with ways to run the IP-family of protocols all the way from the clients to the sensors, via the server architecture. Both of the protocols which implementations are described in this paper are directly related to HTTP, the application protocol that forms a large part of the Internet today. WebSockets upgrade a regular web connection to a duplex, binary communication channel, while STOMP is a duplex mainly textual protocol sharing a lot of similarities with HTTP. Implementing both of these protocols has been used to understand the low-level technicalities and details involved. In itself, this implementation provides an assessment as to whether WebSockets and STOMP are suitable for an implementation on top of the constrained resources that are common place at the edges of sensor networks.

Finally, both protocols share a number of similarities with stream protocols in the sense that they sustain a long-lived duplex connection between the initial client and the server. While maintaining the state of this connection poses requirements on the underlying radio infrastructure, and especially on intermediate nodes in mesh networks, it also avoids the bursts involves in (re)creating the connections between sensors whenever information has to

---

1 Information about Z-Wave can be obtained from the Z-Wave Alliance home page at http://www.z-wavealliance.com/ or from wikipedia at http://en.wikipedia.org/wiki/Z-Wave.

2 Specifications for the ZigBee standards are available from the ZigBee Alliance home page at http://www.zigbee.org/, more information is available at http://en.wikipedia.org/wiki/ZigBee.

3 BTLE is part of the specifications for Bluetooth 4.0 available at https://www.bluetooth.org/en-us/specification/adopted-specifications, more information is also available at http://en.wikipedia.org/wiki/Bluetooth_low_energy

4 The full title of the EnOcean standard is: ISO/IEC 14543-3-10 Information technology -- Home Electronic Systems (HES) -- Part 3-10: Wireless Short-Packet (WSP) protocol optimized for energy harvesting -- Architecture and lower layer protocols, more information available at the EnOcean home page at http://www.enocean-alliance.org/en/home/.

reach the edges while ensuring a higher level of interactivity.

3. Background and Related Work

As described in the previous section, there exist a number of communication protocols targeting or suitable for the Internet of Things. IEEE 802.15.4 based protocols such as ZigBee and 6LoWPAN, Z-Wave, EnOcean, ANT[5], BTLE or even the IEEE 802.11 family of protocols (wifi) are all wireless protocols, operating either in the sub-gigahertz frequency ranges or the crowded 2.4GHz radio spectrum. Given the heterogeneity of the offering, the IEEE is pushing IPv6 and 6LoWPAN, a standard that would allow running IP, the Internet Protocol at all levels.

In this context, CoAP [8] is a proposed standard over UDP that specifically addresses the requirements of the constrained nodes carrying sensors and actuators in many deployments. These nodes usually run specialised operating systems such as Contiki [9] or TinyOS [10]. CoAP focuses on a binary HTTP-inspired open protocol for the implementation of RESTful environments, providing features such as discovery of resources and subscription for a resource (resulting in push notifications). In a similar fashion, MQTT-S is a cutdown version of the MQTT[6] (Message Queuing Telemetry Transport) protocol geared towards lossy radio protocols. MQTT is a protocol proposing a unified publish-subscribe approach for M2M communication. MQTT is a lightweight messaging protocol, designed for constrained devices and low-bandwidth, high-latency or reliable networks.

Apart from MQTT, there exist a number of more generic protocols implementing publish-subscribe patterns, STOMP and AMQP [11] (Advanced Message Queuing Protocol) being two well-known examples. Generic broker services such as RabbitMQ or ActiveMQ use these protocols to ease and scale the deployment of modern cloud services. Some of them make use of WebSockets to make it possible to use queuing protocols such as STOMP or AMQP directly from the web browsers. The combination of all these protocols allows for a unified approach to application development and deployment: from tiny sensors and actuators to clients, via scalable and elastic cloud services.

WebSockets will upgrade a regular HTTP connection, as initiated from the client, to a duplex binary long-lived connection. As such, WebSockets will typically present an initial textual header of "subsequent" size following the rules of the HTTP specification, together with the handshaking specified in RFC 6455. Consequently, initiating a WebSocket connection will typically represent a burden on an existing sensor network, while later packets will allow applications to use most of the network packet size for their data. As WebSocket technically upgrade an existing web connection, they are typically suitable for passing through firewalls whenever needed. In addition, the specification requires a heartbeat facility that will keep the connection alive through, for example, network equipment implementing NAT solutions. The work described in this paper is partly based on a server-side implementation of the

[5] ANT is a wireless protocol mostly targeting the sports and outdoor activity domain. More information is available at http://www.thisisant.com/.

[6] MQTT has been proposed as an OASIS standard, the specifications are openly published and made available at the following web site: http://mqtt.org/.

WebSocket protocol that was made available as part of the Tcl web server wibble[7].

STOMP stands for the Simple (or Streaming) Text Oriented Messaging Protocol. The protocol provides an interoperable wire format so that STOMP clients can communicate with any STOMP message broker to provide easy and widespread messaging interoperability among many languages, platforms and brokers. STOMP is loosely modeled after the HTTP protocol: messages will typically start with an uppercase command (like `GET` in HTTP), followed by a number of textual headers in a format similar to HTTP and possibly followed by a body. Connections are client initiated, but messages can flow in both directions. STOMP, similarly to WebSocket specifying heartbeating mechanisms to keep connections opened at all time. However, heartbeating is handshaked at connection time, allowing for all types of situations, including applications where no heartbeating is required. The core of STOMP specifies publish-subscribe mechanisms where clients subscribe to topics (compare to a path in HTTP) and will be notified whenever messages have been sent to that topic. STOMP specifies a number of delivery mechanisms in order to implement different degrees of reliability. In the context of sensor networks, the shortness of commands and headers leaves enough room to application data. Together with implementations in, for example, JavaScript this opens for the use of STOMP at all levels of an architecture, including at the edges formed by the browser or the sensors. tStomp [12] is a SNIT-based client library partially implementing v 1.1 of the specification in Tcl. tStomp provides a basic level implementation, leaving aside some features such as authentication, virtual hosting, receipts, message acknowledgements or heart-beating.

4. WebSockets

The `websocket` library is a pure Tcl implementation of the WebSocket specification covering the needs of both clients and servers. The library offers a high-level interface to receive and send data as specified in RFC 6455, relieving callers from all necessary protocol framing and reassembly. It implements the ping facility specified by the standard, together with levers to control it. Pings are server-driven and ensure the liveness of the connection across home (NAT) networks. The library has a number of introspection facilities to inquire about the current state of the connection, but also to receive notifications of incoming pings, if necessary. Finally, the library contains a number of helper procedures to facilitate the upgrading handshaking in existing web servers.

Central to the library is a procedure that will “take over” a regular socket and treat it as a WebSocket, thus performing all necessary protocol framing, packetisation and reassembly in servers and clients. The procedure also takes a handler, a command that will be called back each time a (possibly reassembled) packet from the remote end is ready for delivery at the original caller. Another procedure allows callers to send data to the remote end in transparent ways. The procedures can be used from both servers and clients, even though the protocol is not entirely symmetric. A great deal of the implementation of these procedures originates from the initial wibble implementation.

[7] Original wibble code is available on the wiki at http://wiki.tcl.tk/26556.

Even though these procedures form the core of the library, they will seldom be used as clients and servers can benefit from a second layer of API at a higher level. Typically, clients will open a connection to a remote server by providing a WebSocket URL (`ws:` or `wss:` schemes, `wss:` being, as `https:`, encrypted) and the handler described above. The opening procedure is a wrapper around the latest `http::geturl` implementations: it arranges to keep the socket created within the `http` library opened for reuse, but confiscates it from its (internal) map of known sockets for its own use. Therefore, it will only work with the versions of the `http` library that have support for version 1.1 of the HTTP specification.

The following example arranges to connect to the echo server, send a simple text message and to finally close the connection and exit on reception of the message that it had sent to the echo server. The code also exhibits some of the introspection facilities that are built in the `websocket` library.

```
package require websocket

# Maximise loglevel to get detailed information on the console.
::websocket::loglevel debug

# Handler procedure registered as a receiver of all information
# from the server and internal state changes of the library.
proc handler { sock type msg } {
    switch -glob -nocase -- $type {
      co* {
          # Once connected, arrange to show off introspection
          # facilities and to send a simple text message to the
          # echo server.
          puts "Connected on $sock"
          test $sock
      }
      te* {
          # On reception of the text message that we have sent,
          # print it out and disconnect.
          puts "RECEIVED: $msg"
          ::websocket::close $sock
      }
      cl* -
      dis* {
          # Exit on disconnection, i.e. as soon as we've received
          # the message that we had sent to the echo server.
          exit
      }
    }

}
```

```
# Send a single message to the echo server after having printed
# out information about the current websocket connection.
proc test { sock } {
    # Print connection info
    puts "[::websocket::conninfo $sock type]:\
        [::websocket::conninfo $sock sockname] ->\
        [::websocket::conninfo $sock peername]"

    # Send message to echo server.
    ::websocket::send $sock text "Testing, testing..."
}

# Open connection to the echo server and arrange for the handler
# procedure to be called whenever receiving information from the
# server or about the connection.
set sock [::websocket::open ws://echo.websocket.org/ handler]

# Arrange for the event loop to kick-off
vwait forever
```

For servers, the process is slightly more involved in order to account for the differences of their inner workings. Indeed, as the library wishes to take over the socket, it needs to interface with the remaining of the server code to know at which point of the transaction the overtaking should occur. Servers will start by registering themselves and especially their handlers (see central procedure above) to the library. Then for each incoming client connection, they should test the incoming request to detect if it is an upgrade request by providing the path and HTTP headers to a testing procedure. Finally, a server will perform the final handshake to place the socket connection under the control of the `websocket` library and its central procedure. This is exemplified in the following pseudo-code.

```
# Assuming the server is listening on connections on srvSock,
# create a handler for the webserver socket
set srvHandler [::websocket::server $srvSock]

# Provide matching between paths and handlers, this would match
# any path to be handled by the handler command, but there can
# be any number of such declarations, for different paths at
# the server.
::websocket::live $srvSock * handler

...

# At a later time, when a client has connected at sock and all headers
# for the incoming connection have been parsed and are made
# available in the headers dictionary, test if this is a websocket
# upgrade request. If it is, upgrade the socket to a websocket.
if { [::websocket::test $srvSock $sock $url $headers] } {
```

```
    ...
    # Upgrading the socket will arrange to call the handler
    # depending on the path and place the whole socket under
    # the control of the library. This also means that the
    # library will send back some handshaking data on the
    # client socket.
    ::websocket::upgrade $sock
}
```

The `websocket` library is, since a few months back, part of `tcllib`. The mini web server that is part of the `efr-tools`[8] is able to hosts websockets and can serve as a more elaborate example of how servers and the library should interface in order to provide support for WebSockets.

5. STOMP

The STOMP library provides both a client side implementation and a minimal server broker in pure Tcl. Coding constructs are constrained so as to be able to run under jTcl [13] if necessary. The library is composed of a three sub-packages: a messaging package provides core facilities for creating, parsing and sending STOMP messages; the client package is a near-complete implementation of all versions of the protocol and the server package provides a minimal broker implementation in pure Tcl, ready for integration in any existing application.

The messaging package provides procedures to create messages, set and get their various parameters and components. STOMP Messages are composed of a command, a set of headers (loosely similar to HTTP headers) and a body. The library makes it possible to strictly follow the message constraints as imposed by the protocol, i.e. control which header are mandatory and optional for a given command. The messaging package also offers procedures to send and receive messages to and from a STOMP server. Reception is implemented via a "reader" context as messages can arrive at any time from a server on a socket. The reader context contains a handler that will be called once incoming messages have been parsed and validated. Finally, the messaging package can keep alive a connection by sending (almost) empty data at regular intervals. It watches that a remote end continuously sends heartbeats, and provides a callback whenever the remote is deemed to have disconnected, i.e. when no heartbeats have been received for a given time period.

The client package encapsulates all traffic to a remote server into a single object. The layer provides an implementation that follows the v1.2 of the specification, except that it does not provide a high-level support for transactions. The library is able to open connections to remote servers, while respecting the initial connection handshake that will establish how heartbeats will be exchanged between the client and the server. It also implements facilities

---

[8] `efr-tools` is a google code project hosting both a number of libraries, but also the context manager [14], a cloud service for IoT applications. The project is available at https://code.google.com/p/efr-tools/ and it contains an experimental copy of the websocket library.

to keep the connection alive at all times, continuously attempting to reconnect whenever the connection has been lost. The client library provides callbacks to follow the current state of the connection (in progress, connected, disconnecting, etc.), but also to be notified of the reception of any message. Sending messages to the remote end is a high-level wrapper around the messaging package, a wrapper that will take care of reconnections, header assignments, etc. The client package offers a procedure to subscribe to data coming from the server and to arrange for callbacks to be delivered each time a message matching the subscription is received from the server. Subscriptions are represented by a context and can be ended at all time, in cooperation with the server. Finally, the client library is able to request for receipts, to be called back on reception of the receipt and to perform graceful disconnections from the server, i.e. disconnections in cooperation with the server. A basic level of security is ensured by supporting authorisation, but also by some basic security mechanisms against packets that would be too long.

The following code exercise the library by connecting to a remote server, subscribing to a topic, sending messages and verifying that even binary messages can transit between clients and servers.

```
package require stomp::client

# This code supposes that the global variable dta contains the
# binary content of a Windows .ico file (anything else would do)
# and will check that what has been sent to the server is also
# receive, even when sending larger binary messages.

# Print out reception acknowledgment
proc received { cid rid } {
    puts "Server has received message, id: $rid"
}

# Handler called on reception, print the command and headers
# contained in the message, and if it was an icon, compare it
# to what we had sent. This provides examples for how to use
# the messaging package part of the library.
proc incoming { msg } {
    global dta
    puts "Incoming message: [::stomp::message::getCommand $msg]"
    set type [::stomp::message::getHeader $msg content-type]
    if { $type eq "image/x-icon" } {
        puts "Comparing: [string eq $dta [::stomp::message::getBody $msg]]"
    }
}

# Unsubscribe from the only topic that we've ever subscribed to,
# which demonstrates how to look for existing subscriptions if any
proc stop {} {
    global s
```

```
    set sub [lindex [::stomp::client::subscriptions $s /queue/a] 0]
    ::stomp::client::unsubscribe $sub
}

# Connect to a STOMP server, these credentials are the default one
# on the Apache Apollo implementation of STOMP
set s [::stomp::client::connect -user admin -password password]

# Arrange to stepwise in the near-future, subscribe to a queue,
# send a text message, send a binary message, unsubscribe from the
# topic, verify we've stopped listening for that topic and finally
# to disconnect.
set ops [list \
       1000 [list ::stomp::client::subscribe $s /queue/a \
                    -handler incoming] \
       2000 [list ::stomp::client::send $s /queue/a -body "Hello world" \
                    -receipt received] \
       4000 [list ::stomp::client::send $s /queue/a \
                    -type image/x-icon \
                    -body $dta] \

       6000 stop \
       7000 [list ::stomp::client::send $s /queue/a -body "Gone away?"] \
       30000 [list ::stomp::client::disconnect $s] \
       ]

foreach { when what } $ops {
    after $when $what
}
vwait forever
```

Similarly to the client library, the server broker implements heart-beating and simple message receipts. The broker will fan out incoming messages to all clients that have expressed interest via a subscription. It implements basic security mechanisms to discard messages from non-connected clients, to discard messages that would be too long or to check for user authorisation. Finally, the server supports virtual hosting.

6. Conclusion and Future Work

This paper has described the design and implementation of two Tcl libraries targeting the use of Web(-like) protocols in sensor networks applications. The implementation served as a an assessment of the suitability of the protocols to the few resources available on sensors. As most sensor networks use 16-bits microcontrollers, running Tcl on top of these hardware constrained devices is difficult[9]. However, the implementations discussed in this paper have been tested for longer active sessions on small hardware platforms such as the

[9] Running Tcl(-like) languages on small hardware platforms can however be achieved through languages such as Jim [15] or Hecl (see http://www.hecl.org/).

BeagleBoard-XM[10] or the Raspberry Pi[11], both as servers and clients. Given the low price tag and the presence of GPIOs on the Raspberry Pi, this opens up for the use of Tcl at all levels of sensor applications, i.e. not only in the cloud services and clients, but also within sensors. Stepping away from Tcl, C-based WebSocket client code has already been integrated into the Contiki OS and is part of Thingsquare Mist, thus demonstrating the suitability of WebSockets as a low-level protocol down to the sensors. WebSockets exhibit a larger header at connection establishment, while keeping protocol overhead to a minimum in subsequent message exchanges. STOMP uses plaintext headers, though keeping them to a minimum which makes it a possible alternative to WebSockets if ever needed. At the time of writing, the STOMP library is in the half-bakery on the wiki[12] and integration to the context engine [14] is in progress.

This work has been sponsored by the ARTEMIS project me^{3}gas and the Swedish project Intelligent Energy Services. Many thanks to all colleagues at SICS and especially Joakim Eriksson for lively and interesting discussions along the development of these libraries and their purpose. Finally, hats off to Andy Goth for the initial version of the WebSocket implementation and to Immanuel Patzschke for bug testing and fixing of the WebSocket library.

7. References

[1] "*The WebSocket Protocol*", I. Fette and A. Melnikov, RFC 6455, IETF.

[2] "*STOMP Protocol Specification*", available at http://stomp.github.io/stomp-specification-1.2.html.

[3] "*IPv6 over Low-Power Wireless Personal Area Networks (6LoWPANs): Overview, Assumptions, Problem Statement, and Goals*", N. Kushalnagar, G. Montenegro, C. Schumacher, RFC 4919, IETF.

[4] "*A Development Platform for Integrating Wireless Devices and Sensors into Ambient Intelligence Systems*", M. Eisenhauer, P. Rosengren, P. Antolin, Proceedings of the 6th Annual IEEE Communication Society Conference on Sensor, Mesh and Ad Hoc Communications and Networks Workshops, June 2009.

[5] "*Ad-hoc Composition of Pervasive Services in the PalCom Architecture. In Proceedings of International Conference on Pervasive Service*" D. Svensson Fors, B. Magnusson, S. Gestegård Robertz, G. Hedin and E. Nilsson-Nyman, Proceedings of ACM CPS09, London July 2009.

[6] "*Zero-programming Sensor Network Deployment*", K. Aberer, M. Hauswirth, A. Salehi, Proceedings of the IEEE Service Platforms for Future Mobile Systems (SAINT 2007), Japan, 2007.

[7] "*Role of Middleware for Internet of Things: A Study*", S. Bandyopadhyay, M. Sengupta, S. Maiti, S. Dutta, International Journal of Computer Science & Engineering Survey (IJCSES), Vol. 2, no. 3, August 2011.

[8] "*Constrained Application Protocol (CoAP)*", Z. Shelby, K. Hartke, C. Bormann,

[10] BeagleBoards are a family of low-cost, fan-less single-board open source computers featuring an ARM cortex core and expansion facilities. More information about the boards is available at http://beagleboard.org/.

[11] The Raspberry Pi is comparable to BeagleBoards, but packages a less powerful ARM core to an ever lower price. More information available at http://www.raspberrypi.org/.

[12] More information about the various stomp implementations can be found at http://wiki.tcl.tk/38103.

draft-ietf-core-coap-18, June 2013.

[9] "*Contiki - a lightweight and flexible operating system for tiny networked sensors*", A. Dunkels, B. Grönvall, T. Voigt, Proceedings of the 29th Annual IEEE International Conference on Local Computer Networks, Nov. 2004.

[10] "*The Emergence of Networking Abstractions and Techniques in TinyOS*", P. Levis, S. Madden, D. Gay, J. Polastre, R. Szewczyk, A. Woo, E. Brewer, D. Culler, Proceedings of the 1st USENIX/ACM Symposium on Network Systems Design and Implementation (NSDI), 2004.

[11] "*Advanced Message Queuing Protocol*", S. Vinoski, IEEE Internet Computing, Vol. 10, no. 6, Nov/Dec 2006, pp 87-89.

[12] "*New Siemens Open Source Contribution for TCL: tStomp Messaging library. Why and how to use TCL in a very large scale Software Development*", D. Münchhausen, Talk at EuroTcl'2012.

[13] "*JTcl and Swank: What's new with Tcl and Tk on the JVM*", B. Johson, T. Pointdexter, D. Bodoh, Proceedings of the 18th Tcl/Tk conference, Manassas, 2011.

[14] "*Bringing Context To the Internet of Things*", Emmanuel Frécon, Proceedings of the 19th Tcl/Tk Conference, Chicago, Sept. 2012.

[15] "*Jim Tcl - A Small Footprint Tcl Implementation*", S. Bennett, Proceedings of the 18th Tcl/Tk Conference, Manassas, 2011.

A State-Driven, Service-Oriented Dynamic Web Development Framework

Stephen E. Huntley
stephen.huntley@alum.mit.edu

Abstract

I introduce a Tcl-based framework for development of dynamic web sites. It was written as an attempt to get away from object-oriented web development paradigms which have largely failed to deliver the advantages that dynamic scripting tools ought to provide. It leverages some of Tcl's unique features, such as hierarchical namespaces, module-based package management and extensive call stack introspection; in order to provide a hierarchy of composable dynamic services in response to a URI, inspired by service-oriented programming techniques.

1. Introduction

The subject of this paper is a collection of Tcl packages designed to work together as a simple, modular web application framework; specifically it is designed to bring to the task of authoring and delivering a dynamic web site the relative ease, flexibility, reliability and empowerment associated (by those who know it well) with development of a Tcl software program.

The last decade has seen a tremendous increase in complexity of programming techniques used in the most popular web application frameworks. These include heavy reliance on object-oriented programming, model-view-controller design patterns and object-relational mapping for database access. The Ruby on Rails framework is probably the most high-profile embodiment of these trends, with packages such as Spring and Hibernate in Java and Zend and CodeIgniter in PHP taking similar approaches and reaching similar levels of adoption and mindshare.

The appeal of such products is the promise of rapid prototyping and fast delivery of database-driven web sites achievable by designers with relatively little experience.

The design approaches and associated hype typified by these frameworks have become so widespread and ingrained in programming culture that I have encountered younger programmers who have expressed surprise that other means of designing a dynamic web site are even conceivable.

The drastic downside of these trends in web site engineering is that the promise of quick prototyping and fast early results has been bought with introduction of intractable medium-to-long term issues of code

draft-ietf-core-coap-18, June 2013.
[9] "*Contiki - a lightweight and flexible operating system for tiny networked sensors*", A. Dunkels, B. Grönvall, T. Voigt, Proceedings of the 29th Annual IEEE International Conference on Local Computer Networks, Nov. 2004.
[10] "*The Emergence of Networking Abstractions and Techniques in TinyOS*", P. Levis, S. Madden, D. Gay, J. Polastre, R. Szewczyk, A. Woo, E. Brewer, D. Culler, Proceedings of the 1st USENIX/ACM Symposium on Network Systems Design and Implementation (NSDI), 2004.
[11] "*Advanced Message Queuing Protocol*", S. Vinoski, IEEE Internet Computing, Vol. 10, no. 6, Nov/Dec 2006, pp 87-89.
[12] "*New Siemens Open Source Contribution for TCL: tStomp Messaging library. Why and how to use TCL in a very large scale Software Development*", D. Münchhausen, Talk at EuroTcl'2012.
[13] "*JTcl and Swank: What's new with Tcl and Tk on the JVM*", B. Johson, T. Pointdexter, D. Bodoh, Proceedings of the 18th Tcl/Tk conference, Manassas, 2011.
[14] "*Bringing Context To the Internet of Things*", Emmanuel Frécon, Proceedings of the 19th Tcl/Tk Conference, Chicago, Sept. 2012.
[15] "*Jim Tcl - A Small Footprint Tcl Implementation*", S. Bennett, Proceedings of the 18th Tcl/Tk Conference, Manassas, 2011.

A State-Driven, Service-Oriented Dynamic Web Development Framework

Stephen E. Huntley
stephen.huntley@alum.mit.edu

Abstract

I introduce a Tcl-based framework for development of dynamic web sites. It was written as an attempt to get away from object-oriented web development paradigms which have largely failed to deliver the advantages that dynamic scripting tools ought to provide. It leverages some of Tcl's unique features, such as hierarchical namespaces, module-based package management and extensive call stack introspection; in order to provide a hierarchy of composable dynamic services in response to a URI, inspired by service-oriented programming techniques.

1. Introduction

The subject of this paper is a collection of Tcl packages designed to work together as a simple, modular web application framework; specifically it is designed to bring to the task of authoring and delivering a dynamic web site the relative ease, flexibility, reliability and empowerment associated (by those who know it well) with development of a Tcl software program.

The last decade has seen a tremendous increase in complexity of programming techniques used in the most popular web application frameworks. These include heavy reliance on object-oriented programming, model-view-controller design patterns and object-relational mapping for database access. The Ruby on Rails framework is probably the most high-profile embodiment of these trends, with packages such as Spring and Hibernate in Java and Zend and CodeIgniter in PHP taking similar approaches and reaching similar levels of adoption and mindshare.

The appeal of such products is the promise of rapid prototyping and fast delivery of database-driven web sites achievable by designers with relatively little experience.

The design approaches and associated hype typified by these frameworks have become so widespread and ingrained in programming culture that I have encountered younger programmers who have expressed surprise that other means of designing a dynamic web site are even conceivable.

The drastic downside of these trends in web site engineering is that the promise of quick prototyping and fast early results has been bought with introduction of intractable medium-to-long term issues of code management, stability, security and scalability. Attempts to fix these issues have led to increases in the complexity of the frameworks themselves, often thereby leaving behind the inexperienced programmers the frameworks were originally intended to appeal to. Dynamic web development has come to resemble the dispiriting slog of enterprise architecture programming, rather than the quick and satisfying scripting experience that programmers turned to the lighter-weight, non-compiled languages for in the first place.

As a capper to these struggles, which have been simmering for some time, in the beginning of 2013 a series of catastrophic security flaws were found in the software of the Ruby on Rails framework[1]. These bugs make total takeover of web servers running the software trivially easy for attackers. The revealed flaws were so deeply entwined in the code that they appeared to some expert observers to herald a whole new class of bugs; where, even if the immediately known issues were patched, it might take years to track down the underlying vulnerabilities, if they do not in fact turn out to be inherent in the object-oriented, object-relational architectural approach (and thus ultimately ineradicable).

All this is by way of saying that the past ten years or so of web authoring progress is today looking like something of an evolutionary dead end. A total rethink of how to design small to medium-sized dynamic websites, which might have seemed like an indulgence just a year ago, now importunes more like a matter of urgent importance.

This program is a serendipitous result of attempts to solve a number of pressing web design and delivery problems encountered by me professionally over the past several years. These problems relate to issues of code deployment, identity management, role-based access to resources, workflow and collaboration. Despite the intensifying complexity of the mainstream application frameworks, the state of the art in grappling with these issues has hardly budged in the Twenty-first Century.

The code attempts to leverage Tcl's natural strengths: its hierarchical namespaces, its strong package management features, its string-oriented data processing paradigm, its event loop and its call stack introspection features, all map exceptionally well to the problem spaces presented by the HTTP protocol and its stateless, hierarchically-indexed, string-based orientation. Thus the program is able to pursue the goal of mapping the design of a dynamic web site to the well-understood task of writing a Tcl program as encapsulated in a collection of packages.

As a result of its serendipitous creation, the program is something of a mutant hybrid; I hope that like some other mutant hybrids, it will prove fitter for survival in the wild than other more purebred species.

2. Design Approaches: Service-orientation and Hierarchical Indexing

The code relies on a simple central design axiom: the URI of a request from an external client to a web server can be used internally by the server as a master index to control access to the range of heterogeneous information sources a web framework is today expected to access and coordinate to fulfill the external request.

The simplest example is mapping of a HTTP query's URI to a Tcl procedure, which is programmed to return the desired dynamic response. In this instance comparison may be made to Tclhttpd's "application direct URL" feature[2]. This feature allows the developer to register URIs as keys and procedure names as values in a global array. On receipt of a query with a matching URI, the correspondingly mapped procedure is called. Tclhttpd additionally decodes the query's named values and calls the procedure with the values mapped to the appropriate arguments.

This is a handy feature, but the mappings of URI to code are arbitrary, and no structure is provided for organization or marshaling of the procedure code within the project.

The new code does a similar mapping of URIs to procedures, but does so without the need for maintenance of any key-value arrays; there is in fact no need for any metadata superstructure at all -- it instead simply leverages Tcl's hierarchical namespace feature and maps the nodes of the URI to a namespace path, which is presumed to exist or be loadable from a package module. Like Tclhttpd, it also decodes query strings (and REST-format values as well) and goes on to do a smart best-fit mapping of the lot to procedure arguments.

The program takes a few additional steps in management of the mapping of URI to procedure. In order to prevent inadvertent unintended access to code, at startup it requires specification of a namespace path prefix which defines the space of allowable procedure mappings. It requires exporting of specific procedures (via the [namespace export] command) as a prerequisite for being called as a means of declaring them "public." It also carries forward the concept of hierarchically-indexed access to services by looking for and loading Tcl package modules in the module filesystem path space if a procedure suitable for mapping is not already loaded in the interpreter.

This behavior illustrates how as an alternative to the dominant but flawed object-oriented design paradigm, this project looks for inspiration to concepts associated with the approach known as "service-oriented programming." Service-oriented programming is typically used by large enterprises in pursuit of "service-oriented architecture," which aims to coordinate a large number of disparate heterogeneous networked computer resources by strictly segregating them and letting them interact via a simplified, structured API schema.

To quote Wikipedia[3]: "In SOP [service-oriented programming]... software modules are strictly encapsulated through well-defined service interfaces that can be externalized on-demand as web service operations." In addition: "a service can be composed of other nested services in a hierarchical manner."

While making no attempt to conform to any official definitions or protocols, the code attempts to follow the service-oriented approach by casting Tcl package modules in the role of the aforementioned "software modules," with namespaced and exported procedures stored in the modules as the "well-defined service interfaces."

If generalized away from its enterprise programming origins, service-oriented programming might be seen as an abstraction of the "Unix way;"[4] that is, a means of fulfilling programming goals by using small code units each of which performs simple tasks well and interacts with the others via simple text-based interfaces. This project tries to iterate that abstraction by recognizing that a web server's function has evolved into that of a coordinator and collator of a variety of resources and information nodes, and thus the service-oriented approach is applicable reflexively both to the server's external role as a fulfiller of information requests on a hierarchized global network, and to the web framework's internal data marshaling challenges.

Now the beginnings of a hierarchy of services within the web framework can be envisioned, all leveraging the tools naturally available and used by the Tcl programmer in assembling a sophisticated software installation. The request URI maps to a procedure well-encapsulated in a hierarchical namespace. The namespaced procedure exists in a package which is stored in a Tcl package module file whose name by convention reflects the namespace path. The package module is stored in a filesystem directory path that mirrors the module name.

The program code transparently manages all these levels in search of the appropriate service mapping that will fulfill the web client's request. Thus the process of designing a dynamic web site boils down to tasks that feel quite natural to the experienced Tcl programmer: creating namespaced packages containing publicly-declared interfaces of exported procedures. The developer need only write such a package and drop the package file into the defined module library path space in order to instantiate a new web service API. The program takes care of all the rest: determining package availability, loading package modules, mapping procedures and arguments to inborne URIs, executing the procedures and returning results.

3. Additional Facilities

The code is formatted as a collection of packages. The project files are laid out so that they may be delivered as a Starkit, as a single package with sub-packages included in an internal library directory and loaded as needed, or as a traditional application with a bin subdirectory containing an rc file and a configuration file.

Included is the pure-Tcl web server Wibble, and may be started as a stand-alone web server. Or, it can be accessed via gateway protocols such as CGI or SCGI from a third-party web server.

3.1 Package: tserver

As stated, the program is a collection of packages, and its operation may be best explained in more detail by closer examination of the individual packages:

The package named tserver coordinates and controls the other packages. In addition, it manages startup and configuration tasks. By design tserver server code listening on a port plays nicely with other event-generating code that may be running in the interpreter. Unlike Tclhttpd, which keeps its configuration values in global variables and has a complex interrupt protocol if the developer wants to make use of event programming independent of the web server's function, tserver keeps its configuration state in the namespace in which it was started; and all event-level state is kept within the event's call stack.

Thus the framework can run multiple listener ports with the same configuration in the same namespace, or it can run listeners with completely different configurations in separate namespaces.

The tserver package manages event-level state by providing "getter" and "setter" procedures which are call stack-aware. The getter procedure can access server-level state from the controlling namespace. The setter uses the [info frame] command to introspect which call stack it occupies in the event-loop structure, and sets arbitrary desired values in a place restricted to the call stack's scope. Once a call stack-level value has been set, the getter will always retrieve that value, even if there is a server-level value with the same name. Thus code executed in response to a query can customize the call stack's state; a variety of independent services can contribute to construction of a response, and a coordinating procedure can finally collate the information contained in the event-level state into a response.

3.2 Package: Wibble

The tserver package makes use of the pure-Tcl web server package Wibble[5], written by Andy Goth. The version used is customized to eliminate use of coroutines in order to allow pre-Tcl version 8.6 use and for performance, and other optimizations.

Thus the program can be used as a stand-alone web server, or can be configured to accept straight redirects from another server or reverse proxy without additional processing. Since the flow of code in Wibble is well-encapsulated via use of dictionaries, it is fairly easy to write new front ends for the Wibble code which accept different input protocols, simply by constructing a custom request state dictionary and injecting it into the Wibble code flow. For example, an SCGI front end has been written.

Wibble uses its own controller/dispatcher for matching query URIs to procedures. It utilizes a table of "zone handlers," where a zone is a URI prefix and the handler is a procedure, with optional custom state variables added to the request dictionary before dispatch. The framework own dispatcher function is constructed as a Wibble zone handler, so calls to it can be restricted to the domain of one or more specified URI prefixes.

The zone handler table is one of Wibble's most innovative and useful features. It is superficially like Tclhttpd's application direct URL feature (mentioned above); but instead of an array of keys and values, with one match opportunity, Wibble's dispatcher runs down the whole table and calls every procedure whose associated URI prefix matches the incoming query. Thus configuration of the table offers creative opportunities for multiple pre- and post-processing phases, and pipelining of response structures through multiple procedures. How this facility interacts felicitously with the framework service-handling architecture will be elaborated on further below.

3.3 Package: pkgTree

The package named pkgTree provides the controller and dispatcher procedures sketched above in section 2, as well as utilities for managing the package modules which contain the service code.

The package is so named because of the way the Tcl package module feature provides an alternate way of storing code packages: in a tree-structured filesystem directory location. (N.B. The "package module" feature is distinct from the classic package storage and discovery method; i.e., putting packages and their pkgIndex.tcl files in subdirectories of a directory which is listed in the global auto_path variable.)

Thus for example the module file for package textutil::string version 0.7.1, instead of being stored in a package library directory along with a pkgIndex.tcl file to control how it is sourced, is stored in a subdirectory of a module directory determined by the package name; i.e., <tm>/textutil/string-0.7.1.tm

The new(ish) package module feature provides a convenient and visually meaningful way to organize web server API code, since the pkgTree dispatcher assumes that the directory layout of the specified module path location mirrors the valid URIs of the server's API.

Thus, for example, if the dispatcher is initialized with the package prefix "API" and receives a query of the form:

http://example.com/document/statistics/wordcount?doc=tutorial.txt

then it will use the [namespace which] command to see if the procedure:

::API::document::statistics::wordcount

exists. If it does not, the dispatcher looks for the package:

API::document::statistics

and loads it. The dispatcher checks again if the procedure "wordcount" exists in the package, and additionally checks if the procedure is exported. If so, and the procedure has an argument named "doc", then the procedure is called with the argument appropriately set.

The combination of checking for the prefix ("API"), and for exported procedures only, ensures that only procedures the developer intends to be available are called.

Since REST-type calls are supported transparently, if the URL had been of the form:

http://example.com/document/statistics/wordcount/tutorial.txt

the dispatch process would have proceeded in the same way.

These facilities all come together when the developer comes to want to expand the API; for example to support the call:

http://example.com/document/transforms/translate?doc=tutorial.txt&lang=german

then the developer would simple create a package module called:

API::document::transforms

containing the exported procedure "translate" and drop the module file in the location <tm>/API/document/transforms-0.1.tm. Once that module exists the new API call is live, and the dispatcher takes care of loading and executing it, no server restarts or reloads necessary.

In line with the concept of using the URI as an index into different services, the pkgTree package also contains the procedure "resource". The resource directory allows an API procedure to retrieve static files from the filesystem without having to specify an explicit pathname.

The resource procedure is initialized with the location of a directory laid out as a mirror image of the API package module directory; that is, with sub-directories corresponding to

URIs supported by the API. If the resource procedure is called within an API procedure, it uses introspection to discover the namespace and procedure name of its caller, and retrieves the contents of the static file located in the resource directory corresponding to the URI path. If the retrieved file contains template code, the code will be executed and the final result returned.

Thus if a query of the form:

http://example.com/account/statement.html

were received, the procedure:

::API::account::statement.html

would be called. If this procedure were simply to contain a call to the procedure **::pkgTree::resource,** then the file **<resource>/account/statement.html** would be retrieved. This file could contain template code for returning customized information to the caller, which the resource procedure would see to executing.

4. Using Framework Features to Drive a State Machine

An advantage of mapping URIs to namespaces is that the pkgTree package's dispatcher can use the [namespace path] and [namespace which] commands to determine quickly which procedures are visible and executable. This approach contributes significantly to the performance, security and logical clarity of the code.

For the sake of security, the pkgTree dispatcher was designed with the requirement that it be initialized with a call to the [namespace path] command in the dispatcher's namespace to set a namespace value which acts as a prefix. The value set by the [namespace path] command is analogous to the PATH environment variable in a UNIX operating system, it determines the visibility of procedures as the PATH value determines the visibility of executable files. Thus no procedure that doesn't share the [namespace path] prefix will be callable by the dispatcher, so it is impossible for malicious hackers to construct a URL that would result in execution of code that was not intended to be part of the web server API.

Although not a design goal, the potential for a useful hack quickly became evident. There is no reason the namespace prefix set at startup time has to stay at the same value -- the [namespace path] command can be called at any time to set the visibility of code dynamically, and so the range of reachable procedures can be customized on a per-connection basis.

Given this capacity, it's not hard to envision the desirability of sometimes restricting a visitor's access to the API to a limited subset, depending on privileges or role. It's not hard to take the imaginings further to an API design that's segregated into logical groupings, even placed into entirely separate package module paths meant to satisfy different usages.

All that's needed to complete this scenario is an easy way to set the namespace path for an incoming connection, in a way that is clear and straightforward and thus not prone to confusion which would jeopardize security.

I have found, serendipitously, that the Wibble zone handler feature is the perfect tool for setting per-connection server state. It both allows creative configuration options and ensures the transparency necessary for high confidence in correctness of configuration. As stated above, the zone handler table can contain multiple entries that match a single URI, and each matching handler procedure is called in succession unless and until a procedure specifically calls an interrupt routine that terminates processing.

There is of course no necessity for any single handler procedure's code to address the contents of the server response, any desired task can be performed. Thus it is near trivially simple to segregate identity-validating, state-setting, and response-compiling operations in separate zone handlers.

And thereby an order of execution can be set up: an initial zone handler can validate identity by checking cookie values, session ID number or any other standard means. The handler can use the tserver package's per-connection state setting features to set an identity variable. A second zone handler can map an identity to a namespace path or set of paths, thus restricting the visibility of API procedures by the pkgTree package to a desired subset. Thus the different packages of the web framework leverage one another to restrict access to server resources using well-understood Tcl features. Finally, another zone handler can actually call the pkgTree dispatcher, which will only execute the requested API procedure if the dispatcher can detect its presence via the [namespace which] command.

Given the ability to specify such an order of execution, a namespace path can be utilized as more than a token of role-based access, its utility can be taken further to represent a session state that persists across visits. For example, a client interaction that requires sequential filling out of three separate forms can be controlled by using a pre-processing zone handler to restrict the visitor's access to the correct form at each point, and a post-processing handler that monitors if the form was completed successfully and storing in the session state the permitted namespace path of the next visit by the client. This would make problems like backtracking and double form submitting impossible.

In this way, a server built around this framework can be cast in the role of a state machine, with the API namespace defining the total state space, and zone handlers controlling state transitions, driving visitors through a custom state sub-space on a per-session basis.

A state machine framework promises to make it easy to attain some web programming goals that have been difficult or impossible with other frameworks, such as workflow programming, sophisticated collaboration scenarios, and programmable virtual servers mediated within the framework.

4.1 Additional State Configuration Options

The above section presents one detailed scenario for controlling access to server resources. But access to virtually every other information source can be similarly programmed.

As stated, the tserver package allows configuration of server state on a per-connection basis. This includes for example the value of the "docroot," the default location for static files. Instead of such complex and error-prone tools as htaccess files, the docroot can be given a default value of a directory containing only publicly accessible files, and only reset to a directory of more sensitive files after identity validation. There is thus no chance of misconfiguration causing leakage of access to restricted files, because the restricted files are simply invisible to the server until the validation step.

The custom version of the Wibble server package also includes a feature allowing the ability to reload the entire zone handler table and restart processing of handlers. Thus whole categories of function or complex workflows can be modularized and segregated in their own handler tables, and loaded as needed.

5. Conclusion

The aim of this paper is two-fold. First, to introduce this new framework and its architecture. Second, to communicate the observation that the experience of designing this program made it clear anew to me that Tcl's feature set makes it particularly well-suited to interfacing with the World Wide Web and serving the demands of the HTTP protocol. The failure of object-oriented design practices to deliver reliable solutions leaves a gaping need on the part of computer professionals who need to operate reliably and securely on the Internet. Tcl deserves to be seen as newly relevant in this space, not just as a good general-purpose scripting tool with potential for application to the WWW, but as the language and environment best suited to delivering on the usage goals of dynamic web development frameworks.

of more sensitive files after identity validation. There is thus no chance of misconfiguration causing leakage of access to restricted files, because the restricted files are simply invisible to the server until the validation step.

The custom version of the Wibble server package also includes a feature allowing the ability to reload the entire zone handler table and restart processing of handlers. Thus whole categories of function or complex workflows can be modularized and segregated in their own handler tables, and loaded as needed.

5. Conclusion

The aim of this paper is two-fold. First, to introduce this new framework and its architecture. Second, to communicate the observation that the experience of designing this program made it clear anew to me that Tcl's feature set makes it particularly well-suited to interfacing with the World Wide Web and serving the demands of the HTTP protocol. The failure of object-oriented design practices to deliver reliable solutions leaves a gaping need on the part of computer professionals who need to operate reliably and securely on the Internet. Tcl deserves to be seen as newly relevant in this space, not just as a good general-purpose scripting tool with potential for application to the WWW, but as the language and environment best suited to delivering on the usage goals of dynamic web development frameworks.

confidence in correctness of configuration. As stated above, the zone handler table can contain multiple entries that match a single URI, and each matching handler procedure is called in succession unless and until a procedure specifically calls an interrupt routine that terminates processing.

There is of course no necessity for any single handler procedure's code to address the contents of the server response, any desired task can be performed. Thus it is near trivially simple to segregate identity-validating, state-setting, and response-compiling operations in separate zone handlers.

And thereby an order of execution can be set up: an initial zone handler can validate identity by checking cookie values, session ID number or any other standard means. The handler can use the tserver package's per-connection state setting features to set an identity variable. A second zone handler can map an identity to a namespace path or set of paths, thus restricting the visibility of API procedures by the pkgTree package to a desired subset. Thus the different packages of the web framework leverage one another to restrict access to server resources using well-understood Tcl features. Finally, another zone handler can actually call the pkgTree dispatcher, which will only execute the requested API procedure if the dispatcher can detect its presence via the [namespace which] command.

Given the ability to specify such an order of execution, a namespace path can be utilized as more than a token of role-based access, its utility can be taken further to represent a session state that persists across visits. For example, a client interaction that requires sequential filling out of three separate forms can be controlled by using a pre-processing zone handler to restrict the visitor's access to the correct form at each point, and a post-processing handler that monitors if the form was completed successfully and storing in the session state the permitted namespace path of the next visit by the client. This would make problems like backtracking and double form submitting impossible.

In this way, a server built around this framework can be cast in the role of a state machine, with the API namespace defining the total state space, and zone handlers controlling state transitions, driving visitors through a custom state sub-space on a per-session basis.

A state machine framework promises to make it easy to attain some web programming goals that have been difficult or impossible with other frameworks, such as workflow programming, sophisticated collaboration scenarios, and programmable virtual servers mediated within the framework.

4.1 Additional State Configuration Options

The above section presents one detailed scenario for controlling access to server resources. But access to virtually every other information source can be similarly programmed.

As stated, the tserver package allows configuration of server state on a per-connection basis. This includes for example the value of the "docroot," the default location for static files. Instead of such complex and error-prone tools as htaccess files, the docroot can be given a default value of a directory containing only publicly accessible files, and only reset to a directory

References:

[1] http://www.kalzumeus.com/2013/01/31/what-the-rails-security-issue-means-for-your-startup/

[2] http://tcl.activestate.com/software/tclhttpd/#advanced

[3] http://en.wikipedia.org/wiki/Service-oriented_programming

[4] http://c2.com/cgi/wiki?UnixWay

[5] http://wiki.tcl.tk/23626

Tcl 2013
New Orleans, LA
September 23-27, 2013

Session II

September 25, 2013
1:15-2:45pm

Integrated Tcl/C Performance Profiling

Brian Griffin and Chuck Pahlmeyer
Mentor Graphics
8005 SW Boeckman Road
Wilsonville, OR 97070
brian_griffin@mentor.com
chuck_pahlmeyer@mentor.com

ABSTRACT

We present an approach to combine compiled (C) and interpreted (Tcl) call stack information for profiling purposes. We have integrated Tcl proc and C function calls into combined call stack information to provide a more complete picture of program state at profile sample times.

1. Introduction and Motivation.

According to mathematician Richard Hamming, "The purpose of computing is insight, not numbers." (Hamming, 1962). In that light, we use performance profiling to gain insight into where our program is spending time. The goal is to provide that "Ah ha!" that leads to finding and correcting a performance problem. To that end, we have devised a method to provide greater insight in our profiling results.

What is the problem?
Adequate performance is an important attribute for many software applications. Profiling is a useful tool to provide insight into where a program is spending time. A statistical profiler records the program call stack at regular intervals and collates information to provide statistics on number of samples encountered in various parts of the program. Examples of statistical profilers include Zoom, Oprofile, gprof, google-perftools and Intel® VTune™. Even gstack and gdb can be used as crude statistical profilers; simply do "gstack <pid>" a number of times during program execution or interrupt execution and retrieve the call stack periodically in gdb. Additionally there exist instrumenting profilers which work by modifying function entry and exit. These events are recorded during program runtime and later collated into reports of time and function call count. Examples of this include callgrind, DTrace and gprof (gprof uses both statistical as well as instrumented approaches).

There are also Tcl-specific performance profilers. Although the authors are unaware of any statistical Tcl performance profiler, the ActiveState® Tcl Dev Kit includes a Tcl profiler. DTrace can also be used for Tcl profiling. These profilers instrument the code and record information about every call. This information is summarized into various profile reports.

However, Tcl applications often have a combination of C and Tcl. A section of call stack of C code representing execution of Tcl code shows up in a standard profiler as shown in Figure 1. This provides very little insight into the Tcl language calls that were being executed.

```
Tcl_Eval
  Tcl_EvalEx
    TclEvalObjvInternal
      Tcl_IfObjCmd
        Tcl_EvalObjEx
          TclCompEvalObj
            TclExecuteByteCode
              TclEvalObjvInternal
                Tcl_CatchObjCmd
                  Tcl_EvalObjEx
```

Figure 1 Sample call stack representing Tcl code evaluation

Why is it interesting and important?

To understand what portion of a program is involved in time consuming activities, it is essential that the profile results provide reference to the original source code, whether that code was compiled (e.g. C) or interpreted (e.g. Tcl). Existing profilers provide information for either the compiled or interpreted code, but not both together.

Why is it hard?

The Tcl interpreter is a collection of C functions that execute Tcl command. Tcl command execution shows up in a standard call stack as a series of C function calls with names like `TclExecuteByteCode` and `TclEvalObjvInternal`. The difficulty in providing an integrated call stack is in knowing which C functions in the call stack are executing which Tcl procs. The C call stack alone provides insufficient information for this.

What are the key components of this approach and results?

In order to provide integrated C and Tcl call stack information, it is necessary to reference auxiliary information about the state of the Tcl call stack. Our approach uses a standard statistical profiler which collects and processes program call stacks at intervals during program execution. In addition, we maintain a representation of the Tcl call stack as Tcl calls are being made. When a C call stack is processed to include Tcl command entries, the Tcl call stack information is used to replace entries on the C call stack with the appropriate Tcl commands. We correlate position in the C call stack with position in the Tcl call stack by tracking how many `TclEvalObjvInternal` calls have been encountered in processing the call stack. This allows us to present profile results with a combination of C functions and Tcl procs.

2. Integrating Tcl procs into call stacks

Mentor Graphics' Questa® simulator has a built-in statistical performance profiler. It uses a timer-driven mechanism to collect call stack information at regular intervals. It provides a user interface to allow interactive exploration of profile results. However, prior to this work, it reported only C-language call stacks, providing limited usefulness for our application which is written in Tcl and C. To get better insight into program hotspots, we sought to integrate Tcl procs into C call stacks.

2.1 Overview

To collect and store Tcl call stacks, we utilize `Tcl_CreateObjTrace` to set up a trace function for Tcl command execution. For each Tcl command that is executed, a call to our specific trace function is made. In the trace function, we store a textual version of the command at the level-th location in a static array. When we process a C call stack, we can replace every `TclEvalObjvInternal` call with the corresponding Tcl command. We maintain correlation between the C and Tcl call stacks by matching on each `TclEvalObjvInternal` call—that is, each `TclEvalObjvInternal` call maps to an entry in the `tcl_stack`. A counter is incremented for each `TclEvalObjvInternal` call—the counter value is used to address into the static array of Tcl procs. Figure 2 provides an overview of the processing involved. Simplified code segments in Section 2.2 below provide more detail.

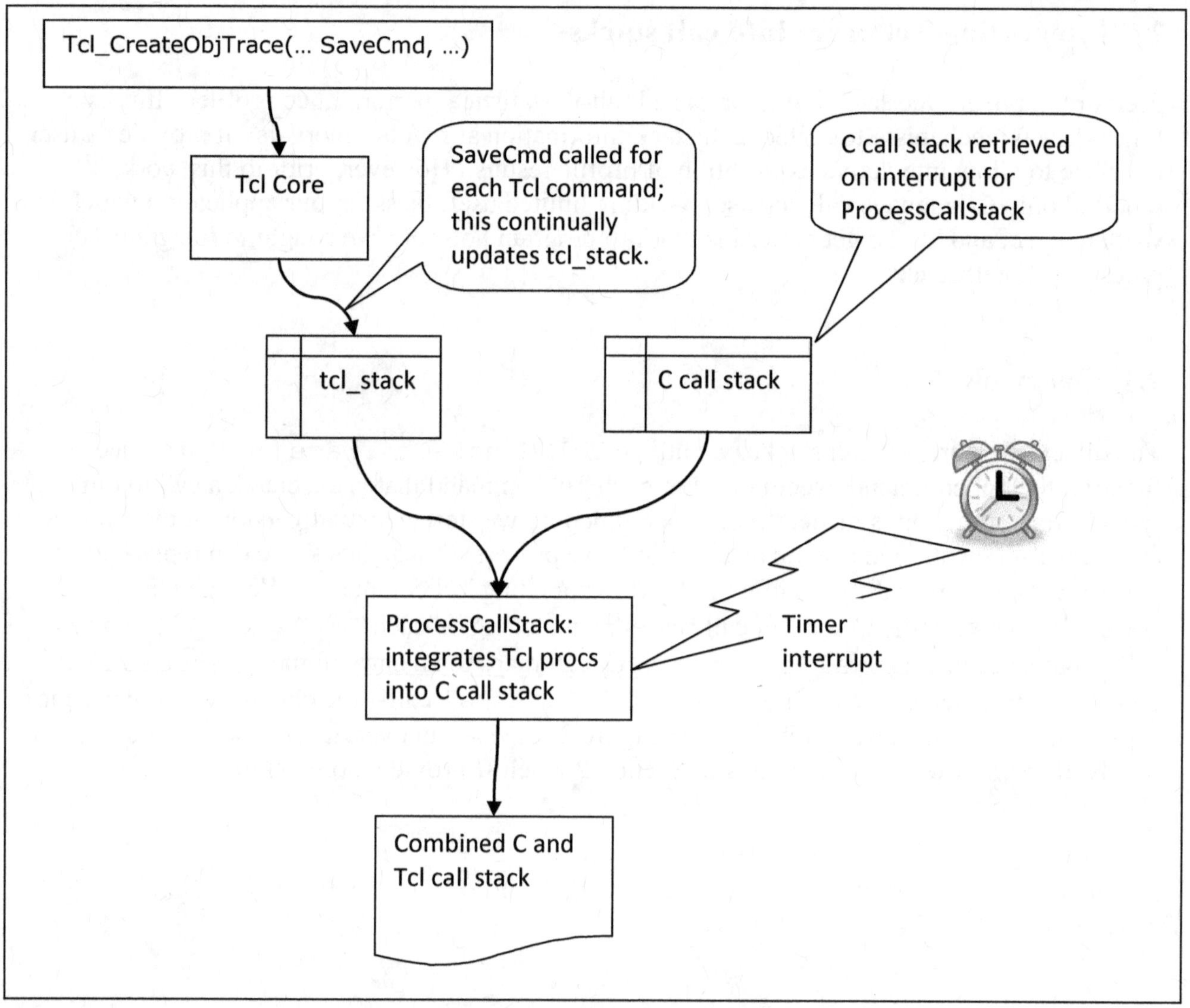

Figure 2 Flowchart indicating overview of profiling operation

2.2 Implementation

The Tcl call stack (`tcl_stack`) is stored in this compact structure (Figure 3); it consumes only a few tens of KB.

```
typedef struct t_tcl_stack {
    char command[80];
} s_tcl_stack, *p_tcl_stack;
s_tcl_stack tcl_stack[300];
```

Figure 3 Storage for Tcl stack

A simplified version of the trace function is shown below in Figure 4. `tcl_stack_max_loc` is a global variable indicating the maximum depth of the Tcl call stack at any moment. This variable is used in the call stack processing routine (`ProcessCallStack`). Note that the processing required in the trace function is small; this is essential since this function is called for each Tcl command that is evaluated. In the example in Section 3 below, about 2,800 profile samples were collected. During this process, `SaveCmd` was called about 21,000,000 times. The vast majority of entries that `SaveCmd` made into `tcl_stack` were unused. The calls to `SaveCmd` were necessary, though, to keep `tcl_stack` current because a profile sample could be taken at any time.

```
int SaveCmd(
    ClientData clientData,
    Tcl_Interp* interp,
    int level,
    const char *command,
    Tcl_Command commandToken,
    int objc,
    Tcl_Obj *const objv[] )
{
    /* There are cases where Tcl trace skips levels in the call stack
     * callback.  Fill any intermediate levels with entries that will be
     * skipped in ProcessCallStack(). */
    for (i=tcl_stack_max_loc+1; i<level && i<300 ; ++i) {
        strcpy(tcl_stack[i].command, "SkippedTclStackEntry");
    }

    if (level < 300) {
        strcpy(tcl_stack[level].command, command);
    }
    tcl_stack_max_loc = level;
    return TCL_OK;
}
```

Figure 4 SaveCmd trace function implementation

A simplified version of the call stack processing routine is presented in Figure 5 below. This function is executed for each call stack that is collected and processed. Processing of the call stack starts from the root (e.g. "main" (or "vish_inner_loop" for Questa)) and proceeds toward the leaf function call. The `while` loop processes each entry of the call stack. Each entry is handled in one of three ways:

- We replace `TclEvalObjvInternal` with the corresponding Tcl proc name. We do some manipulation of the reported text depending on the Tcl command being processed. For example, if a `string` command is being processed, we add one or two arguments to make a more informative entry. Also, some Tcl commands like `if` and `foreach` are ignored because we felt that they didn't add useful information to the call stack.
- Items on the call stack that match "Tcl*", "Itcl*", etc. are ignored as they don't add to our understanding of the processing.
- Other C function name entries are taken as-is.

```
static int ProcessCallStack()
{
    int tcl_stack_loc = 1;
    char *name, *proc;

    while (more entries in call stack) {
       name = name of call stack entry;
        if (name == "TclEvalObjvInternal") {
            char *cmd[4] = { 0 }, lcmd[80];
            strcpy(lcmd, tcl_stack[tcl_stack_loc].command);
            ++tcl_stack_loc;

            cmd[0-3] = first 4 tokens of lcmd

            if ((cmd[0]==0)    ||  (cmd[0][0]==0)                           ||
                (strcmp (cmd[0], "::"                               )==0) ||
                (strcmp (cmd[0], "if"                               )==0) ||
                             ...
                (strncmp(cmd[0], "Transcript::ReturnKey",      21)==0)) {
                proc = NULL; /* Ignore these Tcl commands */
            } else {
                /* Manipulate names for better info in displayed callstack */
                if (cmd[1]              &&
                    ((strcmp ("add"    ,       cmd[0])==0) ||
                          ...
                     (strncmp("."      ,     cmd[0],1)==0)))   {
                    proc = dstrPrintf(&ds, "%s++%s", cmd[0], cmd[1]);
                } else if ((strcmp ("string", cmd[0])==0) ||
                           (strcmp ("switch", cmd[0])==0)) {
                    if ((cmd[1][0]=='-')) {
                        dstrPrintf(&ds, "%s++%s++%s", cmd[0], cmd[1], cmd[2]);
                    } else {
                        dstrPrintf(&ds, "%s++%s", cmd[0], cmd[1]);
                    }
                    proc = dstrValue(&ds);
                   ...
                } else {
                    proc = cmd[0];
                }
            }
        } else if ((strncmp(name, "Tcl", 3) == 0)              ||
                   (strncmp(name, "Itcl", 4) == 0)             ||
                      ...
                   (strcmp (name, "WindowEventProc") == 0))    {
            proc = NULL; /* Ignore these functions in callstack */
        } else {
            proc = name; /* Save other non-Tcl C-level code addresses */
        }
        if (proc) addToDisplayedCallStack(proc);
    }
}
```

Figure 5 ProcessCallStack implementation

3. Results

We can compare results using standard C call stacks versus ones with Tcl commands substituted. The Tcl code in Figure 6 was used as a simple test case. It exercises the `tok2column` proc – code built into the Questa simulator. `tok2column` is designed to tokenize a string. The rules for tokenizing are different depending on the HDL language in use; in this case we specify "Verilog" as the language.

```
proc doWork { howMany }  {
    set l [list]
    for {set i 0 }  { $i<$howMany }  { incr i } {
        set l [doWork2  $i]
    }
    puts $l
}
proc doWork2 { i  }  {
    set line "The quick brown fox jumps over the lazy dog."
    set l [tok2column Verilog 23 $line]
    return $l
}
time { doWork 1000000 }
```

Figure 6 Test Tcl code

`tok2column` is a small routine that runs quickly (less than 50 microseconds). Calling it many times allows us to collect profile statistics and analyze it. In this case we call `tok2column` 1,000,000 times in 44 seconds collecting about 2,800 samples in the process.

3.1 Profile Results

The contents of the table below (Figure 7) show the `ProcessCallStack` processing for a portion of a representative call stack. The three columns in the table are:

- The C call stack entries. The `TclEvalObjvInternal` entries are shown in red; these are the items on which we base our C function to Tcl proc mappings.
- The processing done for each entry:
    - "-->" means that the C function was taken verbatim.
    - "X" means that the entry was filtered out.
    - "map to …" means that the entry was mapped to a Tcl command. Note that two Tcl commands (`time` and `for`) were suppressed though.
- The entries in the combined C and Tcl call stack.

Note the difference in length of the two call stacks. The combined C and Tcl call stack is much more compact.

C function only call stack entry	ProcessCallStack action	Combined C and Tcl call stack entry
vish_inner_loop	-->	vish_inner_loop
Tk_MainEx	-->	Tk_MainEx
Tk_MainLoop	-->	Tk_MainLoop
Tcl_DoOneEvent	X	
Tcl_ServiceEvent	X	
WindowEventProc	X	
Tk_HandleEvent	X	
TkBindEventProc	X	
Tk_BindEvent	X	
Tcl_EvalEx	X	
(lines of Tcl*)	X	
TclEvalObjvInternal	map to Tcl command	.vcop++Action
(lines of Tcl*)	X	
Tcl_CatchObjCmd	X	
TclEvalObjEx	X	
TclCompEvalObj	X	
TclExecuteByteCode	X	
TclEvalObjvInternal	map to Tcl command	EvalUserCmd
tclprim_UserEval	-->	tclprim_UserEval
Tcl_EvalObjEx	X	
TclEvalObjEx	X	
TclCompEvalObj	X	
TclExecuteByteCode	X	
TclEvalObjvInternal	map to "time", but suppress	
Tcl_TimeObjCmd	X	
Tcl_EvalObjEx	X	
TclEvalObjEx	X	
TclCompEvalObj	X	
TclExecuteByteCode	X	
TclEvalObjvInternal	map to Tcl command	doWork
TclObjInterpProc	X	
TclObjInterpProcCore	X	
TclExecuteByteCode	X	
TclEvalObjvInternal	map to "for", but suppress	
Tcl_ForObjCmd	X	
TclEvalObjEx	X	
TclCompEvalObj	X	
TclExecuteByteCode	X	
TclEvalObjvInternal	map to Tcl command	doWork2
TclObjInterpProc	X	
TclObjInterpProcCore	X	
TclExecuteByteCode	X	
TclEvalObjvInternal	map to Tcl command	tok2column
TclInvokeStringCommand	X	
tclprim_tok2column	-->	tclprim_tok2column
lang2lang_type	-->	lang2lang_type
Tcl_Eval	X	

Figure 7 Processing of example C call stack to combined C and Tcl call stack

The outputs in Figures 8 and 9 are profile results from the Questa simulator. The contents consist of

1) function name,
2) number of samples in and beneath the function (Under column), and
3) number of samples in the function (In column).

The indentation of the function names indicates calling hierarchy. For example, if function A called function B, B would be shown indented one space with respect to A. The number of samples is used to understand the cost of that function, with and without its children.

This output in Figure 8 shows the depth of a standard C call tree report; multiple call stacks collated together form a call tree. The items hand-annotated with “>>>” prefix and in larger font are Questa-supplied C routines. Note that 110 and 50 lines of “Tcl*” entries were suppressed for readability. Without that substitution, the report would be 224 lines long.

```
Name                                                                         Under(raw)  In(raw)
----                                                                         ----------  -------
vish_inner_loop                                                                    2795        0
 Tk_MainEx                                                                         2795        0
  Tk_MainLoop                                                                      2795        0
   Tcl_DoOneEvent                                                                  2795        0
    Tcl_ServiceEvent                                                               2795        0
     WindowEventProc                                                               2795        0
      Tk_HandleEvent                                                               2795        0
       TkBindEventProc                                                             2795        0
        Tk_BindEvent                                                               2795        0
         Tcl_EvalEx                                                                2795        0
          (110 lines of Tcl* suppressed)
           Tcl_CatchObjCmd                                                         2787        0
            TclEvalObjEx                                                           2787        0
             TclCompEvalObj                                                        2787        0
              TclExecuteByteCode                                                   2787        0
               TclEvalObjvInternal                                                 2787        0
>>>>>>>>>> tclprim_UserEval                                                        2787        0
                 Tcl_EvalObjEx                                                     2787        0
                  TclEvalObjEx                                                     2787        0
                   TclCompEvalObj                                                  2787        0
                    TclExecuteByteCode                                             2787        0
                     TclEvalObjvInternal                                           2787        0
                      Tcl_TimeObjCmd                                               2787        0
                       Tcl_EvalObjEx                                               2787        0
                        TclEvalObjEx                                               2787        0
                         TclCompEvalObj                                            2787        0
                          TclExecuteByteCode                                       2787        0
                           TclEvalObjvInternal                                     2787        0
                            TclObjInterpProc                                       2787        0
                             TclObjInterpProcCore                                  2787        0
                              TclExecuteByteCode                                   2787        0
                               TclEvalObjvInternal                                 2787        0
                                Tcl_ForObjCmd                                      2787        3
                                 TclEvalObjEx                                      2747        4
                                  TclCompEvalObj                                   2743        7
                                   TclExecuteByteCode                              2712       20
                                    TclEvalObjvInternal                            2679       10
                                     TclObjInterpProc                              2442        0
                                      TclObjInterpProcCore                         2436        3
                                       TclExecuteByteCode                          2399       17
                                        TclEvalObjvInternal                        2381       13
                                         TclInvokeStringCommand                    2082        2
>>>>>>>>>>>>>>>>>>>>>>>>>>>> tclprim_tok2column                                   2072        1
>>>>>>>>>>>>>>>>>>>>>>>>>>>>> lang2lang_type                                      1843        4
                                           Tcl_Eval                                1750        3
                                            (50 lines of Tcl* suppressed)
                                            sprintf                                  28        0
                                             _IO_vsprintf                            28        2
>>>>>>>>>>>>>>>>>>>>>>>>>>>>> HDLTextTok2Col                                       221        3
>>>>>>>>>>>>>>>>>>>>>>>>>>>>>> yylex                                               173       39
>>>>>>>>>>>>>>>>>>>>>>>>>>>>>>> is_keyword                                          96       54
                                         TclCheckInterpTraces                       163       10
                                          Tcl_Release                                41       41
                                          Tcl_Preserve                               37       37
                                         GetCommandSource                            41        2
                                         Tcl_ReturnObjCmd                            28        0
                                     TclCheckInterpTraces                           125        8
                                      Tcl_Release                                    38       38
                                      Tcl_Preserve                                   34       34
                                 Tcl_ExprBooleanObj                                  34        0
                                  Tcl_ExprObj                                        34        2
                                   TclExecuteByteCode                                32       15
```

Figure 8 Profile results with C call stack entries only

The profile report in Figure 9 below is one in which our approach has been used to replace "Tcl*" entries with the actual Tcl procs that were being evaluated. This is a screen shot of one of the profile windows in the Questa user interface; the profiler windows allow user interaction with profile data to better manage what is viewed. In this figure, C functions and Tcl commands can be distinguished by the different icons associated with each. The same six entries of Questa supplied C-code can be easily found. Note the interleaving of C functions and Tcl procs. For example, `doWork`, `doWork2` and `tok2column` are implemented in Tcl, `tclprim_tok2column` and `lang2lang_type` are C functions, `lang2lang_type` calls Tcl proc `::MtiFS::IsVerilogLanguage`, etc.

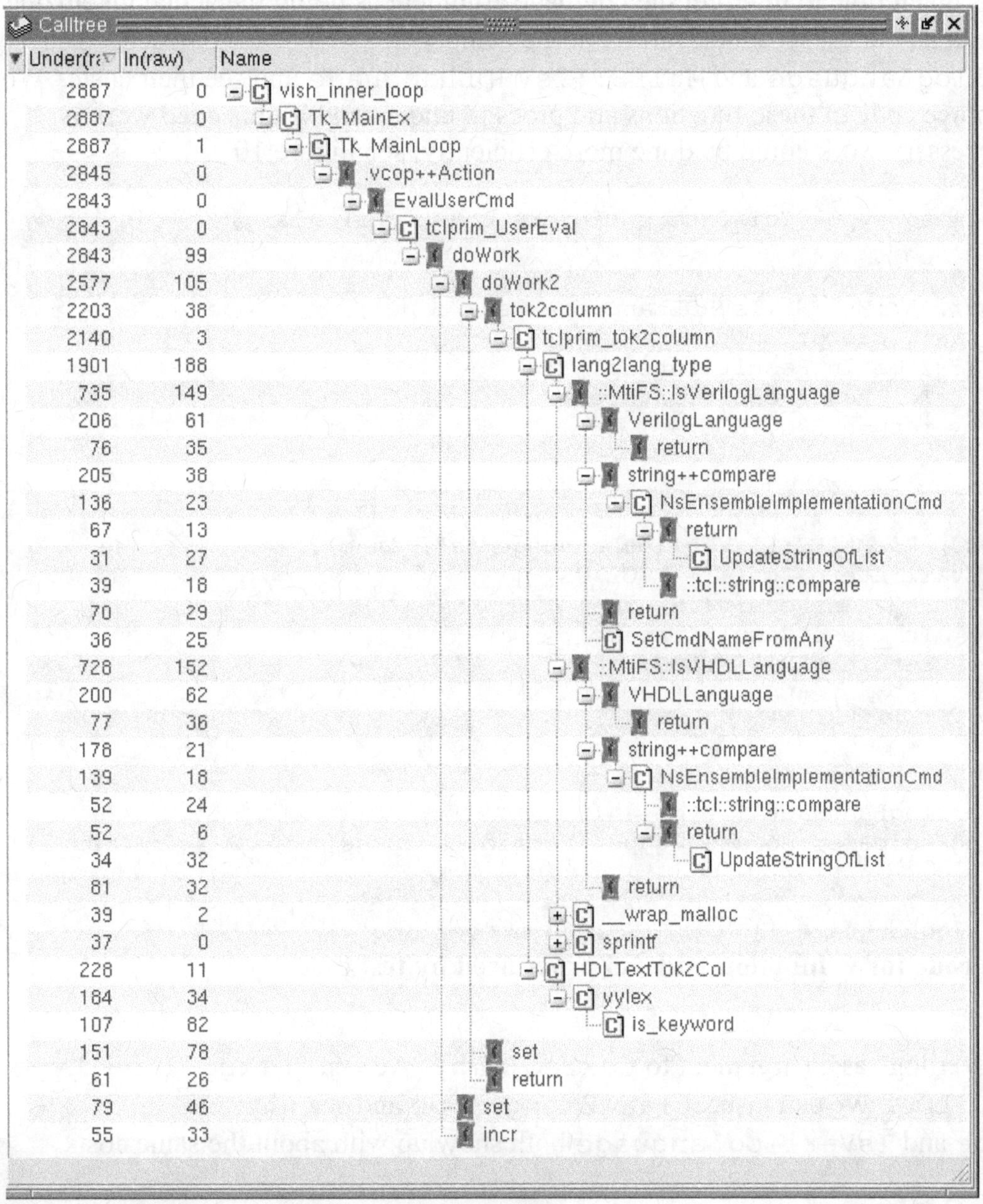

Figure 9 Call tree with Tcl and C entries

3.2 Using Profile Results to Analyze Performance

We can use this profile data to analyze performance of the tok2column proc. In looking at the children of Tcl proc tok2column, we see that C function tclprim_tok2column takes the majority of tok2column's time. We see that tclprim_tok2column spends time in two child routines: lang2lang_type and HDLTextTok2Col. The lang2lang_type routine is designed to determine the language type of the incoming language argument; HDLTextTok2Col does the actual tokenizing. We can see that lang2lang_type takes 1901 samples while HDLTextTok2Col takes only 228 - tclprim_tok2column is spending 8 times as much time to interpret the language argument as doing the actual tokenizing that the routine nominally does! We look further at the components of lang2lang_type: MtiFS::IsVerilogLanguage and MtiFS::IsVHDLLanguage and see their costs. We can examine the source code of these functions and procs to understand if unneeded work is being done or if necessary work could be done more efficiently; see Figure 10.

```
static int lang2lang_type (Tcl_Interp *interp,const char *lang)
{
      char buf[256];
      sprintf(buf, "::MtiFS::IsVHDLLanguage %s", lang);
      if ( Tcl_Eval(interp, buf) == TCL_OK) {
            if (Tcl_GetIntResult(interp)) {
                  Tcl_ResetResult(interp);
                  return LANGVHDL;
            }
      }

      sprintf(buf, "::MtiFS::IsVerilogLanguage %s", lang);
      if ( Tcl_Eval(interp, buf) == TCL_OK) {
            if (Tcl_GetIntResult(interp)) {
                  Tcl_ResetResult(interp);
                  return LANGVERILOG;
            }
      }
     . . .

proc MtiFS::IsVerilogLanguage { type } {
      if {[string compare -nocase $type [VerilogLanguage]] == 0 } {return 1}
      return 0
}
proc MtiFS::VerilogLanguage {}        { return "verilog" }
```

Figure 10 Source code for C function and Tcl procs used by test case

Since we specify "Verilog" as an argument to tok2column, we expect lang2lang_type to return LANGVERILOG. We can inspect lang2lang_type and see why IsVHDLLanguage and IsVerilogLanguage both show up with about the same costs.

The invocation of Tcl procs from C code to determine language type is time-consuming. With this insight into where time is spent in `tok2column`, we can easily reimplement `lang2lang_type()` as a strictly C function to speed `tok2column` considerably.
This example demonstrates the utility of combining Tcl and C routines into a single call tree for performance analysis. Note that `tclprim_tok2column`, `lang2lang_type` and `HDLTextTok2Col` do show up in the first (C function only) profile output (Figure 8). Without the context of the surrounding Tcl procs, though, it is more difficult to understand their role in the overall performance picture.

We have used this profiling feature to track a number of issues in the Questa simulator. For example:

- Tracking GUI sluggishness at a remote customer site. The developer initially suspected the message viewer was involved due to a high number of messages being processed. However, the profiler showed that code that scans simulation events was actually consuming the majority of the time. With this information, the developer was able to understand and address the real problem.
- We've recently integrated the Scintilla editor. Certain of our regression tests ran quite slowly using this editor. The profiler was able to point to the portion of the code that was consuming excess time.

4. Limitations and Notes

Our approach required a few small changes to the Tcl core code in order to get a consistent value for `numLevels` that could be matched to depth of `TclEvalObjvInternal` on the call stack. However, these changes weren't completely compatible with other uses of the notion of `numLevels` in the Tcl library. We're using these modifications in the Questa simulator version of Tcl, but they haven't been propagated to the public Tcl version.

We found that if `TCL_ALLOW_INLINE_COMPILATION` was specified in the flags argument to `Tcl_CreateObjTrace()`, the alignment assumptions made for this process were violated. That is, the assumption of number of times that `TclEvalObjvInternal` appeared in a call stack didn't match the depth of the Tcl call stack.

In our testing, doing profiling in this way caused a doubling to tripling of overall execution time. This is due to two primary factors:

- The cost of maintaining the Tcl call stack at all times via the trace functionality. The trace call is somewhat expensive due to internal overhead.
- Deoptimization of the Tcl code due to not specifying `TCL_ALLOW_INLINE_COMPILATION` to `Tcl_CreateObjTrace()`.

Although this is a non-trivial performance cost, the information it provides is generally worthwhile.

The filtering done in `ProcessCallStack` works well for our needs. Different rules could be used to support profiling in a different application or with interest in aspects of the Tcl library itself.

There were places where the trace function `SaveCmd` didn't appear to be called for every level of Tcl command that was executed. For example, the trace function might be called with `level=12` followed by a call with `level=15`. In this case, we'd enter the value `SkippedTclStackEntry` into the entries 13 and 14 of the Tcl call stack (`tcl_stack`) so that a known value is present on the stack all the way to `tcl_stack_max_loc`, the deepest level of the Tcl call stack. This didn't occur frequently, but did require the handling we provided.

Certain techniques described in this paper are patent-pending as a patent application has been submitted to the US Patent Office.

5. Future work

In the Tcl 8.5 environment, it could be useful to have a lighter-weight function to record Tcl command calls. The `Tcl_CreateObjTrace` approach had a large overhead due to mutex locks that were used around each trace call.

In the Tcl 8.6 environment, "stackless evaluation" has been introduced. This will require a different mechanism to record location in Tcl command call stack for correlation with C call stack.

Acknowledgements

We would like to thank Mark Young of Mentor Graphics for engaging discussions when developing this functionality. We would also like to thank the Questa GUI development team for testing this functionality.

Bibliography

Hamming, R. (1962). *Numerical Methods for Scientists and Engineers.* McGraw-Hill Education.
Tcl Library. (n.d.). Retrieved August 2013, from Tcl Developer Xchange!: http://www.tcl.tk/man/tcl8.5/TclLib/contents.htm

Characterizing and Back-Porting Performance Improvement

Clif Flynt
Noumena Corporation
clif@noucorp.com

Phil Brooks
Mentor Graphics Corporation
phil_brooks@mentor.com

Don Porter
NIST
donald.porter@nist.gov

September 4, 2013

Abstract

The Tcl interpreter is constantly being modified and improved. Improvements include new features and performance boosts.

Everyone wants to use the latest releases with the newest improvements, but corporate users with large code bases may not be able to do this. Reworking an extremely large code base can take longer than the interval between Tcl releases. These users may need a change to be back-ported to the version of Tcl that they are using.

A Tcl release includes many changes and identifying the modification that caused a particular performance boost isn't always simple, particularly if the performance boost of interest was a side-effect of other improvements.

This paper describes the discovery of a thread-performance issue in Tcl 8.4 which was fixed in 8.5, a semi-automated technique for tracking down the code modification that improved the performance, and a discussion back-porting the improvement.

1 Introduction

The first rule for carpenters and seamstresses is "Measure twice, cut once". For software engineers the rule for optimization is just "Measure First".

Work reported at the Tcl Conference in 2005 and 2012 identified an area where Tcl performance was not living up to expectations and provided the critical benchmark to measure the interpreter performance behavior with multiple threads.

1.1 Tcl-2005: 'Pulling Out All the Stops'

Phil Brook's 2005 Tcl conference paper discussed implementation of Calibre LVS's Device TVF feature, in which a highly efficient, though quite limited, calculation engine is given the ability to make calls to a Tcl program allowing for more sophisticated programming capabilities.

1.2 Tcl-2012: 'Pulling Out All the Stops - Part II'

The follow up 2012 paper discussed implementation of threading capabilities on the 2005 calculation engine and identified a bottleneck that is present especially when the calculation engine is creating many strings and formatting numbers into strings. The behavior in the application was reproduced in a stand alone C++/Tcl test program that similarly created many strings from numbers. The application behavior and that of the stand alone benchmark bore telltale signs of a locking problem:

- Real time execution scaling tapers off and even gets worse with additional threads.
- System time required escalates with the number of threads as additional kernel intervention is required to resolve lock contention.

The following graph compares MT scaling across Tcl versions 8.4.19, and 8.5.14:

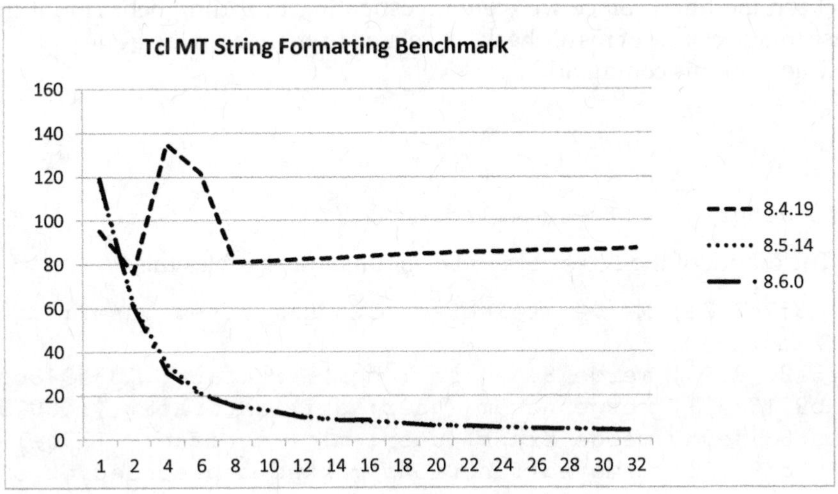

Figure 1: Application run time vs threads for Tcl 8.4, 8.5 and 8.6

When the stand alone test program was run against Tcl 8.5 and Tcl 8.6, the contention issue was not observed. That led to the question: What changed in Tcl that improved multi threading execution time? One other observation between Tcl versions 8.4, 8.5 and 8.6 was that the simple use of expr in a for loop was significantly slower in Tcl 8.5 and again slower in Tcl 8.6. This fact, along with the difficulty of porting a major application with over 1 million lines of Tcl code onto Tcl 8.5 or 8.6 led us to investigate finding the optimization and looking at the possibility of porting it back to Tcl 8.4.

2 Procedure

The benchmark program developed by Phil Brooks was used to characterize several Tcl check-ins. This benchmark performs a number of float-to-string conversions and allows the user to select the number of threads to use to perform the conversions.

The basic flow for performing the benchmarks was

```
For revision in List_Of_Fossil_Identifiers
  Checkout revision
  Build Tcl libraries
  Link benchmark with new libraries
```

```
Run benchmark and record results
```

The `fossil finfo` command will return a list of check-ins in which a file has been modified. Since we were investigating threading behavior, it made sense to collect a set of fossil check-ins related to changes in the `generic/tclThreadAlloc.c` module with this command.

```
> mkdir tcl
> cd tcl
> fossil open ../tcl.fos
> fossil finfo generic/tclThreadAlloc.c >../ThreadFiles.fo
```

The output of the `fossil finfo` command resembles this:

```
2012-11-26 [1d357d342e] Merge (selected bits of) novem (user: dgp, artifact:
        [2314c6d7b8])
2012-11-26 [45a2eb8ff0] merge 8.5 (user: dgp, artifact: [58f949bc42])
2012-11-26 [ab9713b5f1] merge novem (user: dkf, artifact: [1b8015a219])
2012-11-26 [cdc837ae05] merge trunk (user: mig, artifact: [59ce13b7e5])
2012-11-26 [6b2cf92413] Removed functions marked deprecated or obsolete for a
        long time: Tcl_Backslash, Tcl_EvalFile, Tcl_GlobalEvalObj,
        Tcl_GlobalEval, Tcl_EvalTokens. Remove Tcl_FindExecutable from
        ...
```

The useful lines are the ones that start with a date stamp. The numbers inside square braces are the identifier for this check-in. This set of numbers can be used with `fossil checkout` to check out a specific version of the Tcl source code.

This set of code examines the `finfo` output and checks out Tcl revisions in the order that they were checked into fossil.

```
set top $pwd
foreach l [split $d \n] {
  cd $top

  # extract first 10 characters
  set dt [string range $l 0 10]

  # Sudden death tests - if not date, or no values, skip
  if {[catch {clock scan $dt}]} {continue}
  if {[string trim $dt] eq ""} {continue}

  # If the line starts with a date, get the ID number
  set num [string range $l 12 21]

  # Clean up a folder for new checkout
  catch {exec rm -rf tcl}
  file mkdir tcl
  cd tcl
```

```
# Checkout
exec fossil open ../tcl.fos
exec fossil checkout $num
```

Tcl development is a continuous process on all of the active releases and branches. The chronology of check-ins does not reflect the release or position within a release.

This code snippet opens the `tcl.h` file in the newly checked out sources to find the version number associated with this code.

```
cd tcl
set if [open generic/tcl.h r]
set tclh [read $if]
close $if

regexp {TCL_VERSION[^"]*"([^"]+)} $tclh all rev
```

Once the code is extracted, it needs to be compiled. This is trivial with the TEA based make system and is easily automated.

While Tcl releases are very stable, not every check-in is guaranteed to work, or even compile, so the `make` is executed within a `catch` command.

```
cd unix
exec ./configure --enable-threads -enable-shared=0
set fail [catch {exec make} rtn]
```

The `fail` value is used to determine whether or not to build the benchmark. An application is not guaranteed to be linkable after the components have been successfully compiled, and an application that links doens't necessarily run. The `catch` command gets a lot of use in the sections of the script that make and run the benchmark.

```
  cd $benchFolder

  # Modify Makefile for current release
  exec sed s/REL/$id/g <Makefile.in >Makefile

  # Clean and rebuild benchmark
  catch {exec make clean}
  set fail [catch {exec make}]

  for {set ii 0} {$ii < $runCount} {incr ii} {
    set t1 [clock seconds]
    set fail [catch {exec ./mt_example_$id -tcl -s $count1} rtn]
    regexp {.*REAL TIME=([^ ]+) .*} $rtn aa measure

    # Calculate average
  }
```

The Tcl `time` command was used to evaluate the run time for the benchmark. To protect from system inconsistencies, the benchmark was run multiple times and the average time was used to calculate the ratio between 2 and 6 threads.

The process of checkout, compile and test is time consuming, but will complete in a single night. Once the results were collected, they were graphed as shown below, demonstrating the dramatic performance improvement.

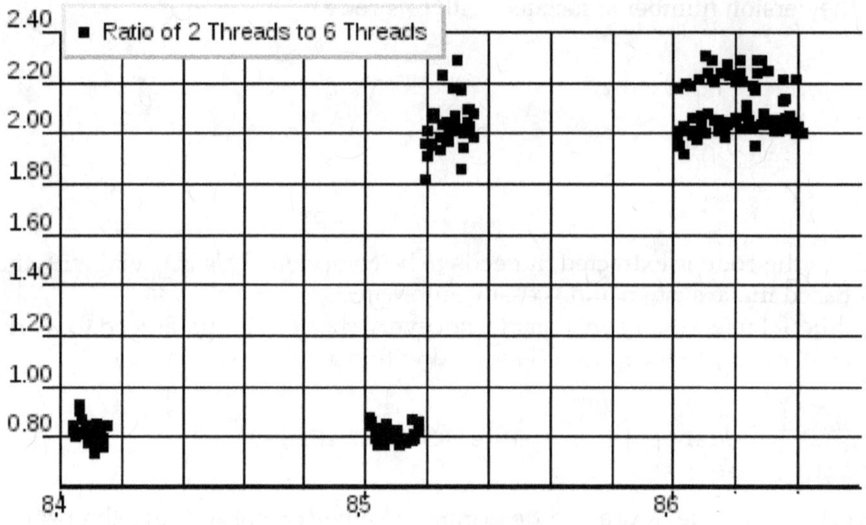

Figure 2: Runtime Ratio vs Tcl Release

The graph is nice for visualization, but does not show where the change occurred.

The raw data, however makes it fairly obvious:

```
...
3af2919289 8.5 RATIO 2.0
7ff2693241 8.5 RATIO 2.0
1cc2336920 8.5 RATIO 2.0
751ccc1989 8.5 RATIO 0.7
edf99c3880 8.5 RATIO 0.8
83aa957ebe 8.5 RATIO 0.8
...
```

In an ideal world, using 6 threads instead of using 2 threads would be result in a runtime reduced by a third, and the ratio would be 3. In the real world there are issues involved with making sure the threads don't collide, switching overhead, etc. The best improvement seen in this set of testing was a bit over 2.

However it's obvious that between the 751ccc1989 check-in and the 1cc2336920 the performance was improved. Examining the code changes, it turned out that the improved thread performance did not come from an improvement in the thread management code, but was a benefit from the merge of a large numerics reform branch.

2.1 Back-port

At this point, the search could easily continue by iterating the automated performance testing script on the merged numerics reform branch to find the precise change responsible. However, having narrowed the matter down to the changes in number handling was sufficient. For someone familiar with the structure and history of that portion of the Tcl source code, it is clear that the problem lies with the treatment of the `::tcl_precision` variable, and the improvement came with a strong move away from using that variable. Searching tools are a great assistant, but knowing the code-base is a key contributor as well.

The `::tcl_precision` variable has a long history in Tcl. It arrived in Tcl 7.0. Setting the variable to an integer value between 1 and 17 specified how many decimal digits of precision should be used when the routine `Tcl_PrintDouble` generates the string form of a floating point value. It had some value as a means to tune performance, with `sprintf()` presumably taking less time to generate shorter strings (and in the days when every value truly was a string, that could matter). However, its greater purpose is to shield unsophisticated Tcl programmers from some of the harsher realities of floating point arithmetic.

```
% expr {1.0/10}
0.10000000000000001
```

The aim is not unreasonable, but the error was in placing this feature in the heart of the value stream of Tcl, and not on the periphery where it would govern display matters only. The consequence over time was a large number of bug reports rooted in the fact that the operation of `::tcl_precision` was at odds with Tcl's value model that "Everything Is A String" (EIAS). An extreme example serves to demonstrate.

```
% set tcl_precision 1
1
% set third [expr {1.0/3}]
0.3
% set compare "0.3"
0.3
% string equal $third $compare
1
% expr {$third == $compare}
0
```

Two equal string values get treated as unequal by some Tcl commands. This is contrary to Tcl's value model that the string representation holds all the value there is to hold.

In the development of Tcl 8.5, one of the goals set and achieved was to make numeric values in Tcl properly conform to EIAS. Strictly speaking this is impossible to fully achieve while the `::tcl_precision` variable still exists and Tcl continues to follow the documented response to its value for sake of compatibility with existing scripts making use of it. (The example above uses a Tcl 8.6.0 interpreter.) However, the continued use of `::tcl_precision` is discouraged in the strongest terms, and the default setting is one that upholds EIAS and also avoids most of the shocking results that motivated its preservation through many earlier calls for its elimination.

```
% set tcl_precision
0
% expr {1.0/10}
0.1
```

Starting in Tcl 8, Tcl values are stored in a `Tcl_Obj` struct, and the `Tcl_PrintDouble` routine is normally only called for producing the string representation of a value of the `double` Tcl_ObjType. In this context, there is no Tcl_Interp to refer to, and so no way to pull a value out of any particular `::tcl_precision` variable. Consequently, in the Tcl 7 to Tcl 8 transition, the actual value controlling precision came to be stored outside of any interp, as one common static variable shared by the entire application. All the `::tcl_precision` variables in all the interps became ways to read and write that common global value through the magic of traces.

Then in Tcl 8.1, as the source code was revised to support multi-threaded operations, the common static variable holding an application wide value for controlling precision came to be shared among all threads, with mutex locking added to guarantee that all writes *and reads* of that value are serialized.

At this point the reader seasoned in multi-threaded programming is thinking "Aha! Of course multi-threaded performance collapses when every thread has significant amounts of double to string conversions to do!" The whole double to string machinery funnels through a serialization bottleneck. Relief came only in the development of Tcl 8.5, when two things happened. First, the entire subsystem for generating the decimal string representation of a floating point value was rewritten, changing the patterns of locking in a way that reduced the scaling problem. Second, an additional design change replaced the application-wide global value for controlling precision with a set of values, one for each thread. This eliminated any need for locking altogether.

Having identified the cause of the performance bottleneck, and the reasons that Tcl 8.5 and later avoid it, the next issue is what can be done in Tcl 8.4 to correct the problem. The solution came into 8.5 as part of a major subsystem rewrite. Forcing that into a patch release of Tcl 8.4 is contrary to the practice of making such major rewrites only with new minor versions. A simpler solution would be to back-port the shift from a single global value to a set of precision control values, one for each thread. However, this solution was avoided because it represents a level of compatibility change that exceeds the normal practice for patch level releases. The amount of incompatibility involved is just too great for those scripts that would notice.

Instead, a new solution was crafted, preserving the global precision control value, and improving performance by replacing the expensive simple-minded serialization scheme with a somewhat more complex scheme, but one far better matched to the actual needs and resulting in far better performance. In practice, the reads from the global precision control value are far more frequent than writes. A locking scheme that reduces the need for locking when only reading the value is highly effective in improving performance. The machinery to make this happen is an adapted back-port of the `ProcessGlobalValue` utility already used in Tcl 8.5 to manage other application-wide values like `[info hostname]` and `[info nameofexecutable]`.

A `ProcessGlobalValue` maintains a master string value, and also keeps a cached copy of that value in a Tcl_Obj for each thread. A master integer epoch value is also maintained, and a cached value of that epoch in each thread as well. When the master value is written, full mutex locks are used to serialize writes. The new master value is stored, and the master epoch is incremented. When there is a need to read the value, however, a scheme of epoch checking avoids the need for locks most of the time. The cached epoch value is compared with the master epoch value and so long as they are the same, the cached Tcl_Obj value is still valid, and the thread proceeds making use of it. Only when an epoch mismatch indicates that the master string value has been written since the last epoch check in a thread does the expense of a lock and a recopy from the master value to the thread cache take place, along with an update of the thread epoch value. This mechanism preserves the single global value that is a feature of Tcl 8.4, while bringing the cost of it down significantly. The patch to make this change was added, tested, and released as part of Tcl 8.4.20.

The change was incorporated into the original Calibre application and the resulting application performance clearly shows an improvement in scaling and continues to scale incrementally even with 32 threads running on a 32 way system as shown in the following graph:

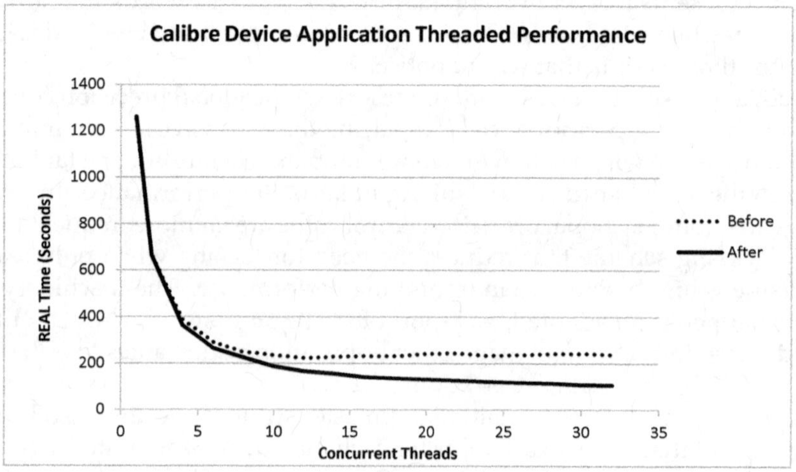

Figure 3: Application run time vs threads

2.2 Conclusion

Keeping Tcl users happy and improving the performance of the kernel is always good. What is interesting in this particular case is the techniques used to identify the time when a performance change occurred using a scripted set of checkouts and builds, and the cooperation of three entities (the three authors) in identifying the problem, reducing the problem set, and fixing the issue.

The technique of using a set of scripts to checkout, configure, build, test is fairly obvious and is applicable to any performance study. The scripts that checked out versions of the Tcl interpreter and built multiple copies are relatively simple.

2.3 Future Work

The scripts used to run this set of benchmarks have been modified and extended in a larger study of the behavior of Tcl with the `tclbench` suite to characterize Tcl behavior over a larger number of subsystems.

Tcl 2013
New Orleans, LA
September 23-27, 2013

Session III

September 25, 2013
3:00-4:30pm

TAO/TK

A TclOO Based Toolkit for GUI Design

Presented at the 20th Annual Tcl Developer's Conference (Tcl'2013)
New Orleans, LA
September 23-27, 2013

Sean Deely Woods
Senior Developer
Test and Evaluations Solutions, LLC
400 Holiday Court
Suite 204
Warrenton, VA 20185

Table of Contents

Introduction

In this paper, I will describe TAO/TK, a comprehensive architecture for implementing user interfaces, control systems, and machine learning. TAO is a dialect of TclOO. TAO builds on TclOO and adds its own notations and policies in a way that allows it to interact with other TclOO code.

TAO adds features that are required to make complex systems of related classes easier. TAO's main feature is passing data through inheritance as well as code. TAO/TK extends TAO into a more familiar set of widget and megawidgets.

TAO/TK requires Sqlite and Tcl 8.6.

Interoperability with TclOO

Behind the scenes, TAO classes are really TclOO classes. They just have a few extra methods, and additional introspection via the TAO internal database. It is perfectly reasonable to have a TAO object list a TclOO object as a superclass, and *vice versa*.

```
oo::class create foo {
}
::tao::class bar {
  superclass foo
  method someop args {
    return some
  }
}
oo::class create baz {
  superclass bar
}
```

All of the TclOO introspection tools are usable on TAO objects and classes:

```
info class definition bar someop
> args {
>   return some
>}
```

In short, TAO is intended to be an additive extension to TclOO. It does not break or otherwise force the user to alter his/her way of doing things if they are already familiar with TclOO.

TAO Parser

Some of you may remember my paper from 2006 on my concept of TAO. TAO, then, was my answer to problems I had encountered with [Incr Tcl], and was essentially Pure-Tcl code, with a syntactic sugar parser, and held together with Sqlite.

And aside from the name and the fact that, yet again I seem to have invented a syntactic sugar parser held together with Sqlite, there aren't many similarities between the two projects.

The code that can be implemented is not the real code, after all. ;-)

TAO has been reinvented using TclOO at it's core. To introduce new keywords and design patterns all TAO code passes through the TAO Parser. The TAO Parser borrows heavily from the TclOO parser. Several TclOO keywords are intercepted and their contents logged into an in-memory sqlite database. Wholly new keywords string together a series of TclOO calls and sql queries to produce TAO code.

The TAO parser operates in it's own namespace: ::tao. The ::tao::class command works like a combination of ::oo::class create and ::oo::define. It will either create a new class, or modify an existing one.

```
::tao::class foo {
  # Works just like TclOO class
  # definitions
  method noop args {
    return {}
  }
}
::tao::class bar {
  superclass foo
  method someop args {
    return some
  }
}
```

Unlike in TclOO, the command tao::class is not actually an object. It's a procedure that implements the parser. If you didn't know already, in TclOO the very keyword used to create a class is itself a class, thus why you have to give it a method to work on. (Either create or new.)

Operation of the Tao Parser

The TAO parser operates in 3 main phases:

Parse the incoming class

Code submitted to the **tao::class** command is passed to the **::tao::parser** namespace for digestion. Each keyword is read, and a picture of the new class is developed. At the same time, the raw TclOO form of the new class is being built using **oo::define**.

Apply dynamically generated methods.

Once the picture of the new class is developed, the parser adds dynamically generated methods. These methods include the **property** method and method ensembles.

Update affected classes

After the class is parsed, built, and the dynamic methods area applied, the parser looks to see if the new definition of the class will affect any already existing decedents of this class. It then regenerates the dynamic methods for all of those descendents.

Properties

```
::tao::class animal {
  property tkingdom Animalia
  property has_spine 0
}
::tao::class vertebrate {
  superclass animal
  property torder Chordata
  property has_spine 1
}
::tao::class mammal {
  superclass vertebrate
  property tclass Mammalia
  property has_fur 1
}
::tao::class carnivore {
  superclass mammal
  property torder Canivora
}
::tao::class feline {
  superclass carnivore
  property tfamily Felidae
}
::tao::class felis {
  superclass feline
  property tgenus Felis
}
```

In a complex system where a rule has to be written to handle a range of different classes of objects, it is often useful to be able to refer to some meta-information within the object. It is also helpful to have that meta-information inherited along with the methods.

In this above example, we are creating the taxonomic classification of the common housecat. In that classification, we are seeding some useful traits that will be passed along to descendents of the class above.

The idea being that by the time we get down to putting together the final leaf classes, the code is simply:

```
::tao::class housecat {
  superclass felis
  property tspecies domesticus
}
```

And should a question arise, all objects of that class can answer based in information inherited by ancestral classes.

```
housecat create Thomas
Thomas property torder
> Chordata
Thomas property has_fur
> 1
Thomas property has_backbone
> 1
```

Inheritance

The inheritance mechanism for TAO mimics the behavior of inheritend in TclOO. Under TclOO, when searching for a method implementation, the last method defined is the method that is used. Because the parser runs outside of TclOO, TAO must recreate that process for database queries.

The routine essentially calls **[info class superclasses]** on the subject of inquiry. Because **[info class ancestors]** returns only the immediate heritage specified by the **superclass** keyword, TAO must repeat the process on every ancestor, and ancestor's ancestor.

Every class we have scanned is added to our result, but only the first time it is encountered. If an ancestor is inherited through multiple paths, subsequent references it is ignored.

The result is a list starting from the most advanced, and stepping back to the most primitive of every class that has had an impact on the present class.

The implementation is here:

```
proc ::tao::class_ancestors {
  class {stackvar {}}
} {
  if { $stackvar ne {} } {
    upvar 1 $stackvar stack
  } else {
    set stack {}
  }
  if { $class in $stack } {
    return {}
  }
  stack push stack $class
  if {![catch {
    ::info class superclasses $class
  } ancestors]} {
    foreach ancestor $ancestors {
      class_ancestors $ancestor stack
    }
  }
  if {![catch {
   ::info class mixins $class
  } ancestors]} {
    foreach ancestor $ancestors {
      class_ancestors $ancestor stack
    }
  }
  return $stack
}
```

TAO performs a database query on every property defined for each ancestor, in the order given by **tao::class_ancestors**. A new property is added to a data structure for the class we are parsing if no such property was defined before:

```
proc ::tao::dynamic_methods_property {
  class ancestors
} {
 set info {}
 foreach ancestor $ancestors {
   ::tao::db eval {
SELECT property,type,dict FROM property
WHERE class=:ancestor and defined=:ancestor
} {
    if {
      [dict exists $info $type $property]
    } continue
    dict set info $type $property $dict
   } ; # End of query
 } ; # End of foreach
 # At this point $info contains the complete
 # picture
```

Property Types

Constant properties, being the most common, have the simplest notation. However, constant properties are just one type that TAO supports. To use one of the other property types, specify an additional argument. When the property keyword sees 4 arguments, the third is interpreted as the type of property.

```
::tao::class housecat {
 property dob option {
  storage date
 }
 property age eval {my Age}

 method Age {} {
   set dob [date_to_julian [my cget dob]]
   set now [today_julian]
   return [expr {($now-$dob)/365}]
 }
}
Thomas configure -dob 2010/01/01
# Assuming we ask on 2013/09/01
Thomas property age
> 3
```

A complete table of supported types is as follows:

Type	Description
`const`	A property that always returns a constant
`eval`	A property whose value is generated by evaluating a command run within the object's namespace.
`subst`	A property whose value is generated by evaluating an expression run through subst.
`variable`	A property whose value is retrieved from an internal variable of the same name.
`option`	A property which is treated as an option. See ***Option Handling***.
`signal`	A property which is treated as a signal. See Signals.

Method Ensembles

For large projects, it is often useful to be able to clump similar functions together. At the same time, it's nice to be able to pop and swap chunks of that ensemble to handle the intricacies of your class system.

TAO has a method ensemble system. If the parser detects a method with a "::" in the name, it assumes the portion before the "::" is the ensemble, and after the "::" is the submethod. Method ensembles submethods are inherited by descendents, and descendents can override or extend the ensemble with their own submethods.

```
::tao::class vertebrate {
 superclass animal
 method has::spine {} {
   return 1
 }
}
::tao::class human {
 superclass vertebrate
}
::tao::class politician {
 superclass human
 # ^ Though that may be debatable
 method has::spine {} {
   error {Define "spine"}
 }
}
```

Because Method Ensembles are dynamically generated, a method ensemble will trump a normal method. Any attempt to implement "has" as a bare method in a descendent will simply be ignored:

```
::tao::class lawyer.honest {
  superclass lawyer
  method has {field value} {
    if { $value eq "spine" } { return 1 }
    …
  }
}
layer.honest create mrsmith
mrsmith has spine
> ERROR: Define "spine"
```

Method Ensemble Implementation

Ensemble submethods are tracked and catalogued by the TAO database. After the class is parsed, TAO builds a series of dynamically generated methods. Method ensembles are built during this stage.

Structurally, method ensembles are really a switch statement. Each body of the switch statement is the version of the submethod from the most recent ancestor that defined one.

The default for an ensemble is to throw an error when given an unknown submethod. This can be overridden by providing a **default** submethod. The **default** submethod is guaranteed to be the last evaluated. The method that was given on the command line is preserved as the **$method** variable.

```
# An example catch-all for the has method
::tao::class moac {
  method has::default {} {
    return [string is true -strict \
      [my property $method]]
  }
}
```

If we peer inside the **has** method, we can see how it works:

```
info class definition politician has
{method args} {
switch $method {
  <list> { return {spine} }
  spine {
::tao::dynamic_arguments {} {*}$args
   error {Define "spine"}
  }
  default {
    return [string is true -strict \
      [my property $method]]
  }
}
```

As you can see, in addition to the submethods we have defined in the parser and **default**, our ensemble includes an additional submethod **<list>**. **<list>** provides a list of all of the valid submethods for the ensemble for this particular class.

Method Ensemble Argument Handling

From our code listing above, you well see a call to **tao::dynamic_arguments**. **tao::dynamic_arguments** is a routine that reads the arguments beyond the method name given to the ensemble, and converts them into the local variables. The intent is to mimic the argument handling behavior of the **proc** command. If too many arguments, or not enough arguments are given, **tao::dynamic_arguments** will throw an error.

If the *arglist* ends with *args*, any number of arguments beyond the mandatory ones will be added to a list called args. If the *arglist* ends with *dictargs*, any arguments beyond the mandatory ones are placed into a key/value list called *dictargs*. If one argument is given to *dictargs*, that argument is assumed to be a key/value list.

The following example demonstrates the various ways Method Ensembles will accept input via *dictargs*. The **::character::bio** method parrots back the input it is given.

```
::tao::class show {
 method character::bio {who dictargs} {
   if {[dict exists $dictargs phrase]} {
     set phrase [dict get $dictargs phrase]
   } else {
     set phrase {}
   }
   puts [list $subject says $phrase]
 }
}
# Not enough arguments
show create addams
addams character bio
> ERROR: Usage: who ?dictargs?

# Arguments given after the mandatory.
addams character bio fester \
  phrase {Light Bulb}
> fester says {Light Bulb}

# Arguments packed into a key/value list as
# the first args
addams character bio lurch \
 {phrase {Good Evening}}
> lurch says {Good Evening}

# And it even does dashes!
adama character bio mortisha \
  -subject {Mon Cher}
> mortisha says {Mon Cher}
```

Class Methods

The **class_method** keyword creates a method which operates only on the class object itself. It's like calling **oo::objdefine**, and defining an instance method for the class object. But unlike **oo::objdefine**, **class_method** is passed on to descendents of the class.

A modified version of the ***property*** method is included with all TAO classes. It provides the meta-data and constant value properties of the object version. It doesn't, however, supply any of the properties that require gazing into the state of the object.

The most immediate example if a class method I have is in taotk's user widgets. We trap the **unknown** handler, and detect if the first argument, instead of being create or new is a tkpath:

```
# Example
taotk::frame .foo
```

```
tao::class taotk::frame {
  class_method unknown args {
    set tkpath [lindex $args 0]
    if {[string index $tkpath 0] eq "."} {
      if {[winfo exists $tkpath]} {
        error "Bad path name $tkpath"
      }
      set obj [my new $tkpath \
         {*}[lrange $args 1 end]]
      if {![winfo exists $tkpath]} {
        catch {$obj destroy}
        return {}
      }
      $obj tkalias $tkpath
      return $tkpath
    }
  }
}
```

This could also work if we did it such:

```
oo::class create Frame {
}
oo::define Frame method unknown args {
  method unknown args {
    set tkpath [lindex $args 0]
    if {[string index $tkpath 0] eq "."} {
      if {[winfo exists $tkpath]} {
        error "Bad path name $tkpath"
      }
      set obj [my new $tkpath \
         {*}[lrange $args 1 end]]
      if {![winfo exists $tkpath]} {
        catch {$obj destroy}
        return {}
      }
      $obj tkalias $tkpath
      return $tkpath
    }
  }
}
```

The idea being that with either case, the class behaves like a Tk command:

```
taotk::frame .foo
Frame .bar
```

The difference comes in when we assume this behavior is inherited by descendents:

```
tao::class create taotk::customFrame {
   superclass ::taotk::frame
}
oo::class create CustomFrame {
   superclass Frame
}

taotk::customframe .baz
CustomFrame .bang
> ERROR. Uknown command .baz.
> Valid: create new
```

Like properties and method ensembles, Class Methods are tracked in the database and applied with the other dynamically generated methods.

The DB Backend

TAO uses an in-memory database to index classes and track classes, methods and properties. The database uses sqlite, and can be accessed directly via the **::tao::db** command. A complete schema is available in Appendix, under TAO DB Schema.

If we combine class properties with database backend, we can do some useful searches throughout our library of classes.

```
# Example, find all animals that are
# carnivores
set result {}
tao::db eval {select name from class} {
  if {
    [$name property torder]
    eq "Canivora"
  } {
    lappend result $name
  }
}
```

You may be asking, "Why didn't you just pull the property from the database directly?" Ok:

```
Select class from property where
property='torder' and dict='Carnivora';
> carnivore
-- We only get back the one class where the
-- property was defined
select property,dict from property where
class='carnivore';
> torder|Carnovora
-- We only defined the one property for
-- that class
```

Now, if we ask the property method:

```
carnivore property const dict
> tkingdom Animalia torder Chordata
> has_spine 1 tclass Mammalia has_fur 1
> torder Carnivora
```

We see that the property method's picture includes the most recent ancestor's copy of every property that has been inherited.

Class Regeneration

Every ancestor of every class is indexed in the *ancestry* table, along with which order. That index makes looking up all of the descendents of a class quite simple.

Included with the class table is a simple flag **regenerate**. When the flag is true, the class needs to be regenerated. In the example above, at the conclusion of the **tao::class** command, every class that listed **carnivore** as an ancestors was marked

regenerate=1. After the affected classes are marked, a search is run, and the regenerate flag is rippled out to all descendents of descendents, and so on. When that is complete, the parser re-creates all of the dynamic methods for all classes with the **regenerate** flag. And the process of regenerating the dynamic methods marks each class as **regenerate=0** once more.

Modifications to a class are seemingly instant as far as the Tcl environment is concerned. If we add a property of *has_teeth* to carnivores:

```
tao::class carnivore {
property has_teeth 1
}
carnivore property const dict
> tkingdom Animalia torder Chordata
> has_spine 1 tclass Mammalia has_fur 1
> torder Carnivora has_teeth 1
```

Thomas, our **housecat** several examples, now has teeth:

```
Thomas property has_teeth
> 1
```

If we had asked that before we defined *has_teeth*, the property method would have returned a null.

The Variable keyword

TAO also provides a keyword **variable** that works differently than the **variable** keyword in TclOO. In TclOO, **variable** allows a variable to magically appear in every method of that class (but not descendents.) In TAO **variable** declares a variable and sets it's default. That declaration and default will carry through to descendents. To access that variable, one still needs to use the **my variable** command in methods.

```
tao::class animal {
  variable hungry 0
  method is::hungry {} {
    my variable hungry
    return $hungry
  }
}
Thomas is hungry
> 0
```

The Mother of all Classes

All TAO objects descend from a single class: **moac**, the Mother of All Classes. The **moac** provides methods which enforce TAO policies and design patterns. This next section is intended as an overview of the key features. A complete reference is located in the Appendix.

Default Constructor

The Default constructor for the moac is as follows:

```
constructor args {
  my InitializePublic
  my configurelist \
    [::tao::args_to_options {*}$args]
  my initialize
}
```

The **InitializePublic** method initializes all of the variables declared in the class definition as well as provides default values for all options. The next step is to run **configurelist** on the options fed in through args. Finally, the **initialize** method is called. **initialize** is intended to be a place for developers to be able to insert their code and know that all of the variables have been initialized and the object has been configured, and configurations applied without having to recreate all of the steps in their own constructor or figure out the right incantations of **[next]** to call an ancestral constructor.

Constructor Option Syntax

The **::tao::args_to_options** procedure uses the following rules to allow it to work with this range of inputs:

1. Arguments, beyond the mandatory arguments, are considered options.
2. All options must be given in the form of key/value pairs
3. If a single argument for *args* is given, that argument is assumed to be a key/value list of options.
4. Leading dashes (-) are stripped from keys

Option Handling

Options are tracked as a special kind of property. The "value" for Options are specified in Dict format, because we need to track a lot more than a constant value. For convenience, the **option** keyword was added to the TAO parser as a shortcut.

```
::tao::class housecat {
  superclass felis
  property gender option {
    widget select storage string default {}
    values {{} male female}
  }
  option weight {
    widget scale units kg range {0 10}
  }
}
```

With the modification above, we can specify the animal's weight and gender at creation time:

```
housecat create Thomasina \
 -gender female -weight 8
```

And we can modify an existing object via the **configure** command:

```
housecat configure Thomas \
  -gender male -weight 10
```

Because in large systems one may need to perform a dump of information from a database or some other source, TAO is pretty flexible about the format of options.

```
housecat create Thomas {
  gender male weight 10
}
housecat create Thomasina \
 gender female weight 8
# After a year of snacking
Thomas configure weight 11
# Showing off
db eval {select * from animals where
species='cat'} {
 housecat create ::cat#$uuid [db eval {
    select key,value from attributes where
    uuid=:uuid
 }]
}
```

Option Properties

The TAO parser specifies the following rules for elements given within an option-dict:

Option	Description
class	Reference to another option or option class to clone
default	The default value for the option
default-script	A script to use to generate the default value. If both default and default-script are present, default-script is used. See: `Option Substitution`.
description	A human readable comment.
get-command	Script to retrieve the value in lieu of storing the value internally: See: `Option Substitution`.
set-command	Script to set the value externally in lieu of storing the value internally. See: `Option Substitution`.
storage	Storage type for C, sql, etc.
validate-command	Script used to validate incoming values before they are incorporated into the state of the object.
values	Specifies a finite list of possible values for the option.
values-command	Specified a command to generate the list of finite values. If both values and values-command are specified, values-command is used. See: `Option Substitution`.
widget	Widget to use when generating an automated GUI. See `Dynamic Widgets`

Option Substitution

In Tk what information is sent along with a –command option is often widget specific. Many handlers for options need to work over a range of options. Some need to specify an elaborate path that includes the name of the field, the object, and/or the new value. Rather than force the developer to follow a template, TAO allows the developer to specify how information is sent to scripts in the option dict. It works in a mechanism similar to the substitution used by the Tk bind command:

Field	Substitution
%self%	The object's name
%field%	The field that triggered the script
%value%	The value being input (when appropriate)

```
::tao::class housecat {
  option favorite_food {
    set-command {
 puts {%self%'s favorite %field% is %value%}
    }
  }
}
Thomas configure favorite_food tuna
> ::Thomas's favorite food is tuna
```

Option Classes

Developers often find that options follow a certain template. TAO provides for option templates with the **class** property of options. **class** can specify the name of another option. To create an option which is simply a prototype, use the **option_class** keyword.

```
::tao::class animal {
  option_class variable {
    default {}
    set-command {
   my variable %field% ; set %field% %value%
   puts "%field% is now %value%"
     }
     get-command {
   my variable %field% ;return [set %field%]
    }
  }
}
tao::class housecat {
  option color {
    class variable default black
  }
  method color {} {
    my variable color ; return $color
  }
}
Thomas configure color orange
> color is now orange
Thomas color
> orange
```

Option Event Processing

To keep the outcome of events tied to modifying an option consistent, TAO enforces the following order of operations:

1. **validate-command** is run for all incoming values with the property specified. If an error is thrown, the process is aborted without modifying the object. If the problem is encountered in the constructor, the object is destroyed and an error thrown.
2. The **set-command** is run for all incoming values with the property specified. No local value for the option is kept.
3. For values for which the **set-command** property is null, the new value is saved as a dict element in a local variable *config*.

For calls to the configure command, but not during the constructor, the **Option_set** ensemble is called for all incoming values.

If we want an event to fire off after we set the weight for instance:

```
::tao::class housecat {
   method Option_set::weight newvalue {
     if {$newvalue > 10 } {
       puts "This cat is fat!"
     }
   }
}
Thomas configure -weight 12
> This cat is fat!
```

By default, normal descendents of **moac** will accept unknown options. Descendents of **::taotk::meta::widget** will throw an error on unknown options. The developer can control the behavior of their class with the **options_strict** property.

```
::tao::class housecat {
  property options_strict 1
}
Thomas configure unknownoption 10
> Error unknown option -unknownoption.
Valid: gender weight color favorite_food
::tao::class housecat {
  property options_strict 0
}
Thomas configure unknownoption 10
# No error, and we can retrieve the value
Thomas cget unknownoption
> 10
```

Forwarding and Grafting

The **moac** also provides a set of functions to manage forwarding methods. The simplest is **forward**. Forward is just a simple call to **::oo::objectdefine forward**.

```
Thomas forward puts ::puts
Thomas puts "Hello World"
> Hello World
```

Often times, though, we need to recall what it is we are forwarding to. While TclOO will tell you that a method is a forward vs. any other type of method, it won't tell you where the call is going.

TAO provides the **graft** method, which forwards a command while at the same time recording where it's going. The destination can be retrieved later via the **organ** method.

```
tao::class supertextbox {
  constructor {tkpath} {
     toplevel $tkpath
     my graft toplevel $tkpath
     text $tkpath.text
     my graft text $tkpath.text
  }
  method title newtitle {
    set tl [my organ toplevel]
    wm $tl title $newtitle
  }
  method replacetext {newtext} {
    my <text> delete 0.0 end
    my <text> insert end $newtext
  }
}
```

In the above example, we graft both the toplevel window and the text widget. In the **newtitle** method, we need to pass the path to the window to **wm**. we use the **organ** method to retrieve the value for *toplevel*. In **replacetext** we need to manipulate the text widget. We use the grafted name to address the text widget as though it were one of our own methods.

The **replacetext** method could also have been written:

```
tao::class supertextbox {
  method replacetext {newtext} {
    my text delete 0.0 end
    my text insert end $newtext
  }
}
```

Graft creates two forwarded methods, the original name, and the <original name>. I find marking which methods are going out to a forward somewhat useful. However, we also need the plaintext version because TclOO will not allow a method to be accessed from the public interface if it does not start with a lower case letter.

Locks, Signals, and Notifications

The **moac** defines several methods, and parser keywords to manage locks, signals, and notifications.

Locks

Locks were designed as a guard against an object recursively calling pipeline routines. **lock create** can behave like the classic "up" operator in a semaphore. When you call the lock the first time, the operation returns false. If the lock was already present, it returns true.

```
::tao::class foo {
  method lock_demo {} {
    # Lock create only returns 1 if the
    # lock is already engaged
    if {[my lock create [self method]]} {
      # I must already be running
      return
    }
    … (Some elaborate action)
    my lock remove [self method]
  }
}
```

Because lock is a public method, other objects and system calls can lock and unlock an object.

After the last lock is removed, the object looks to see if it was passed any signals.

Internally, locks are simply a list stored in a variable *ActiveLocks*. The **lock create** method ensures that only one copy of a lock is present in the list at any given time.

Signals

Signals break a menagerie of tasks into discrete pieces that can be received piecemeal and assembled together into a single pipeline of operations.

The **signal** keyword in a class declares a signal. Like options, signals have a descriptor key/value list. Signals are also inherited just like properties and options. Signals have the following properties:

Option	Description
apply_action	Action to perform reflexively when the signal is passed to the object
action	Command to be performed during this stage in the pipeline.
aliases	List of names that this signal will respond to
description	Human readable comment.
excludes	List of signals that this signal prevents from running in the current pipeline.
preceeds	List of signals that this signal must preceed in the pipeline
follows	List of signals that this signal must come after in the pipeline
triggers	List of signals that this signal triggers

For a simple example, let's have an object either fish or cut bait.

```
::tao::class fisherman {
  signal fish {
    follows cut_bait
    triggers cut_bait
    action {my action fish}
  }
  signal cut_bait {
    action {my action cut_bait}
  }
  variable has_bait 0
}
```

As we can see, the fisherman can either be fishing, or he/she can be cutting bait. To fish, the cut_bait signal must be satisfied.

To see our cunning plan in action:

```
::tao::class fisherman {
  variable has_bait 0
  method action::fish {
    my variable has_bait
    if { $has_bait == 0 } {
      error "I have no bait"
    }
    puts "Fishing"
    # Do the fishing
    set has_bait 0
  }
  method action::cut_bait {} {
    my variable has_bait
    set has_bait 1
    puts "Cutting Bait"
  }
}
```

```
fisherman gordan
gordan action fish
> error: I have no bait
gordan signal fish
gordan lock remove_all
Cutting Bait
Fishing
```

Signal_Pipeline

When the last lock is removed from an object, it automatically schedules a call to a method called **Signal_Pipeline**. **Signal_Pipeline** figures out which signals have been called, which signals need to be triggered or suppressed as a result, as well as the order in which they need to be executed. It then executes that plan before returning.

Notifications

Notifications are a message passing system for objects. They are akin to Tk bindings. Objects can both emit and receive notifications.

In the case of emitting an event, it simply passes the message to the TAO message handler. The TAO core then looks through subscriptions to find what objects would be interested in receiving a message of that type from the sender object. With list in hand, TAO goes about calling the **notify** ensemble for each recipient with the sender, type, and content of the message.

If we extend our fisherman example, about, lets add a notification to the fisherman that a fish is on the line.

```
::tao::class fisherman {
 notify::fish_on {snd dictargs} {
   set caught [dict get $dictargs caught_by]
   if { $caught ne [self] } continue
   set fish [dict get $dictargs fish]
   my action catch_fish $fish
 }
}
```

For the fisherman, we need to set up a handler for **fish_on** messages. Because messages are broadcast, we embed the **caught_by** field in the message. Thus, if we overhear another fisherman's **fish_on** we don't do something a rude and uncouth as to harvest it.

Let us assume we have a pond object that is responsible for pairing fish with baited hooks.

```
::tao::class pond {
 method time_step {} {
   foreach fisherman [my list_fishermen] {
     if {![my catch_criterial $fisherman]} {
        # No fish caught
       continue
     }
     # Generate the fish
     set species [my random_species]
     set fish [$species -size random]
     # Hook it on the line
     my event_publish fish_on $fisherman
     set msg {}
     dict set msg fish $fish
     dict set msg species $species
     dict set msg size [$fich cget size]
     dict set msg caught_by $fisherman
     my event generate fish_on  $msg
   }
  }
}
```

The pond sets up a publication with an intended target of the fisherman. It then assembles the outbound message as a dict. And finally it broadcasts the message.

Setup, Cleanup and Renaming

Object names are tracked by the TAO message handling system. As such, the system needs to be notified if an object is destroyed or renamed.

To facilitate this, the TAO parser secretly adds a line to the top of every classes destructor which calls the **::tao::object_destroy** procedure. This procedure scrubs the notification system of all subscriptions, publications, and bindings.

When an object is renamed, developers are encouraged to use the **::tao::object_rename** procedure. This prodedure updates the references in the notification table to the new name.

[namespace code {}]

TAO developers need to take care when binding objects for events. Objects can, and do, change names.

Let's suppose we are binding a command to a button. In pure Tcl, this is easy, we tell the system to call back at a given command name:

```
button .foo -command some_command
```

With namespaces, we need to be a little more elaborate.

```
namespace eval ::foo {
   button .foo -command ::foo::some_command
}
```

Inside of a class method, if the object wants to exercises one of its own methods, it needs to provide a path. The technique that immediately comes to mind for most developers is the **[self]** command.

```
oo::class define myobject {
 method makebutton {} {
   button .foo -command \
     [list [self] some_command]
 }
}
```

I am here to tell you there is a better way. Many of you may not be familiar with the **namespace code** command. **namespace code** captures the environment in which it was called, and provides a globalized return path.

```
oo::class define myobject {
 method makebutton {} {
   button .foo -command \
     [namespace code {my some_command}]
 }
}
```

While an object can change names, it will never change namespaces. (Besides, this is TAO, and the name that can be stored isn't the real name anyway ;-)

Here is a rigged demo of the phenomenon. We have a silly class that can delay calling one of its methods through the Tcl event loop. We will use two different approaches to mapping the global path back to our intended call.

- The **delayed_nspace** method takes in a method as an argument and schedules a callback to that method using **namespace code**.
- The **delayed_self** method takes in a method as an argument and schedules a callback to that method using **self**.

They both also advertise which method sent the event via the **[self method]** mechanism, so we can track what is going on.

```
tao::class silly {
  method gratification {{how {}}} {
    return "[self] Ahhh $how"
  }

  method delayed_nspace m {
   after idle \
 [namespace code [list my $m [self method]]]
  }

  method delayed_self m {
    after idle \
      [list [self] $m [self method]]]
  }
}
```

For normal purposes, both techniques work the same way.

```
silly create whosit
whosit gratification
> ::whosit Ahhhh
whosit delayed_nspace gratification ; update
> ::whosit Ahhhh delayed_nspace
whosit delayed_self gratification ; update
> ::whosit Ahhhhh delayed_self
```

Now we will trigger the events, but change the name before we give the event loop a chance to respond.

```
whosit delayed_nspace gratification
whosit delayed_self gratification
rename whosit whatsit
update
> ::whatsit Ahhhh delayed_nspace
> BGERROR: Invalid command "whosit"
```

namespace code has other advantages. Unlike calls to **[self]**, the event can call private methods.

```
tao::class silly {
  method Gratification {{how {}}} {
    return "[self] AHHH $how"
  }
}

whatsit delayed_nspace Gratification
update
> ::whatsit Ahhhh delayed_nspace
whatsit delayed_self Gratification
update
> BGERROR: unknown method Gratification must
be…
```

TAO/TK

TAO/TK is a GUI extension to TAO, geared toward the creation and operation of graphical user interfaces in Tk. TAO classes come in three distinct forms:

1. *Meta Classes*, intended to be the building blocks for other classes.
2. *User Widgets*, classes intended to be called directly by the end user and behave like a Tk widget.
3. *Dynamic Widgets*, a special class of widgets designed for data entry screens.

Meta Classes

In UI design, there is often the need/desire/lazy tendency to lump similar functions together. Very often though, this code re-use is only helpful on a high-level. Meta classes are method and properties that are inherited by other classes, but which don't make a complete product in their own right.

For coding consistency, TAO/TK meta classes are located in the **taotk::meta** namespace.

User Widgets

User Widgets are designed to be readily useable as a Tk-Like command. Borrowing from the tradition started by tile, TAO/TK widgets are located in their won namespace, **::taotk.** They operate just like any other widget:

```
::taotk::browser .html -title {About:Blank}
```

To make TAO/TK widgets behave like the Tk commands developers are familiar with, we use the unknown handler built into TclOO.

```
class_method unknown args {
  set tkpath [lindex $args 0]
  if {[string index $tkpath 0] eq "."} {
    if {[winfo exists $tkpath]} {
      error "Bad path name $tkpath"
    }
    set obj [my new $tkpath \
       {*}[lrange $args 1 end]]
    if {![winfo exists $tkpath]} {
      catch {$obj destroy}
      return {}
    }
    $obj tkalias $tkpath
    return $tkpath
  }
  next {*}$args
}
```

The **tkalias** method renames the Tk object to something in the object's namespace, and then renames the object to take the Tk object's place. When the object is destroyed, the native Tk object will be destroyed along with it. Even though the Tk object's command has been renamed, it still behaves within TK as if it had never been moved.

```
method tkalias tkname {
  set oldname $tkname
  my variable tkalias
  set tkalias $tkname
  set self [self]
  set nativewidget [::info object \
    namespace $self]::tkwidget
  my graft nativewidget $nativewidget
  rename ::$tkalias $nativewidget
  ::tao::object_rename [self] ::$tkalias
  my bind_widget $tkalias
  return $nativewidget
}
```

The **bind_widget** method ensures that when Tk destroys the widget, the object's destructor is called.

```
method bind_widget window {
  my graft topframe $window
  my graft toplevel \
    [winfo toplevel $window]
  bind $window <Destroy> \
   [namespace code {my EventDestroy %W}]
}
```

The **EventDestroy** method is a sanity check. When <Destroy> goes off, it is possible for a parent to see the <Destroy> event for it's children. Also, there are times where the only notification that goes out to a child window is that the toplevel window to was destroyef. It took a bit of trial and error to get this part right.

```
method EventDestroy window {
  if { [string match "${window}*" $w] } {
    my destroy
  }
}
```

Conversely, our destructor needs to destroy the Tk object when called. But because the developer may have his/her own destructor logic, the smarts for this process have been packed into a private method. It is the destructor's job to call that private method at some point.

Before we destroy the native Tk widget, we use the **unbind_widget** method to remove our bindings to prevent the *<Destroy>* binding for the Tk object from calling the destructor yet again.

```
destructor {
   my Widget_destructor
 }

 method unbind_widget window {
   my variable tkalias
   if {[winfo exists $window]} {
     bind $window <Destroy> {}
   }
   set tkalias {}
 }

 method Widget_destructor {} {
   my variable tkalias
   set alias $tkalias
   if {$alias ne {}} {
     my unbind_widget $alias
   }
   catch {my action destroy}
   # Destroy an alias we may have created
   if { $alias ne {} && \
     [winfo exists $alias] } {
       catch {
  rename [namespace current]::tkwidget {}
       }
   } else {
     catch {
     ::destroy [my organ nativewidget]}
     }
   }
 }
```

Dynamic Widgets

Dynamic Widgets are designed for producing automated data entry screens. They are designed to obey a limited set of commands, and fit into a relatively rigid template

1. Every element to be tracked is an field in a global array
2. For every element, a key/value list of metadata is provided to the constructor.
3. The path specified will become a frame containing the tk objects that implement the UI representation of the element.

The syntax boils down to:

```
taotk::dynamic_widget tkpath fieldname \
   arrayname properties
```

Let's see an example:

```
toplevel .foo
array set ::record {
   message {Have nice day}
}
taotk::dynamic_widget .foo.bar \
  message ::record {}
grid .foo.bar
```

And we get back and entry box (the default if we have no other data):

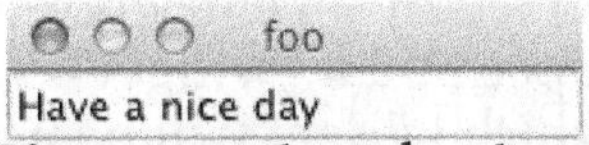

If we just alter the description, we get different behavior.

```
set ::record(weather) sunny

taotk::dynamic_widget .foo.baz weather \
   ::record {
widget select
values {cloudy sunny rainy foggy snowy}
}
grid .foo.baz
```

We now see a combobox:

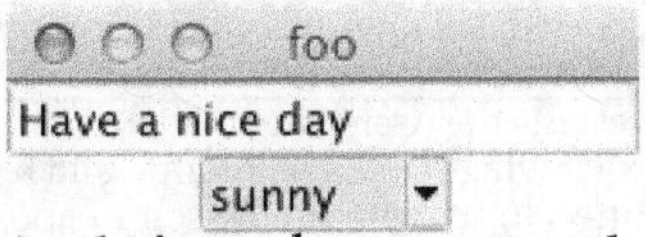

And if you hang around me, soon enough you'll be generating screens that look like this:

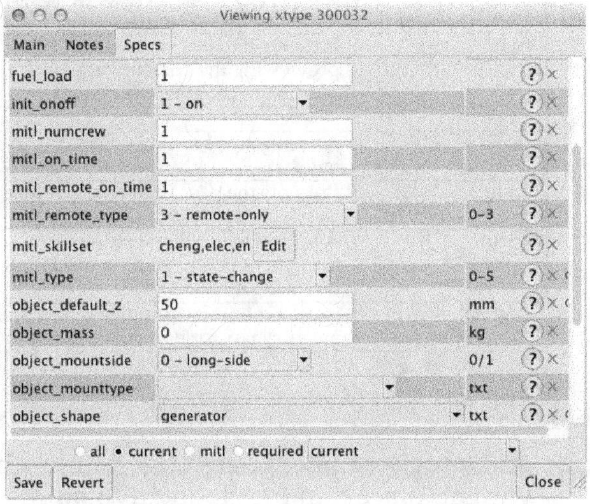

On the project I work with, we have hundreds of "specs" that can be used to describe a piece of equipment, a room on a ship, a doorway, even crew members. We also have dozens of controls that we present to the user to drive the simulator. And even 50 or so visual preferences.

Needless to say, figuring out which properties go on a given screen is hard enough without having to generate the GUI.

Property Inferences

The first step to making a Dynamic Widget is to read through the description. In the absence of any other information, the dynamic system will assume the field is a text string, represented by an entry box.

If the user has specified a "widget" property, that is which widget will be used. Otherwise, the widget has to be inferred. With no widget property, it tries to guess by the presence of a "values" field. If "values" is present, the widget is then assumed to be a selection. With no "widget" or "values" property, the inferencer then looks for a field name "type" or "storage".

Here are the basic dynamic widgets implemented by TAO/TK:

boolean	A checkbox to handle the simple cases of 1 and 0
checkbutton	A checkbutton with stylized properties for controlling on/off values
color	Presents the user with a label previewing the current value and a button to activate the Tk color chooser
entry	An entry box. If the "read-only" property is set to true, reverts to a label.
filename	Presents the user with an entry field for a value as well as a button to launch the Tk file chooser
font	Presents the user with a label previewing the current value and a button to activate the Tk font chooser
label	A label
real	An entrybox, but intended for numerical values
scale	Presents the user with an entry box coupled with a scale slider.
script	A button that, when pressed, presents the user with a popup window with a text widget.
vector	Breaks the entry into pieces and presents an entry box for each component.

Building Custom Dynamic Widgets

To register a new class of dynamic widget, place it in the ::taotk::dynamic namespace. The name you give it in that namespace is the name you reference in the **widget** property of the object description.

The constructor for dynamic widgets is as follows:

```
constructor {
  window fieldname arrayname args
} {
    my InitializePublic
    my configurelist \
      [::tao::args_to_options {*}$args]
    my variable field arrayvar
    set field $fieldname
    set arrayvar $arrayname

    my graft mainframe $window
    my graft nativewidget $window
    my BuildDynamicMethods
    my Build_topframe $window
    my build_widget $window
    my bind_widget $window
}
```

The **BuildDynamicMethods** method adds hooks to TAO/TK's style sheet handler. The **build_topframe** method builds the frame at *window*. The **build_widget** method builds the UI for this element. The **bind_widget** ensures the destruction of the Tk path calls the destructor for the object.

For every dynamic widget developed thus far, I've only had to modify the **build_widget** method.

Implementing an entry box is simplicity itself:

```
tao::class taotk::dynamic::entry {
 superclass taotk::dynamic
 option width {default 0}

 method build_widget window {
  set readonly [my cget readonly]
  set varname [my GlobalVariableName]
  set opts [list \
    -textvariable ${varname} \
    -width [my cget width] \
    -style [my Style label] \
  ]
  if { $readonly } {
    ::ttk::label $window.native {*}$opts \
      -takefocus 1
  } else {
   ::ttk::entry $window.native {*}$opts
  }
  my graft nativewidget $window.native
  grid $window.native -sticky news
 }
}
```

Conclusion

I've gone over quite a bit of material in this paper. In fact, there is quite a bit more on the cutting room floor, including sample projects, and demonstrations. That material as well as the complete sources for TAO/TK and all of its supporting libraries and documentation will be copied to the USB sticks that will be distributed by the conference. I will also be publishing the material online at:

http://www.etoyoc.com/tao2.0

Acknowledgements

This paper would not be possible if it weren't for the work of Donal Fellows to bring TclOO to life, convince the community to use it, and explain its inner workings to me patiently over several years.

I would also like to thank my employer, T&E Solutions, for allowing me to share this research with the community, plus the time to prepare this material and present it at the conference.

I would like to thank my wife, Ginger, for being a code-widow for the past few weeks while I put this paper together.

I would also like to thank Victoria Andrews for proofreading early drafts of this paper.

The random squiggles that I may or may not have completely eliminated from this manuscript are early works of my son, Xavier. Never too early to start them coding, I guess. I just wish he wouldn't have picked Tcl instead of Perl for his first project.

The graphic on the front cover was taken from Mallory Pearce's "Ready-To-Use Celtic Designs" published by Dover Clip Art.

Appendix

TAO Parser Keywords

Keyword: option

Syntax:
```
option fieldname keyvaluelist
```

The **option** keyword defines an option that will be conferred to all object of this class, and passed on to descendents of this class. It is equivilent to:

```
property fieldname option keyvaluelist
```

Keyword: option_class

Syntax:
```
option_class fieldname keyvaluelist
```

The **option_class** keyword defines a set of attributes that can be inherited by other options.

This statement is equivalent to:

```
property fieldname option_class \
 keyvaluelist
```

Keyword: property

Syntax:
```
property fieldname ?type? description
```

The **property** keyword defines a property that will be conferred to all objects of this class, and passed on to descendents of this class.

Keyword: variable

Syntax:
```
variable fieldname defaultvalue
```

The **variable** keyword defines an variable that will be conferred to all object of this class, and passed on to descendents of this class. The difference between the TAO form of the keyword and the standard TclOO usage is that TAO guarantees the variable will be initialized with the default value within the **InitializePublic** method, which is normally called by the constructor.

This statement is equivilent to:

```
property fieldname variable default
```

Keyword: class_method

```
Syntax:
  class_method name arglist body
```

The **class_method** keyword defines a method for the class itself. If no **method** of the same name is defined of the class, the implementation will be copied to the objects of the class.

class_method is equivalent to declaring a local method for the class object via:

```
oo::objdefine class method arglist body
```

A method defined by **class_method** will be inherited by descendents of a class, whereas the above example would not.

The Mother of all Classes

Static Methods

The static methods of the **moac** are methods declared in tao/moac.tcl file, using the conventional manner. They can be superseded and/or replaced by descendents.

Method: cget

```
Syntax:
 OBJ cget field ?default?
```

Returns the current value for option *field*. If "default" is given as the second argument, return the default value for option *field*.

Method: configure

```
Syntax:
 OBJ configure field
 OBJ configure field value ?field value…?
```

If one value given, return the current value for *field*. If two or more arguments given, write new values to options.

Method: configurelist

```
Syntax:
  OBJ configurelist {field value …}
```

Write new values to options.

Method: event cancel

```
Syntax:
 OBJ event cancel handle
```

Cancel any timer events created by **event schedule. handle** can be of any form acceptable to [string match].

Method: event generate

```
Syntax:
 OBJ event generate event args…
```

Generates an event to be published to other objects. Args are intended to be a key/value list describing the event.

Method: event publish

```
Syntax:
 OBJ event publish who event
```

Add a notification subscription for events matching **event** to recipients matching **who**. Both **event** and **who** can be of any form acceptable to [string match].

Method: event schedule

```
Syntax:
 OBJ event schedule handle interval script
```

Schedule for the Tcl event loop to run *script* on the object's behalf after *interval*. Any input valid for [after] is acceptable for *interval*.

Method: event subscribe

```
Syntax:
 OBJ event subscribe who event
```

Add a notification subscription for events matching **event** to senders matching **who**. Both **event** and **who** can be of any form acceptable to [string match].

Method: event unpublish

```
Syntax:
 OBJ event unpublish ?event?
```

Remove all subscribers for this object's notifications matching pattern **event**. **event** can be of any form acceptable to [string match]. If no event is given, all publications for this object are removed.

Method: event unsubscribe

```
Syntax:
 OBJ event unsubscribe ?event?
```

Remove all subscriptions for this object to notifications matching pattern **event**. **event** can be of any form acceptable to [string match]. If no event is given, all subscriptions for this object are removed. (NOTE: It is still possible for the object to still receive notifications if the object matches another object's **publication**.)

Method: graft

```
Syntax:
 OBJ graft stub object
```

Create a link to another object as a forwarded method. Two methods are created: **$stub** and <**$stub**>.

Method: InitializePublic

```
Syntax:
 my InitializePublic
```

Designed to be the first method called by the constructor. This method reads the properties of the object an ensures the default value is loaded for all declared variables and options.

Method: initialize

```
Syntax:
 OBJ initialize
```

Designed to be called by the constructor after the object has initialized all of its variables. The default implementation is empty, it is reserved for developers to perform any higher level initialization that an object may require within the constructor.

Method: morph

```
Syntax:
 OBJ morph newclass
```

Convert this object to be of class *newclass*.

Method: organ

```
Syntax:
 OBJ organ all
 OBJ organ stub
```

If the argument **all** is given, return a key/value list of all stubs for this object and what objects they point to. Otherwise, return the object directed to by *stub*.

Method: private

```
Syntax:
 OBJ private method args…
```

Exercise a private method.

Method: signal

```
Syntax:
 OBJ signal signal ?signal…?
```

Register a signal to be executed during the next *Signal_pipeline*. An "idle" signal will trigger an [after idle] call to **Signal_pipeline** if not locks are active.

Method: Signal_pipeline

```
Syntax:
 my Signal_pipeline
```

Develop and execute a pipeline based on all signal received since the last call to **Signal_pipeline**.

Method Ensembles

Ensemble: action actionname ?args...?

Every submethod is a response to an "event". Actions are expected to be immediate. Developers can feel free to define their own events.

Method: action::pipeline_busy

```
Syntax:
  OBJ action pipeline_busy
```

Commands to run at the start of **Signal_pipeline**, but before the pipeline begins.

Method action::pipeline_idle

```
Syntax:
  OBJ action pipeline_idle
```

Commands to run at completion (or failure) of **Signal_pipeline**.

Ensemble: lock

The **lock** ensemble manages object locks.

Method: lock::active

```
Syntax:
  OBJ lock active
```

Return a list of all locks currently active on this object.

Method: lock::create

```
Syntax:
  OBJ lock create lock ?lock...?
```

Create one or more locks on the object. Returns zero if the all of the locks specified are new. Returns 1 if one or more of the locks was already active.

Method lock::peek

```
Syntax:
  OBJ lock peek lock ?lock...?
```

Returns 1 if one or more of the locks specified is active. Returns 0 otherwise.

Method: lock::remove

```
Syntax:
  OBJ lock remove lock ?lock...?
```

Remove one or more locks on the object. Returns zero if other locks are still present on the object. Returns 1, and calls **lock remove_all** if there are no more locks on the object.

Method: lock::remove_all

```
Syntax:
  OBJ lock remove_all
```

Remove all locks on the object and call the **Signal_pipeline** method.

Ensemble: notify event dictargs

This ensemble is present to allow object to respond to notifications. The only defined notification is *default*, which quietly ignores any event that wasn't already processed.

Ensemble: Option_set option newvalue

Each submethod is the name of an option. The default handler mirrors any option set with an existing internal variable.

Ensemble: SubObject *stub*

Return the name of an object to create for a particular stub. The default hander returns:

```
[namespace current]::Subobject_generic_$stub
```

Dynamic Methods

Dynamic methods are generated by the TAO parser. They are custom produced for each class, and replaced with the next call to **tao::class**.

Method: property

```
Syntax:
  OBJ property property
  OBJ property type property
  OBJ property type <list>
  OBJ property type <dict>
```

This method has several functions depending on the content and number of arguments. A modified form is also created for the class itself, with a subset of all properties that do not depend on the state of an object instance.

```
Usage:  OBJ property property
```

Returns the value of property *field*. If multiple types for *field* are given, the line of succession is as follows: signal, option, variable, subst, eval, const.

i.e. if a class has a signal named *foo* and a constant named *foo* the data returned from

property will be the description for the signal.

```
Usage: OBJ property type property
```

Return the value of property *property* of type *type*.

```
Usage:  OBJ property type <list>
```

Return a list of all properties of type *type*.

```
Usage:  OBJ property type <dict>
```

Return a dict of all properties of type *type*.

TAO DB Schema

Table: ancestry

TAO has to independently track the chain of heredity for classes. It does this by replicating the rules TclOO uses, and then recording the results as a sequence of ancestors from the most advanced, to the most primitive.

```
create table ancestry (
  class string references class,
  ancorder integer,
  parent string references class,
  primary key (class,ancorder)
);
```

Table: class

Each class that has been processed by the TAO parser has an entry in this table. The ***name*** field is the name of the class. The ***package*** field is for future expansion. The ***regen*** field is set to true when an ancestor of the class is modified. See Class Regeneration.

```
create table class (
  name string primary key,
  package string,
  regen integer default 0
);
```

Table: class_alias

As projects grow and evolve, the names of classes can change over time. The ***class_alias*** table is consulted in cases where a new class tries to refer to an ancestor whose name has changed.

```
create table class_alias (
  cname string references class,
  alias string references class
);
```

Table: ensemble

TAO captures information about method ensembles in the ***ensemble*** table.

```
create table ensemble (
  class string references class,
  method string,
  submethod string,
  arglist string,
  defined string references class,
  body text,
  primary key (class,method,submethod)
  on conflict replace);
```

Table: method

TAO captures information about methods in the ***method*** table.

```
create table method (
  class string references class,
  method string,
  arglist string,
  body text,
  defined string references class,
  primary key (class,method)
  on conflict replace);
```

Table: object

Each object that has been spawned by a tao class has an entry. ***name*** is the name of the class. ***package*** is for future expansion. ***regen*** is set to true when the class is modified, and the dynamic methods for the object need to be regenerated.

```
create table object (
  name string primary key,
  package string,
  regen integer default 0
);
```

Table: object_alias

Objects can occasionally change names throughout the course of the program. This table has an entry for all former names an object may have possessed.

```
create table object_alias (
  cname string references class,
  alias string references class
);
```

Table: object_bind

TAO has an independent event handling system, The **object_bind** table is where an object designates which script to call when an event is triggered.

```
create table object_bind (
  object string references object,
  event  string,
  script blob,
  primary key (object,event) on conflict
replace
);
```

Table: object_schedule

TAO has an independent event handling system, The **object_schedule** table is where an object can schedule an event to occur in the future.

```
create table object_schedule (
  object string references object,
  event  string,
  time   integer,
  eventorder  integer default 0,
  script string,
  primary key (object,event) on conflict
replace
);
```

Table: object_subscribers

TAO has an independent event handling system, The **object_subscribers** table is where an object can subscribe which events from which objects it wishes to respond to. Note: ***sender***, ***receiver*** and ***event*** are matched using the same rules as [string match].

```
create table object_subscribers (
  sender   string references object,
  receiver string references object,
  event string,
  primary key (sender,receiver,event) on
conflict ignore
);
```

To make the "example" object listen to all events from "appmain":

```
insert into object_subscribers (
sender,receiver,event
) VALUES (
'appmain','example','*'
);
```

Table: property

TAO stores the input given by the parser's option, property, and signal keywords as records in the ***property*** table.

```
create table property (
  class string references class,
  property string,
  defined string references class,
  type string,
  dict keyvaluelist,
  primary key (class,property,type) on
conflict replace
);
```

Table: typemethod

TAO captures information about class method classes in the ***typemethod*** table.

```
create table typemethod (
  class string references class,
  method string,
  arglist string,
  body text,
  defined string references class,
  primary key (class,method) on conflict
replace
);
```

Scintilla Tk Porting Project

Brian S Griffin
Mentor Graphics Corporation
8005 SW Boeckman Road
Wilsonville, OR 97070
brian_griffin@mentor.com

Abstract

A couple of years ago we decided that the application window used to display program source file text was inadequate in several ways. The basic problem was with the performance of a few significant features: keyword/syntax coloring, inline annotations, and large file load times. There have also been recurring problems with keeping displayed line numbers in sync with the text body. Rather than continuing to attempt repairs on the current implementation, a decision was made to find a complete replacement. After reviewing and testing a number of applications and widgets, we narrowed the field down to two options: customizing the Tk text widget, or porting Scintilla to Tk. This paper will discuss the requirements and implementation challenges with ScintillaTk.

Introduction

In 1995 when development started on our Tk-based GUI, a simple Tk Text widget was used to display program text. The simple Tcl code implementing the source code viewer was more than adequate to meet the needs at that time. As features were added to the application, the demands on the source view grew. The Supertext[1] widget was added to support undo. In 2004, an effort was made to provide a more IDE-like experience in the application; we decided to incorporate a Tcl/Tk based text editor developed for another product in the company. This editor widget gained widespread use across several products.

Although the editor was a bit buggy, the real problems began when we attempted to implement source code value annotations in 2006. Annotations display values above or below variables that appear in the source code. Implementing this using Tcl/Tk is a challenge. Various techniques were attempted until we finally settled on using double-spaced text and overlaid label widgets below each location. This gave a clean presentation and allowed for easy and efficient update to values as they change,

---

[1] Supertext extension of the Tk text widget: http://wiki.tcl.tk/3387

however, when scrolling the text, the labels had to be removed before the scroll and laid back down after the scroll. This leads to slow scrolling performance and a lot of flashing.

After living with the flashing and buggy editor implementation, a decision was made to start over. We searched for existing source code viewer widgets that provided all the necessary features. All possible solutions were considered, from using an external editor to writing a fully custom widget. The Scintilla widget quickly gained favor primarily because of the annotation, line number, and folding features. In this paper, I will describe the project of porting Scintilla to work with Tcl/Tk as a Tk widget, the Scintilla architecture. I will also describe the challenges faced and solved, or not solved as the case may be. In the conclusion I will offer some suggestions for possible improvements to Tk and Scintilla.

Problems with [text]

To begin, I have to say that the Tk text widget is an awesome implementation. It is amazingly fast compared to all other text viewers we've tested. The feature set is really good, especially the powerful tag system. And the peer[2] feature is pretty cool.

There are some things that are hard to do or hard to do right. One of the most common things done with the text widget when displaying source code is to display line numbers along the left hand column. There are at least 3 techniques to do this:

- Insert the line number with the text in the text widget.
```
$text insert $index "$lineno  $text"
```
- Fill a second text widget with line numbers and pack this widget next to the body text widget.
```
while {[$linetext compare end < [$text index end]]} {
    $linetext insert end "${lineno}¥n"
    incr lineno
}
```
- Actively draw line numbers in a canvas packed next to the text widget.
```
set dline [$text dlineinfo ${i}.0]
set y [lindex $dline 1]
$canvas create text 0 $y -anchor nw -text $i
```

The editor was implemented using the second technique – using a second text widget to contain line numbers as well as other indicators, marks and counters. Inevitably, bugs would creep in over time, causing the contents displayed in the two widgets to be

---

2 TIP #169: Add Peer Text Widgets (http://www.tcl.tk/cgi-bin/tct/tip/169.html)

out of sync. Most recently, the change in the text widget to support smooth scrolling caused a synchronization problem in the editor.

The rich tag mechanism is a great feature of the text widget. One of the most visible uses is for syntax highlighting of source code. However, a Tcl-based lexer is not the most efficient way to process large text files. Our current editor employed such a lexer and consequently, the load time performance suffered with very large files.

Annotating the source code with values is a desired feature. We first attempted to make use of tags to implement annotations. We tried to -offset[3] the value text, but without an x (horizontal) offset option, the desired effect could not be achieved. We also tried embedded windows[4] (widgets), but again there is insufficient offset placement control to achieve the desired effect.

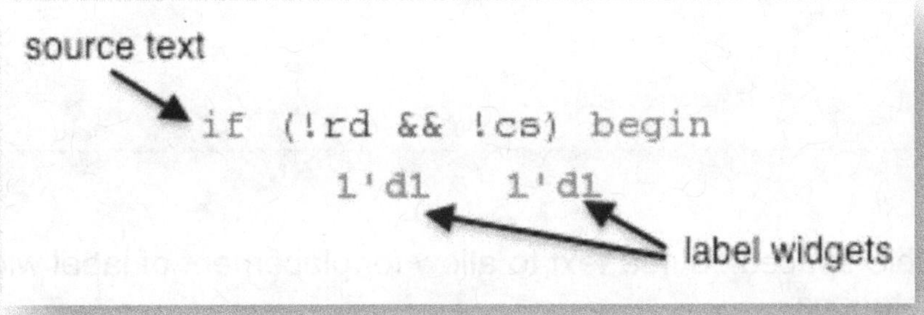

Figure 1. Label widgets placed under the source text to display annotated values. ("1'd" means 1-bit wide, decimal radix followed by the value.)

The solution we settled on was to place label widgets over the double-spaced text widget, using the bounding box information supplied by the text widget. The desired effect was achieved, but with the side effect of flashing when the window is scrolled, since a scrolling operation required removing and replacing the label widgets. In addition, the work involved was too much and delayed the scrolling action. Another undesirable trait of this approach is the double-spacing of the source text, which ends up wasting a lot of screen space, as illustrated in Figure 2a. Ideally, the annotation rendering would be handled directly by the widget so that it is all drawn at one time. Then the annotations would take up space only where they are needed, as shown in Figure 2b.

---

[3] Text widget tag vertical offset option. (http://www.tcl.tk/man/tcl8.5/TkCmd/text.htm#M37)

[4] Text widget embedded window feature. (http://www.tcl.tk/man/tcl8.5/TkCmd/text.htm#M49)

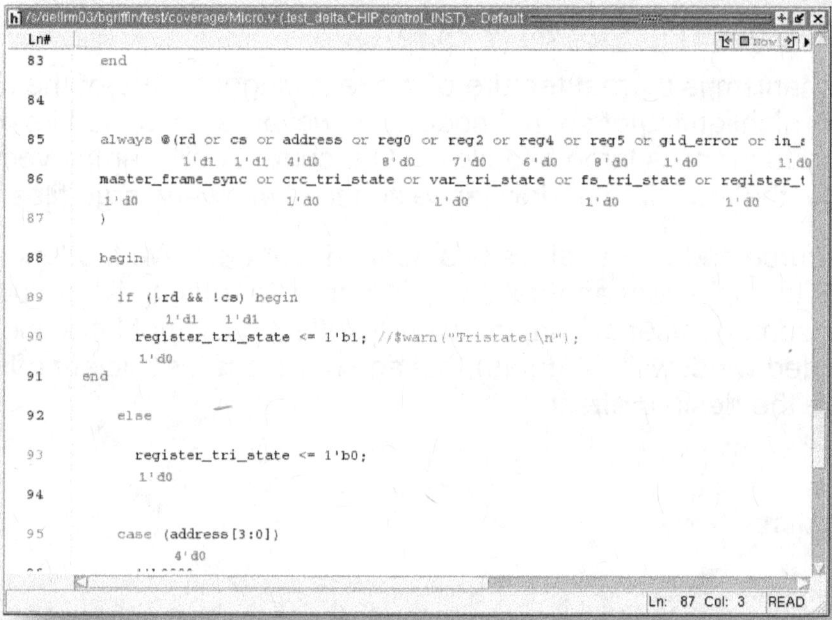

Figure 2a. Double-spaced source text to allow for placement of label widget annotations.

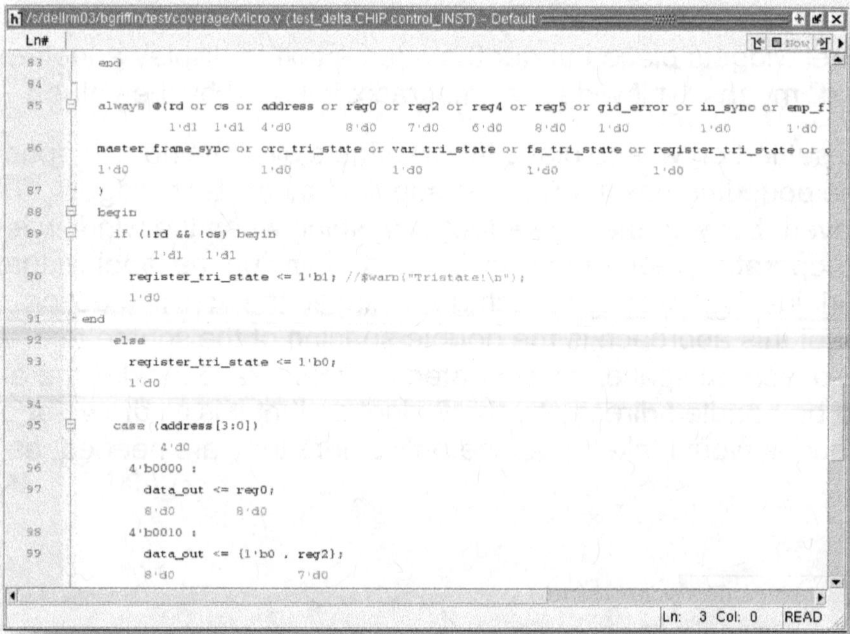

Figure 2b. With vertical space allocated only to annotations, 4 additional lines of source text can be displayed in the same screen space.

Replacement Criteria

In order to improve the user experience with the source code viewer, we identified key requirements that must be addressed.

Fast file load with syntax highlighting

The time to load and display a very large source file with syntax highlighting must be the best possible. A review was conducted of various IDEs and text editors to determine a nominal standard. The review was not exhaustive, but several popular tools were tested.

Embedded Annotations

A highly efficient and flexible mechanism is needed to annotate the source text without getting in the way of display performance or text selection and editing.

Margin Annotations

A mechanism to place marks and other data annotations in a margin to the left side of the text, by line, is required. Some common examples are line numbers, breakpoint symbols, bookmark symbols, and execution counts. At times it may be necessary to have markers overlap and still be recognizable, as shown in Figure 4.

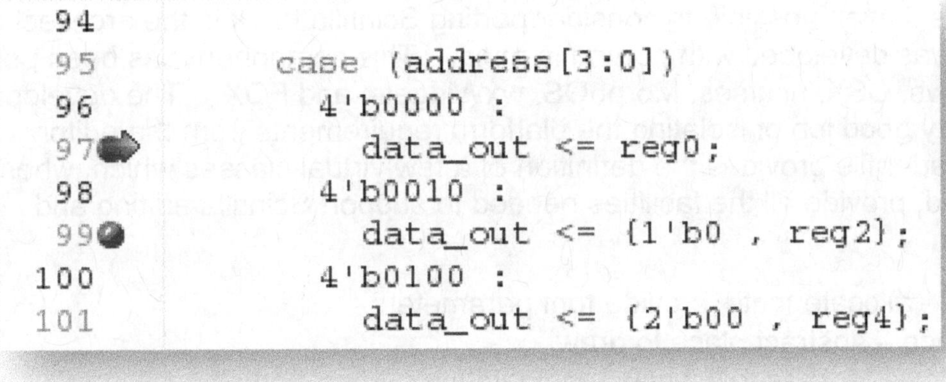

Figure 4. Overlapping markers. Red dots are breakpoints. Blue arrow is the current execution location.

Scope folding

Scope folding is a combination of special margin marks coupled with lexical parsing to identify language scopes. This feature is considered a lower priority, “nice to have” capability.

Solution space

Several possible solutions were considered to satisfy our high priority requirements. We tested several widgets and editors, including the Tk text widget. We even considered writing a text widget from scratch, but that was rejected as too large a project and the performance testing showed that there were several other viable candidates.

Some additional requirements, not listed above: the widget must work with Tk, be easy to implement within our application, and naturally interact with the rest of the GUI. Only the Tk text widget met these criteria. The next best candidate was the Scintilla[5] text widget, an open source code-editing component. Except for not supporting Tk, it meets all of the other required features.

This led us to two possible conclusions:

1. Using the Tk text widget, enhance it to support annotations and margins, C based lexers for syntax highlighting, and scope folding.
2. Port Scintilla to Tk.

Clearly #2 is the easier task as it only has 1 item!

Scintilla Architecture

What makes it even possible to consider porting Scintilla to Tk is the architecture of Scintilla; it was developed with porting in mind. This component has been ported to Gtk, Windows, OSX, ncurses, MorphOS, wxWidgets, and FOX. The developers have done a pretty good job of isolating the platform requirements from the editor. A platform header file provides the definition of a few virtual classes which, when implemented, provide all the facilities needed to support Scintilla editing and presentation.

- Font – allocate fonts, provide font parameters
- Surface – abstract place to draw
- Window – access to window manipulation and properties
- ListBox, Menu – Widgets for menus and dialogs
- ElapsedTime – timer access
- DynamicLibrary – abstract dynamic library loading facility
- Platform – used to retrieve system wide parameters such as double-click speed and chrome color.

---

5 Scintilla is maintained by Neil Hodgson and hosted on Sourceforge. The web site is http://www.scintilla.org

The key interface classes here are Surface, Window, and Font. These provide for the crux of the rendering engine. The Platform, DynamicLIbrary, and ElapsedTime complete the necessary general facilities. The ListBox and Menu widget interfaces are only necessary if the Scintilla editor is going to manage Auto completion or Popup menus, respectively, otherwise, the platform may use other means to implement these behaviors.

All operations on the component are done through a generic message interface that looks like this:

```
    sptr_t sci_cmd(
                    sptr_t ptr,
                    unsigned int iMessage,
                    uptr_t       wParam,
                    sptr_t       lParam
    );
```

As of this writing, there are 645 different messages.

The component also separates the notion of Document from Window; Documents hold the text contents and styling, and a Window presents a Document on the screen, similar to the Tk text peer feature. From the Scintilla documentation:

> "A Scintilla window and the document that it displays are separate entities. When you create a new window, you also create a new, empty document. Each document has a reference count that is initially set to 1. The document also has a list of the Scintilla windows that are linked to it so when any window changes the document, all other windows in which it appears are notified to cause them to update. The system is arranged in this way so that you can work with many documents in a single Scintilla window and so you can display a single document in multiple windows (for use with splitter windows)."[6]

So, how hard could it be to marry Tcl/Tk, a portable GUI toolkit, with Scintilla, a port capable text-editing component?

Implementation

One of the driving goals in implementing this port was to take maximum advantage of the Tk API in order to maximize portability of the port. In other words, we want the widget to work wherever Tk works without having to deal with OS specific platform

---

6 Scintilla Documentation, section Multiple Views (http://www.scintilla.org/ScintillaDoc.html#MultipleViews)

issues within the ScintillaTk port code. After all, that is Tcl/Tk's philosophy[7] as well. In the descriptions below you'll see how this is applied and how successful it is.

Surface

The Surface class was probably the most straightforward to implement. This class has methods like FillRectange and DrawText that align closely with Tk C API calls. Almost every method is implemented with just a few lines of code. The one limitation is the rendering with alpha (transparency) channel in colors. Currently the alpha channel is ignored since the current attempted implementation has poor performance. This is a known limitation in Tk.

Fonts

Fonts are implemented as a wrapper class around the Tk_GetFont() API and a bit of code to manage the font references. Scintilla does require the use of Xft in order to support the Font property requests, which include arbitrary float sizes. Older X11 fonts aren't sufficient and produce less than desirable results.

Images

The Scintilla interface for images is based on a raw 4-plane image data array: rgb color + alpha channel. This format is compatible with Tk_GetImage, however, there is no Tk API to directly draw a raw image to a drawable. To draw the image it must first be put into a Tk_Image. This presents a challenge in managing images from Tcl/Tk since they pass through Scintilla as an unmanaged array. There isn't any way to associate a Scintilla image draw request with a particular Tk_Image.

There are two reasons why I believe Scintilla has a single DrawImage request using raw image data: 1) some of the images drawn are internally created by Scintilla, not supplied by the client or platform, and 2) Scintilla can optimize a redraw by requesting a partial image redraw. This single interface keeps things simple for the components implementation.

It would be helpful if Scintilla defined a class or opaque handle for images and then let the platform implementation manage the resource. It would also be helpful if Tk exposed the TkPutImage() as a public function.

Encodings

Scintilla supports both UNICODE and UTF-8 encodings internally as a runtime configuration option. For the Tk platform, keeping Scintilla set to UTF-8 encoding

---

[7] John K. Ousterhout, Ken Jones, [et al], 2010, *Tcl and the Tk Toolkit – Second Edition*, Addison-Wesley, page xxxii.

makes it simple to interface text between Tcl and the Scintilla Document since Tcl is all UTF-8 internally.

Loadable Lexers

One of Scintilla's features is that it comes with a number of programming language lexers used to perform syntax highlighting. It can also be configured to make lexers loadable dynamically. It is up to the platform implementation to provide the loading mechanism. This was simple to implement using Tcl's Tcl_LoadFile API, however, the set of symbol entry points that Scintilla needs are not the same pair of entry points for which LoadFile was designed. The platform DynamicLibrary class also requires a FindFunction method. We decided to make use of TclpFindSymbol() in the implementation. This is currently a problem since this function is not easily exposed.

Tcl command interface

To complete the porting effort, the Scintilla component needs to act and feel like any other Tk widget. This means integrating the Scintilla component into the Tcl/Tk command & widget infrastructure. The code here constitutes about 80% of the implementation. For this part of the project we set the goal to match the Tk text widget subcommands and options as much as possible within the limits of what Scintilla can support. For example, we matched the scrollbar interface, but since Scintilla does not support embedded windows, that part of the Tk interface is left out. In some cases, code from the Tk text widget was borrowed in order to match the behavior. This was done for the "search" subcommand, for example.

All of the important text widget subcommands have been implemented for managing the widgets' content and display. For the most part, the Scintilla widget is compatible with the Tk text widget. Figure 5 lists the widget subcommands. Those that are underlined in the figure have been added to support Scintilla specific features. Tk text widget subcommands that have not been implemented are shown in the figure printed in grey italic.

A couple of items cannot be supported in Scintilla; they are embedded images and windows. Scintilla simply has no mechanism to duplicate these Tk text widget features, therefore, these subcommands have not been implemented. The tag subcommand implements all the same Tk text widget methods, but a tag's options are different for Scintilla since the styling of text, margins, and annotations diverge from Tk text widgets' design.

annotate	*dlineinfo*	keywords	scisearch	xview
bbox	dump	loadlexer	search	yview
cget	edit	margin	see	zoomin
compare	fold	mark	style	zoomout
configure	get	marker	tag	
count	*image*	*peer*	textwidth	
debug	index	property	*window*	
delete	insert	*replace*	version	

Figure 5. Scintilla widget subcommands. Underlined subcommands are added for Scintilla. Greyed out italic subcommands have not been implemented.

Style vs Tag

In Tk's text widget, formatting of text can be performed by applying a tag to one or more arbitrary ranges of characters. A tag's definition holds the formatting properties to be applied to the text. These properties include color, font, and shading (stippling), but there are also additional controls over things like spacing, margin, justification, offset, and even event binding, a very flexible and powerful mechanism. Scintilla, on the other hand, has the notion of Styles that are applied on a character-by-character basis. Style only affects the look of the character, color, font, weight, etc., and not any other rendering considerations. There are a few predefined styles, and the number of styles is limited to 256.

Since Tk text widget tags are effectively unlimited, this presents a challenge to implementing tags in the Scintilla widget. In order to present the appearance of an unlimited number of tags in Scintilla, a Tag Manger is implemented to keep track of tag names and ranges, and to manage the allocation of styles as needed. One of the heavier uses of tags in the text widget tends to be as meta-data on the text. This use model does not require consuming any style resources since no formatting changes are applied to the tag. So far we have not seen any practical case of hitting the limit on styles. Styles can also be applied to margin text and annotation text. Luckily, these styles can be configured to be a different set from those used in the document body.

Margins, Annotations, Indicators, Markers

Scintilla provides a number of different ways to augment the document body with additional information: margins, indicators, and annotation.

- **Margins and markers**: Scintilla provides for up to five margins. There are three types of margins: symbol, number, or text. The margins are configured using the margin subcommand. Symbols can be set in the margins using either the built-in Scintilla markers, or using Tk images. Markers are configured using the markers subcommand.
- **Indicators**: Indicators are drawn on the text in the document body. An indicator is specified via the tag subcommand.
- **Annotations**: These are read-only lines of text that appear under editable lines of text in the document. The text is styled independently from the document text. Annotations are configured via the annotation subcommand.

Lexers

Scintilla provides a number of built-in lexers for a variety of programming languages. Additional lexers can be dynamically loaded using the loadlexer subcommand. The configure option, -language, is used to set the name of the lexer language to use. The lexer is then configured using the "keywords" and "property" subcommands. Each lexer defines the number of keyword sets, and the names and types of properties. In order to use these subcommands correctly one must become familiar with the particular lexer in use.

Searching

Scintilla provides a search function, as does Tk. Because there are differences in the options and results of these two functions, we decided to provide both search subcommands in the widget. The search method uses the Tk text widget algorithm to perform the search. The code for this was copied from Tk. The second method, scisearch, calls the Scintilla function to perform the search. The differences come about because they use different regular expression engines, and they have different definitions of a word. Rather than trying to accommodate or justify merging the behaviors, providing two subcommands was just easier.

Textwidth and Zoom

Other subcommands provide direct access to Scintilla.

The textwidth subcommand is similar to the [font measure] command in Tk, except that Scintilla performs the calculation.

The zoomin and zoomout methods provide a capability specific to Scintilla.

Not all specialized calls that Scintilla provides have been implemented; to date, only the calls that have been needed have been implemented in the widget interface.

Conclusions

Scintilla has a good foundational architecture that made the porting effort relatively easy. The work here is not complete; there is plenty to do to evolve this widget extension into a powerful text component for Tk.

Some of the remaining work needed to complete the port:

- Complete all Tk text widget configure options and subcommands to improve compatibility.
- Implement event binding for tags.
- Create a custom subset of Tk text widget tests to verify compatibility.
- Complete access to all Scintilla API calls and options.
- The configure script(s) for all Tk supported platforms. The current configure script has only been tested on some Linux machines, and only works on Windows under specific conditions.
- Full html documentation.

There are a few things that could be done in each project that would benefit the integration:

- It would probably be better if all lexers were dynamically loaded as a Tk package, one per language.
- Create TIP's to expose the few internal functions needed to complete the Tk port and keep the ScintillaTk portable and isolated as much as possible.
- I would like to see ScintillaTk brought into the Scintilla project directly since most of the implementation variations will come from Scintilla itself. The platform port intentionally uses Tk's public API (with already noted exceptions), which keeps the port isolated from the Tcl/Tk releases.

Acknowledgments

I'd like to thank the developers who did the porting work: Joe Mueller, John Vella, and Ron Wold. It's their "boots on the ground" that are getting this job done. Thanks, guys!

Dynaforms and Dynaviews:

A Declarative Language for User Dialogs in Tcl/Tk

William H. Duquette
Jet Propulsion Laboratory, California Institute of Technology
William.H.Duquette@jpl.nasa.gov

Abstract

A dynaform is a specification of a dynamic data entry form: one whose content and layout can change based on the input of the user. Consider a GUI for entering rules for filing e-mail messages into folders: each rule can have many different forms, depending on the desired criteria. The user must first select the kind of criteria; each criterion has its own set of parameters, and the user's choices for those parameters might result in a further series of choices. The dynaform mechanism consists of a little language for specifying such a set of related inputs, infrastructure for processing that language, and the dynaview widget, which can display any desired dynaform and accept user input.

1. Background

The Athena Regional Stability Simulation is a model of political actors and the effects of their actions in a particular region of the world. The region is divided into neighborhoods, in which reside civilian groups. The actors have a variety of assets, including money, military and police forces, and means of communication, that they use to achieve their political ends. The extent to which they succeed depends on the attitudes of the civilians, which change in response to current events. The Athena user must enter a wide variety of data about many different simulation entities, and the complexity of the data to be entered has increased with each new version of the software. The dynaform mechanism is our latest approach to providing complex user-friendly easily maintainable data entry forms with a minimum of code.

2. The Problem

In the Athena application, an order is a specialized procedure used to handle user input. An order takes a dictionary of order parameters and values as input, validates them, and either throws a detailed error or performs the desired task. On success it returns an undo script; the application's undo/redo stack is in fact a stack of executed orders.

Some orders are simple, with one or two parameters that are always provided by the application; most are more complicated, and require significant input from the user. As a result, each order requires an order dialog. At present Athena contains 187 orders, and this number is always increasing. It is essential that implementation and maintenance of order dialogs be easy and straightforward.

2.1 Field Widgets

Tk provides a number of widget types useful for entering data, but their APIs often have subtle differences. Athena defines a standard field widget API, and uses Snit wrappers where necessary to make standard widget conform. The API was established early in Athena development, and has been remarkably stable since.

First, every field widget has at least the following options:

`-state` *`state`*
: Sets the widget's *state* to **normal** or **disabled** in the usual way.

`-changecmd` *`command`*
: Specifies a command prefix that will be called whenever the field's value changes for any reason (whether programmatically or due to user input). The *command* is called with one additional argument, the new value of the field.

Next, it has at least the following subcommands:

`field` `get`
: Retrieves the field widget's current value.

`field` `set` *`value`*
: Sets the field widget's *value*, calling the `-changecmd`.

Configuration is naturally field-type-specific, but once the field widgets are created and configured they all work just the same from the point of view of the form infrastructure.

2.2 Order Dialogs: The Mark I Solution

Our original solution to the order dialog problem was to associate enough metadata with each order definition to allow Athena to put together and pop up an order dialog. The first dialogs were quite simple: two parallel columns, with labels on the left and data entry fields on the right, implemented in a Tk grid. There were just a few field types, mostly text fields and combo box-based pull-downs; the metadata specified the list of valid items for the pull-downs.

These order dialogs often required additional code to provide dynamic behavior:

- Enabling or disabling fields based on prior entries in the dialog

- Configuring field widgets based on the state of the application (i.e., setting a pull-down to contain a list of currently defined simulation entities)

- Configuring field widgets based on the state of prior fields in the dialog.

Dynamic behavior was provided by means of a `-refreshcmd` callback associated with the dialog fields. Whenever the content of any field in the dialog changed, whether programmatically or due to user input, the dialog code called each field's `-refreshcmd` callback. The callback could enable or disable the field, or reconfigure it in a variety of ways. The difficulty was that each field was handled individually, when it was often necessary to coordinate changes to multiple fields.

Further, there were multiple reasons why a field might be refreshed, and the appropriate response differed. The callbacks needed to second guess the dialog logic in order to do the right thing. As a result, dialogs were finicky to get right, and when there was a problem it was hard to fix it without introducing problems elsewhere. Worse, the underlying dialog logic was convoluted and hard to follow.

2.3 Order Dialogs: The Mark II Solution

As a result, I rewrote the order dialog code from scratch, separating the main dialog logic from the form logic. I abstracted the form code out into a new `form` widget. The layout was still two parallel columns of labels and fields, but the order dialog code itself no longer needed to concern itself with the layout. The field-specific `-refreshcmd` callbacks were replaced by a single `-refreshcmd` callback that applied to the entire form. It was called with:

- The name of the order dialog, a Snit widget with a variety of introspection and configuration subcommands.

- A list of the names of the order parameters whose fields had changed

- A dictionary of the current values of all fields

The callback would then have to figure out the appropriate dialog configuration given the fields that had changed and the current field values, and update the dialog accordingly. It was now much easier to coordinate configuration changes to multiple fields, since all of the logic was in one callback. This scheme was a great improvement over its predecessor, but also proved to be unmanageable for complex dialogs. The complexity was all in one place—in the `-refreshcmd` callback—but refreshing still occurred for multiple reasons, and the callback code still needed to second guess the dialog logic in order to do the right thing. Writing robust code that caught all of the corner cases was difficult for any but the simplest patterns.

In the meantime Athena continued to grow, the number of orders continued to increase, and the individual orders continued to get more complex.

2.4 Lingering Issues

By this time we had a fairly sophisticated, maintainable set of code; but it was still unpleasantly limited.

- Dynamic behavior was easier to implement than before, but not truly simple.
- Form layout was limited to two parallel columns, and there was no easy way to change it.

3. An Example

As a simple example, the Athena analyst may create a DEPLOY tactic to deploy simulated troops into a neighborhood. He may choose the number of troops to deploy in two ways: he may deploy all remaining troops or he may deploy some specific number of troops; and in the latter case, he may deploy them with or without reinforcement. If he selects all remaining troops, he is done; but if he chooses to enter a specific number, he must enter the number and the reinforcement flag.

With the old system, the dialog looked like this:[1]

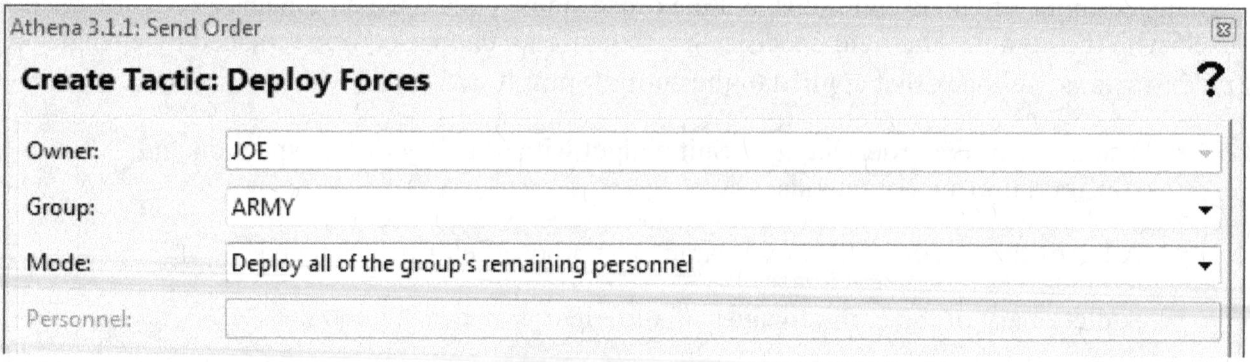

When the user chose to deploy all remaining personnel, the "Personnel:" field was disabled. When the user chose to deploy only some, the "Personnel:" field was enabled again, and the user could type in a number. Note that it was not possible to make the "Personnel:" field disappear when it was not wanted: the underlying "form" widget didn't support that.

[1] The reinforcement flag field is not shown, because it had not yet been added to the underlying order.

4. The Mark III Solution

The Mark I solution had the order dialog widget layout fields in a Tk grid based on the list of order parameters and a little metadata. Any relationships between fields were captured purely in external callbacks.

The Mark II solution made use of a Tk-grid-based form widget, and had the order dialog widget configure it based on the list of order parameters and a little metadata. The layout remained the same, and any relationships between fields were captured, again, in external callbacks.

The Mark III solution is radically different: the order dialog uses a new form widget, the `dynaview` widget, which can display any *dynaform*. A dynaform is a description of the form's fields and layout, including significant relationships between the fields, as captured in a declarative Tcl-based language. A dynaform specification becomes part of each order's metadata, but the dynaform language and infrastructure are independent of the order and order dialog infrastructure. In short, the new infrastructure is useful not only for order dialogs but for other general purpose dialogs.

The Mark III equivalent of the order dialog show above implemented as follows as a dynaform:

```
rcc "Owner:" -for owner
text owner -context yes

rcc "Group:" -for g
enum g -listcmd {group ownedby $owner}

rcc "Mode:" -for mode
selector mode {
    case SOME "Deploy some of the group's personnel" {
        rcc "Personnel:" -for personnel
        text personnel

        rcc "Reinforce?" -for reinforce
        yesno reinforce -defvalue 0
    }

    case ALL "Deploy all of the group's remaining personnel" {}
}
. . .
```

The `text`, `enum`, `selector`, and `yesno` commands each create a field, giving it a name and any required configuration options. The `rcc` commands add labels and layout hints. We'll take them in turn.

4.1 Field Specifications

All field creation commands have the following signature:

```
fieldtype name ?option value...?
```

There are a number of standard field options, and each field type may have its own specific set of options.

The `owner` field names the actor to whose strategy the new tactic will be added. It is defined as follows:

```
text owner -context yes
```

It is a text entry field; the –context option indicates that it is a "context" field: one whose value is set by the application to provide context to those that follow. The value of a context field cannot be edited by the user. Tactics are always created from a browser widget that shows the strategy of one actor at a time, and so the owner field is field in by the browser when the dialog is popped up.

The `g` field is used to enter the name of the force group to be deployed. It is defined as follows:

```
enum g -listcmd {group ownedby $owner}
```

The `enum` command creates an enumeration field, which is rendered as a combo box containing a list of force groups to deploy. Each actor has his own set of force groups, so the content of the list has to be limited to those belonging to the owner. In the Mark II code, this would have been done in a clumsy way by the `-refreshcmd`, which when called would have had to figure out which fields needed to be updated and how. Here, instead, we simply define a `-listcmd`, which returns the desired list. It is called whenever the infrastructure determines that any prior field's value has changed.

Note that the `-listcmd` references the variable `$owner`. Rather than being called in the global namespace, as callbacks usually are, all field configuration callback commands are called in a context in which the form's field values are available as variables. This makes it trivially easy to make a field's configuration depend on a prior field in the same dialog. In this case, the command simply returns all of the groups owned by the tactic's `owner`.

The reinforce field is a Boolean field created using the yesno field type. This is an example of a custom field type; it simply wraps the enum field type with the required configuration options to display "Yes" and "No" and map them to the integers 1 and 0. It was defined by the Athena application itself to streamline this common case.

4.2 Selector Fields

Next we come to the mode field, which specifies how the number of personnel to deploy is to be determined. It is defined as follows:

```
selector mode {
    case SOME "Deploy some of the group's personnel" {
        rcc "Personnel:" -for personnel
        text personnel

        rcc "Reinforce?" -for reinforce
        yesno reinforce -defvalue 0
    }

    case ALL "Deploy all of the group's remaining personnel" {}
}
```

The selector field type controls the form's displayed content in a special way. After any options, it takes a body script which contains case commands; each case command takes a body script which can contain arbitrary dynaform commands.

The mode field will be displayed as a combo box with one item for each of the cases in the selector body. The field's value will be **SOME** or **ALL**, and the combo box will display the associated text, e.g., "Deploy some of the group's personnel". When the user selects a case, the fields defined in that case's body will be displayed. For this dynaform, the dialog will display the personnel and reinforce fields only when the mode is **SOME**.

For example, the dialog looks like this when the mode is **ALL**:

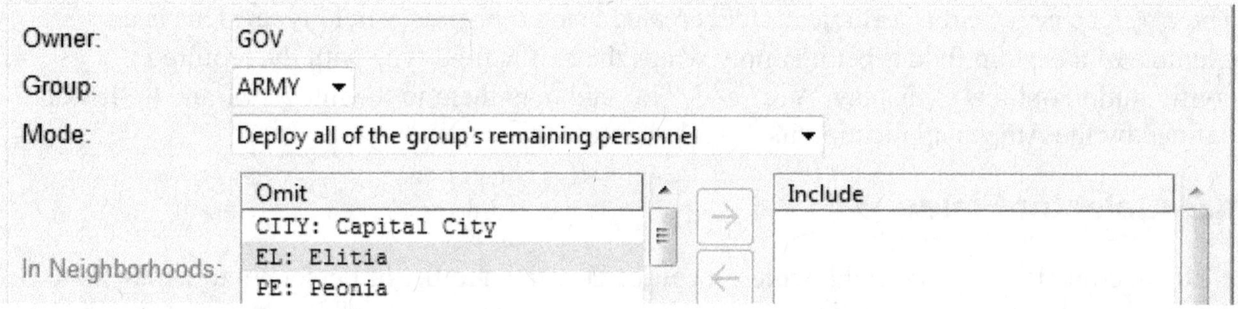

but like this when the mode is **SOME**:

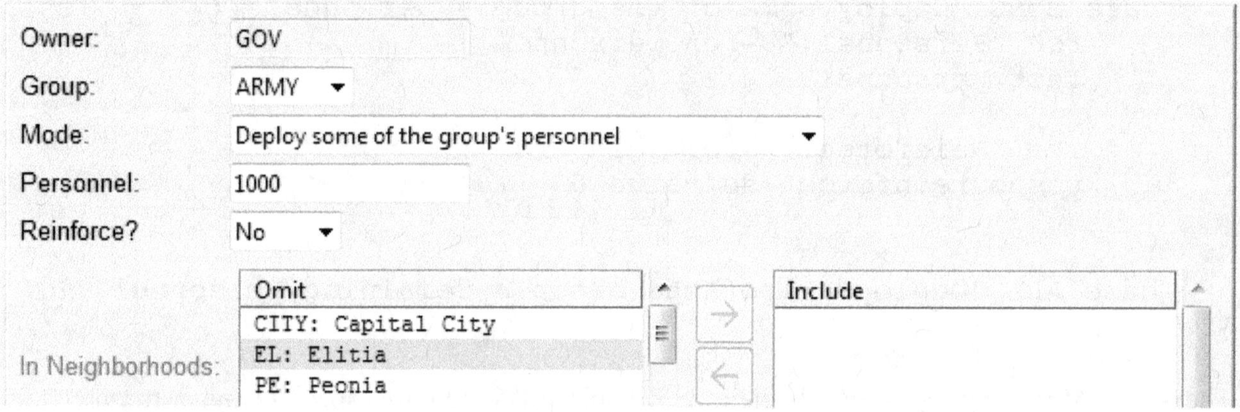

Selector fields can be nested arbitrarily deeply.

4.3 Dynamic Behavior

The Mark I and Mark II versions of the order dialog infrastructure allowed for three kinds of dynamic behavior in response to changes in the content of the fields:

- Changing the configuration of a field, e.g., setting the list of valid items for a pull-down field.
- Loading record data into the dialog when a key field's value changes.
- Changing the layout in some way

Dynaforms support these same behaviors, but in a significantly different way. In the Mark I and Mark II code it was necessary to write `-refreshcmd` callbacks; these callbacks had to contain significant logic to determine what just happened and the current state of the dialog, and make the required changes. This required second-guessing the underlying dialog code, and unless the programmer had a pretty good notion of how that code worked, it was hopeless. Even if the callbacks did mostly what was wanted it was hard to catch all of the corner cases.

With dynaforms, each of the three behaviors listed above is handled in an appropriate way.

Fields that require dynamic configuration do so by a callback that returns the required configuration information given the values of the prior fields in the dialog and the state of the application. The `enum` field, for example, has a `-listcmd` option; the command must return the current list of valid items, which is passed directly to the underlying field widget. The dynaform infrastructure ensures that the callback will be called whenever needed; and the callback need not concern itself with the dialog or second-guess its behavior or state. The command usually can just do a simple data retrieval, without any complex logic.

Key fields are handled by a `-loadcmd` callback; this is an option that can be used with any field type. The callback is called whenever the field's content changes in any way; and its job is to return a dictionary of field names and values to load into the dialog. Again, the command usually just does a simply data retrieval. All of the logic is handled by the infrastructure.

Finally, it is no longer necessary to write custom logic to control the dynamic layout of the dialog. Instead, such dynamic behavior is stated declaratively in the dynaform specification script. No callbacks are involved.

In short, dynaforms get the encapsulation layer in the right place. There are a few things a form might need to know, and callback options are provided so that the dynaform can ask for them; but the application programmer need only provide information. The dynaform's logic is internal, where it belongs.

4.4 Layout Hints and Layout Engines

The remaining commands in the dynaform language create label text and provide layout hints; the `rcç` command does both. For example, the label for the `personnel` field is created as follows:

```
rcc "Personnel:" -for personnel
```

This command assumes that a table layout is being used. It creates a new row and column, places the label "Personnel:" in that column, and then creates a new column for any subsequent content. The `-for` option relates it explicitly to the `personnel` field; when the field's value is invalid, the label will be drawn in red.

The `rcc` command is referred to as a layout "hint" because the dynaform language doesn't presuppose any particular mechanism of laying out the fields; rather, it is aimed at defining the fields and linking them to each other and to the required application data. The hints are there for the use of the GUI when it displays the dynaform, which it is free to do in any way it likes. In particular, the dynaform language does not itself assume the use of Tk; it could in principle be used with Gtk or (on the server side) with HTML or JavaScript displayed in a browser.

4.5 The Item Tree

Consider the following dynaform.

```
label "A:" -for a
text a

label "B:" -for b
selector b {
    case B1 "B1:" {
        label "C:" -for c
        text c
    }

    case B2 "B2:" {
        label "D:" -for d
        text d
    }

    case B3 "B3:" {
        label "C:" -for c
        text c

        label "D:" -for d
        text d
    }
}
```

First there is field a, which is always displayed. Next, there is selector b, which is always displayed. The selector has three cases; the first displays field c, the second field d, and the third both. Each field has an associated label. Each command in the form defines an *item*, and these items form a tree, as shown in the following diagram.

If this were a real form, it would be associated with an order with fields a, b, c, and d, and the processing of fields c and d would depend on the value of field b. Note that there are fields named c and d on several different branches. This is perfectly OK. Laying out the dynaform involves walking this tree, and picking the branches corresponding to the selector values. A field name can appear on any number of branches, just so long as it does not appear twice on the path from the root to any leaf node.

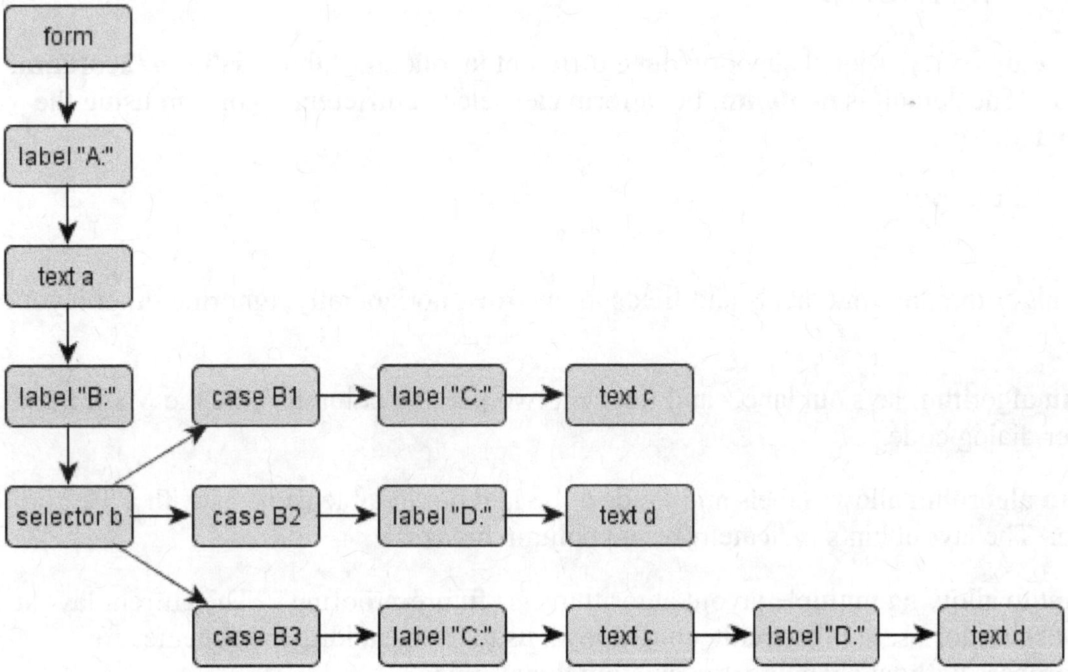

The path from the root to a leaf given the current selector values is called the *current path.*

4.6 Creating a Dynaform

Dynaforms are created using the `dynaform define` command:

```
dynaform define MYFORM {
    # form specification commands
}
```

Most dynaforms in Athena are associated with orders; the form specification is entered as part of the order's metadata and `dynaform define` is called automatically.

5. The Dynaview Widget

Dynaforms are displayed by the `dynaview` widget; the dynaform to display is determined by the `-formtype` option, which names any defined dynaform. The manner in which the form is displayed is determined by the selected layout algorithm. Given the algorithm, the widget follows the current path from the root to a leaf, using or ignoring hints and laying out labels and fields. How the hints are used depends on entirely on the chosen layout algorithm.

5.1 Layout Algorithms

At present, the dynaview widget supports three different layout algorithms: **ribbon**, **2column**, and **ncolumn**. The default is **ncolumn**, but a form can select a different algorithm using the layout command, e.g.,

```
layout ribbon
```

The **ribbon** algorithm lays out labels and fields in one row, horizontally, ignoring other layout hints.

The **2column** algorithm lays out labels and fields in two parallel columns, like the Mark I and Mark II order dialog code.

The **ncolumn** algorithm allows labels and fields to be laid out in table cells, as with a Tk grid or HTML table. The layout hints indicate row and column breaks.

The real point to allowing multiple layout algorithms is "future-proofing". The current layout scheme is working for us, but the architecture allows us to define additional schemes for particular purposes without changing any existing dynaforms.

The underlying geometry manager in each case is a Tkhtml3 widget; thus, the layout algorithm is generally producing HTML text. Tkhtml3 has a number of advantages over a Tk grid; it is easy to include rich text in the form, and lines of label text and field widgets wrap more attractively. However, the dependence of the API on Tkhtml3 is minimal, and future layout algorithms could use a different underlying widget.

5.2 Widget API

The `dynaview` widget has the following options:

`-formtype` *`name`*
Sets the name of the dynaform to display.

`-state` *`state`*
Sets the widget's *state* to **normal** or **disabled** in the usual way.

`-changecmd` *`command`*

Specifies a command prefix that will be called whenever the form's value changes for any reason (whether programmatically or due to user input). The *command* is called with one additional argument, the new value of the form.

`-currentcmd` *`command`*

Specifies a command prefix that will be called whenever the one of the form's fields receives the focus. The *command* is called with one additional argument, the name of the field that received the focus.

Next, it has the following subcommands (among others):

`form` `get`

Retrieves the form's current value: a dictionary of field names and values.

`form` `set` *`dict`*

Sets the values of the form's field widgets given the field names and values in the *dict*, and calls the `-changecmd`.

`form` `current`

Returns the name of the field that has the input focus (or the first field, if no field has the input focus).

`form` `invalid` *`fields...`*

Marks the named fields invalid. The effect is determined by the layout algorithm; for **ncolumn**, for example, the associated fields are colored red.

`form` `clear`

Clears all non-context fields, and fills in default values.

`form` `refresh`

Refreshes all fields from first to last; all fields will now be configured in accordance with the current state of the application.

Note that the `dynaview` widget adheres to the field widget API described in section 2.1. This is often useful when a field's value isn't a simple scalar value. Instead, a custom field type can be defined based on the `dynaview` widget and an appropriate dynaform.

5.3 The dynabox Command

The dynabox command pops up a modal dialog containing a dynaform, with "OK" and "Cancel" buttons. On "OK" it returns the value of the dynaform (i.e., `[$form get]`); on "Cancel" it returns the empty string. It is roughly similar to the standard tk_messageBox command, but displays an arbitrary dynaform. Thus, dynaforms can be used for general data entry, not simply for order dialogs. This is another advantage of dynaforms over the Mark I and Mark II solutions.

6. Dynaform Language

This section gives a rough overview of the dynaform language. We divide the commands in the language into two sets: content and layout.

6.1 Content Commands

The content commands are as follows:

`fieldType name ?option value...?`

Adds a field of the given type with the given *name* to the form. There are a number of predefined field types, including `text` and `enum`, as described above, and the application programmer can add more. The options are used to configure the field. The following options can be used with any field type.

`-context flag`

If *flag* is true, the field is a read-only "context" field. It provides context to the user, and its value might be used by field configuration callbacks.

`-defvalue value`

Specifies a default value for the field; the value is placed in the field when the form is cleared.

`-invisible flag`

If *flag* is true, the field is invisible, i.e., is not displayed in the dialog. This allows the application to provide context data for use by field configuration callbacks without making it visible to the user.

`-loadcmd command`

This command is called when the field's value changes; its purpose is to load data into the dialog when a key field's value changes. It is given the field's current value and other configuration data, and returns a dictionary containing field names and values. Any field whose name matches a dictionary key is updated with the value from the dictionary.

`-tip text`

Specifies tool-tip text for the field. This option is a layout hint, and how the text is used depends on the layout algorithm.

`label text ?-for field?`

Adds the *text* to the form; it can contain rich text in the form of HTML markup. If the `-for` option is included then the text is a label for the named *field*, and may be highlighted (i.e., colored red) when the field's content is in error.

`selector name ?options...? selscript`

The selector command adds a special pull-down field that controls the content of the dialog. It has the given *name* and takes all of the standard field options. The *selscript* contains one or more `case` commands; the user selects the case from the pull-down.

`case case label script`

This command can only appear in a `selector` field's *selscript*, where it adds another case to the selector. The *case* is a symbolic constant used as the `selector` field's value when the case is selected, and the *label* is corresponding text that appears in the pull-down. The *script* contains any arbitrary dynaform commands (fields, labels, and layout hints); the form items in the *script* are displayed when the case is selected by the user.

`when expr tscript ?else fscript?`

This command is like a selector case in that it controls the items that will be displayed; however, it is not a field. Instead, *expr* is a Boolean expression that may reference upstream fields by name (as well as arbitrary commands). If the expression is true, then the items in the *tscript* will be laid out; otherwise those in the *fscript* (if any) will be laid out.

6.2 Layout Commands

`layout algorithm ?options...?`

Specifies the layout algorithm to use. Currently, the choices are **ncolumn** (the default), **2column**, and **ribbon**. The choice of algorithm determines how the layout hints are used. Most existing hint commands are used only by the **ncolumn** algorithm.

`br`

Adds a line break to the form.

`c ?label? ?options...?`

For **ncolumn** layouts, starts a new column. If *label* is given, a label is added as the first item in the column.

`-for` *`field`*

Relates the label to a field, as for the `label` command.

`-span` *`n`*

The new column will span *n* table columns; defaults to 1.

`-width` *`width`*

The desired column width, in HTML length units, e.g., "3in" or "100pxi".

`cc` *`label ?options...?`*

For **ncolumn** layouts, starts a new column, places the *label* text in it, and starts a second column. The options are the same as for the `c` command.

`para`

Adds a paragraph break to the form.

`rc` *`?label? ?options...?`*

For **ncolumn** layouts, starts a new row and column. The arguments are as for the `c` command.

`rcc` *`label ?options...?`*

For **ncolumn** layouts, starts a new row and column, places the *label* text in it, and starts a second column. The options are the same as for the `cc` command.

7. Examples

This section gives a number of additional examples of dynaforms and the resulting dialogs.

7.1 Dynaform with Help Text

The following dynaform is designed to contain help text so as to be immediately understandable to the user. It is used to enter inputs for a Boolean condition called "DURING":

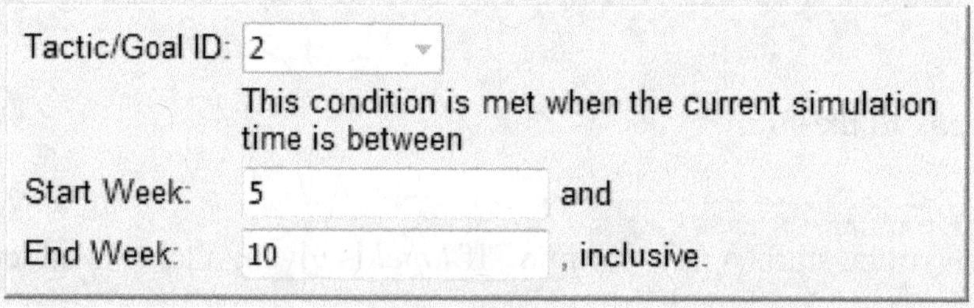

The form specification is as follows; `condcc` is a custom field type.

```
rcc "Tactic/Goal ID:" -for cc_id
condcc cc_id

rcc "" -width 3in
label {
     This condition is met when the current simulation time
     is between
}

rcc "Start Week:" -for t1
text t1
label "and"

rcc "End Week:" -for t2
text t2
label ", inclusive."
```

7.2 Dynaform with "When" Conditions

The following dynaform grows depending on the user input. It is used to enter some number of casualties to a group in the simulation.

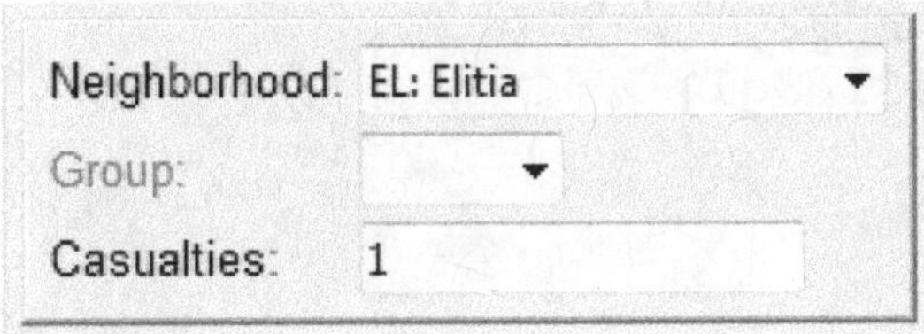

First the user must select a group. If it's a civilian group, then Athena wants to know what force group is responsible for the casualities (if any). A "Responsible Group" field appears.

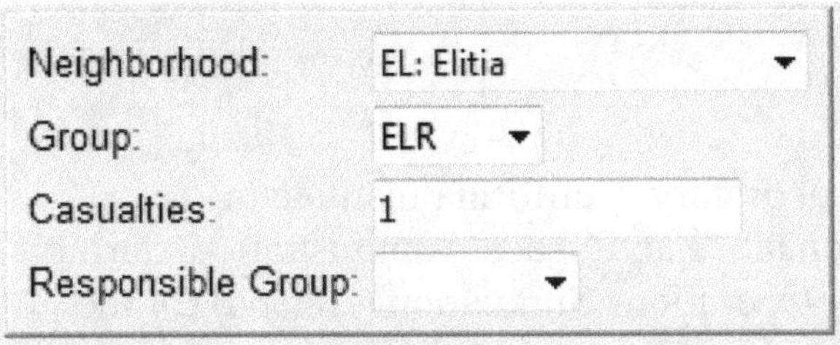

For historical reasons, Athena allows there to be up to two responsible force groups. If a name is chosen for the first, a second "Responsible Group" field appears.

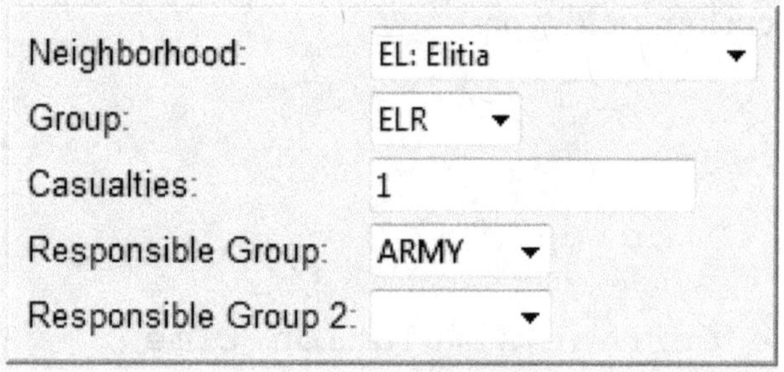

The dynaform specification is as follows; `nbhood` and `frcgroup` are custom field types.

```
rcc "Neighborhood:" -for n
nbhood n

rcc "Group:" -for f
enum f -listcmd {::aam GroupsInN $n}

rcc "Casualties:" -for casualties
text casualties -defvalue 1

when {$f in [::civgroup names]} {
    rcc "Responsible Group:" -for g1
    frcgroup g1

    when {$g1 ne ""} {
        rcc "Responsible Group 2:" -for g2
        enum g2 -listcmd {::aam AllButG1 $g1}
    }
}
```

8. References

[1] Duquette, William, Snit Object Framework, found in Tcllib, `http://tcllib.sourceforge.net/doc/snit.html`.

9. Acknowledgements

This research was carried out at the Jet Propulsion Laboratory, California Institute of Technology, under a contract with the National Aeronautics and Space Administration, during the development of the Athena Stability & Recovery Operations Simulation (Athena) for the TRADOC G2 Intelligence Support Activity (TRISA) at Fort Leavenworth, Kansas.

Tcl 2013
New Orleans, LA
September 23-27, 2013

Session IV
September 26, 2013
10:45-12:15am

A 1Ghz digital Oscilloscope in (mostly) Tcl

Ronald Fox
National Superconducting Cyclotron Laboratory, Michigan State University
640 S Shaw Lane
East Lansing, MI 48824-1321
CAEN Technologies
1140 Bay Street Suite 2C
Staten Island, NY 10305
ron@caentech.com

ABSTRACT

The transition of nuclear and particle physics data acquisition systems to high speed wave form digitization technology allows a great deal of simplification in electronics setups. There are trade-offs however. So-called 'digital data acquisition systems' require higher data transmission bandwidths and can be challenging to set up for the uninitiated.

This paper will address a software product that is being developed to address the first stages of setup. In this work the large and unfamiliar parameter space of the waveform digitizer is hidden behind a cognitive model that is familiar to most experimenters, that of a digital oscilloscope.

1. INTRODUCTION

Traditional nuclear and particle physics data acquisition systems made use of 'feature digitizers'. These devices perform an analog analysis of a waveform and provide a single value to the host/readout software. For example a Wilkinson ADC captures the height of the waveform peak and provides a number that is proportional to that height.

Traditional nuclear and particle data acquisition systems often require a significant investment in analog electronics to condition the signals presented to the digitizer. For example to use a TDC (Time to Digital Converter), an external discriminator is required to convert both the inputs and some reference signal to digital signals.

In recent times, however, improvements in the performance of high speed flash ADCs (FADCs) and high capacity field programmable gate arrays (FPGAs) have ignited a transition from feature digitizers to the use of waveform digitizers coupled with FPGAs in which are embedded digital signal processing algorithms. Indeed there are detector systems such as arrays of segmented germanium detectors which cannot be analyzed fully in any other way.

In experimental Nuclear Physics data acquisitions systems based around these FADC/FPGA combinations are called "Digital Data Acquisition Systems" (DDAS).

These advances do not come without a cost, however. During at least some part of the system setup, and during system diagnostics, it is common to need to transmit raw waveform data from the front end electronics to the online diagnostics software. This requirement drastically increases the bandwidth requirements of these systems since typical digitization speeds may exceed several hundred MHz.

Furthermore, to productively take data from digital data from a DDAS a large number of parameters must be optimized for each channel. These parameters range from those that allow the raw signal to be properly digitized to parameters that affect the digital signal processing performed by the FPGA firmware associated with each ADC channel. This can be challenging and frustrating for users new to the DDAS paradigm.

This paper will describe a project that provides researchers with a simplified familiar cognitive model that makes one set of these parameters more approachable. The scope of this project is limited to helping researchers set up the digitizer to properly accept waveforms from their detectors.

It turns out that early stages of the setup of a digitizer channels are analogous the process of setting up an oscilloscope. Therefore we provide users with digital oscilloscope software that operates by setting appropriate digitizer parameters.

This software is largely written in Tcl/Tk. The paper will discuss:

- The cognitive model being provided to the user
- The wrapping of the C API with a Tcl command ensemble, and how digitizer model differences are handled.
- The considerations behind the choice of a graphics package and its implications.
- The application's functionality and user interface.
- Issues uncovered and solutions arrived at in packaging the software in Starpack format.
- Future work.

2. COGNITIVE MODEL

In past efforts by CAEN to provide support for visualizing waveforms, presented the digitizer parameters to he user without interpretation. These parameters have names like "post-trigger", "trigger level", channel mask, and sample window. New users were often confused about the meaning of parameters and how each parameter impacted data acquisition. As such users often had trouble getting meaningful waveforms to appear in the waveform display.

Acquiring and displaying waveforms is, however something that most users have done in the past. Almost all users were knew how to set up and use a digital oscilloscope to display the signals that they then were going to digitize with their ADC.

We therefore decided to try to model the software after the controls in a digital oscilloscope. The detailed digitizer parameters and their internal names could then be hidden from the user behind more familiar controls such as trigger threshold, channel select, trigger delay.

We were also tempted to add a setup wizard, however wizards can be frustrating to users who already know how to use these devices. What we did instead was provide a guide at the bottom of the oscilloscope user interface led inexperienced users through the process of setting up the digitizer while allowing experts to bypass steps in the process, or the entire process. At each step, a subset of the 'scope' controls are enabled, while in the 'expert' mode all controls are enabled.

3. THE API ITS WRAPPER AND MORE

CAEN provides a layered set of libraries[1] that hides most of the model-to-model differences from the programmer. This allows digitizers to be programmed at a basic level without caring which digitizer the application is using.

The first step of producing the scope application was to produce a Tcl wrapping of the digitizer libraries. The libraries include data types that are not suitable to a swig wrapping, so this wrapping was done by hand. The wrapper is built on top of both the digitizer library and the Tcl++ library that was described elsewhere [2].

The wrapper library appears to the Tcl programmer as a command ensemble in the **::CAEN::** name space with the base command **digitizer**. Sub commands each wrap a specific digitizer library function. The parameters of each function have, where necessary been made Tcl friendly, for example enumerated types are converted back and forth between string representations (e.g. a value like CAEN_DGTZ_XX724_FAMILY_CODE which is a value in the digitizer family enumerator is mapped in Tcl to the string "xx724".

3.1 Module capabilities

While the CAEN digitizer libarary does a good job of insulating the programmer from most model specific issues, some model-to-model differences are not, however, transparent to the programmer. These include but are not limited to:

- Connection between the host and the digitizer.
- Sampling frequency of the digitizer
- Buffer organization of the digitizer.
- Number of channels.
- Input voltage ranges

The API does provide a mechanism to query the digitizer model family and model version (a model version is a particular digitizer model within a family). With the exception of the input voltage range, the model family and model version are sufficient to select the properties of a module.

3.2 Representing module capabilities

Module capabilities are stored in an SQLite database. A package in the software can convert database information for a module to a dict. Child records of a module's master record are represented within the dict as lists of values or sub-dicts depending on whether or not the sub-record has multiple fields that need to be represented.

A small Tk application has also been written to maintain the module database. This application allows the database to be maintained by device designers.

3.3 So you want to take data too?

The digitizer modules have multi-event memories. While some connection types (e.g. CONET and CONET connected VME bus interfaces) support interrupts, others (USB Connected VME bus interfaces and desktop digitizers with USB interfaces) do not and must be polled.

Furthermore the API presents interrupts to the user as events which must be polled. Thus the intent is for the API to be polled by the application for events which then are read out of the digitizers.

This model provides three implementation alternatives within a Tcl/Tk application driven by an event loop:

1. Drive the poll from a self-resetting **after** timer, or the libTcl API equivalent (Tcl_CreateTimerHandler).
2. Create a new event source for the Tcl/Tk event loop.
3. Run the polling in a thread and post and event to the main application thread when data are ready. This can be done either at the C level or via the tcl thread package.

The alternative chosen was to use the Tcl thread package to implement option 3. Since the CAEN digitizer library is thread safe this option does not pose too much difficulty, except for the edge case of application exit with the trigger loop active.

The trigger thread is therefore structured as a one shot. When the application is able to respond to a trigger, It tells the trigger thread to begin polling. The polling thread then polls for data available and posts and event back to the main thread when data is available. The main thread processes the event and then signals the poll thread to resume trigger polling.

When the process exit is requested, if data taking is enabled, a software trigger is generated to ensure the polling thread sees data. Once that trigger is posted back to the main thread, the handles open on the digitizer can be closed and the exit operation completed.

4. REAL-TIME GRAPHICS.

The scope program is a graphically intensive program. For each trigger, the program must draw as many as 8 traces of typically several thousand points each. At high rates, it is not necessary that the software capture every trace, however the updates appear smooth and the user interface must be responsive.

The following packages were considered for trace plotting:

1. BLT

2. Refactored BLT Components (RBC).
3. Plotchart
4. Roll-your-own canvas graphics.
5. The remainder of this section will briefly describe each of these packages, the pros and cons of using them within this application. A concluding sub-section will describe the choice and what was needed to get the choice to work.

4.1 BLT

BLT is a Tcl/Tk extension written and maintained by George Howlett [3]. It is a complied extension that features a wide variety of sophisticated graphical components.

Pros:

1. As a compiled extension its performance is very good.
2. Its design lends itself easily to time varying graphics. Each trace could be represented as a vector and updating the plot would simply be a matter of updating the points in the vector.
3. Support for expansion, coordinate transformation and feature picking is very good.
4. The author has used BLT in other work and was familiar with it.

Cons:

1. BLT is not stubs enabled and the intent from the beginning was to embed this application in a starpack. Note however that TclKits that contain BLT do exist.
2. BLT has not kept up with Tcl/Tk. While patches exist to make it work on Tcl/Tk 8.5, and while the repository shows that work is being done on the project (last update at the time this paper was going through first draft was April 30, 2013), it is not clear that the software author is able to commit the resources needed to continue to evolve the software.
3. BLT has a few dirty hooks into Tcl/Tk which would make 'self-maintenance' of the software difficult in case the project were abandoned.
4. As a compiled extension (I know I called this an advantage earlier), embedding the software in a Starkit/Starpack results in some challenges (see section 6).

4.2 Refactored BLT Components

The Re-factored BLT Components project (RBC) [4] is a project that is run by Bob Techentin. It is a fork of the BLT project. The intent of the project was to remedy the short-comings of BLT by producing a stubs compatible BLT that was decoupled from the internals dependencies that the original BLT suffers from.

Pros:

1. RBC does work with Tcl 8.5 (this author has no experience attempting to use RBC with 8.6 releases although the project pages says that it has been used with 8.6 beta releases).
2. The author has used parts of RBC with a project that used BLT and needed to migrate to Tcl 8.5 with success.
3. RBC is highly compatible with BLT so the author's knowledge of BLT could be used directly with RBC.

Cons

1. Bob classifies the software as "ready for an alpha release" which indicates there may be some pitfalls if used in a demanding environment.
2. RBC still has linkages to Tcl/Tk internals.
3. RBC has not yet been tested with Starkit/Starpacks.
4. The most recent set of releases dates back to late 2009 and the most recent set of commits were documentation commits in 2011. Unfortunately this project seems likely to be dead.

4.3 Plotchart

Plotchart [5] is a pure Tcl scientific plotting package written by Arjen Markus. Plotchart is distributed as part of the Tklib.

Pros

1. Arjen is very responsive to questions about Plotchart and very willing to make changes and bug-fixes on request.
2. Since Plotchart is pure Tcl/Tk, self-maintenance of the package in the event Arjen is not able to continue his work on it is easier.
3. Since Plotchart is a pure Tcl/Tk package, including it in a Startkit/Starpack is trivial.
4. Plotchart provides primitives for coordinate transforms that, together with event handling can add the ability to interact with the plot.

Cons

1. Plotchart's pure Tcl nature (I know I said this was an advantage too) leads to concerns about performance.
2. Plotchart's focus is on static graphics. As such it is not clear it can be easily adapted to Scope's need for dynamically changing graphics (See section 4.5 below).
3. This author was not familiar with Plotchart and therefore there would be a learning curve to using it effectively.

4.4 Roll Your Own Canvas Graphics

This option means creating my own graphics package designed for and adapted to the needs of the scope program.

Pros:

1. The resulting package will be well suited to my needs.
2. The resulting package will be something I can easily understand and be maintainable by me.

Cons

1. Time spent creating and debugging this package would detract from time that could be spent on the main application.

4.5 Decision and Consequences

None of these choices is ideal. The most attractive of all of them, however was Plotchart. Some performance testing was done by plotting a randomly phase shifted sine wave and a randomly phase shifted saw-tooth to see how quickly Plotchart could update the plot.

Plotchart's performance was deemed acceptable, although a couple of emails back and forth with Arjen were needed to fix some issues with the package that popped up as a result of this test.

As stated in section 4.3, Plotchart is not really designed for the dynamic graphics that would be produced by the scope application. For example, Scale changes that, in BLT are performed by simply changing options in the plot widget, require a complete regeneration of the plot.

As development progressed, it was useful to encapsulate the plots used by Scope in a SNIT [6] container that would transparently recreate the plot as needed, as well as provide other services required by the scope application such as markers and a key of markers. At the end of the day, however I think Plotchart was a good choice.

5. Functionality and User Interface

This section will describe the user interface of the scope program in some detail.

When starting the program, the first thing that must be provided is information about the connection to the digitizer. This is currently done via a dialog shown in Figure 1 below. The drop down menu on the left allows the user to select between the communications interfaces available and provide parameters that allow the specific digitizer module to be selected from the set attached to that interface.

Once connection has been established with a digitizer, the software reads its model family and model instance and looks up its characteristics in an SQLite database. The database is part of the Starpack's VFS, however it is copied into a temp directory based on where the operating system likes to put such things. See future work however.

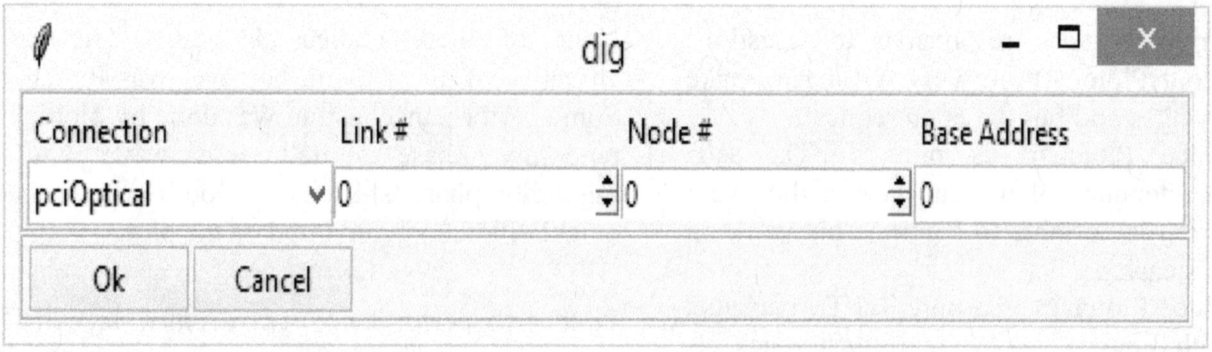

Figure 1: Connection parameter prompt

Unfortunately, the input voltage range of the digitizer is an option that cannot be determined. For each model family and model instance, there are a set of possible input ranges the user specifies when ordering the module.

The model family, model instance and serial number uniquely identify a module. The serial number is also read from the device. These are used to attempt to locate the module in another SQLite data base that is stored in the user's home directory tree (again the exact location of this database depends on the operating system). If the module has been used before, its database record provides a voltage range as a low and high limit pair.

If the module has never been seen before, the set of possible voltage ranges are presented and the user must select the correct voltage range for the module. This information is stored in the user's database and the same user will never again be prompted for this information.

Figure 2 below shows the full user interface. In this section I will describe in turn:

- The channel and trigger selection panes,
- The Scope controls pane
- The Guide pane
- The ways in which the user can interact with the plot itself.
- The menu commands.

5.1 Channel and trigger selection

The number of channels is one of the properties of the module family/module instance. The database lookup of this information is used to generate the grid of channel selection and trigger selection checkboxes and trigger selection. While the digitizer is continuously sampling, an external trigger and channel triggers are used to determine when to store a trace for readout by the host computer. The external trigger is exactly that, a logic input whose falling edge is used to indicate a waveform should be stored. The channel triggers are driven by the FPGA firmware associated with each channel. These provide a leading edge discriminator which can be set to fire when the rising or falling edge of a channel crosses a threshold value. The scope controls section (5.2) will provide more information about how the trigger parameters are set.

Triggers can only come from checked channels in the trigger selection pane. Note that this is a hardware/firmware trigger enable, not a software filter from amongst a more inclusive set of triggers. The module trigger is the logical or of all contributions to the trigger.

When the scope is triggered, only the checked channels are plotted. Where possible, the module is programmed to disable the transfer of unchecked channels to optimize data transfer performance.

In addition to the external and channel hardware triggers, the software can force a trigger at any time. While this feature seems useless, its purpose and usefulness will become clear in the subsequent sections.

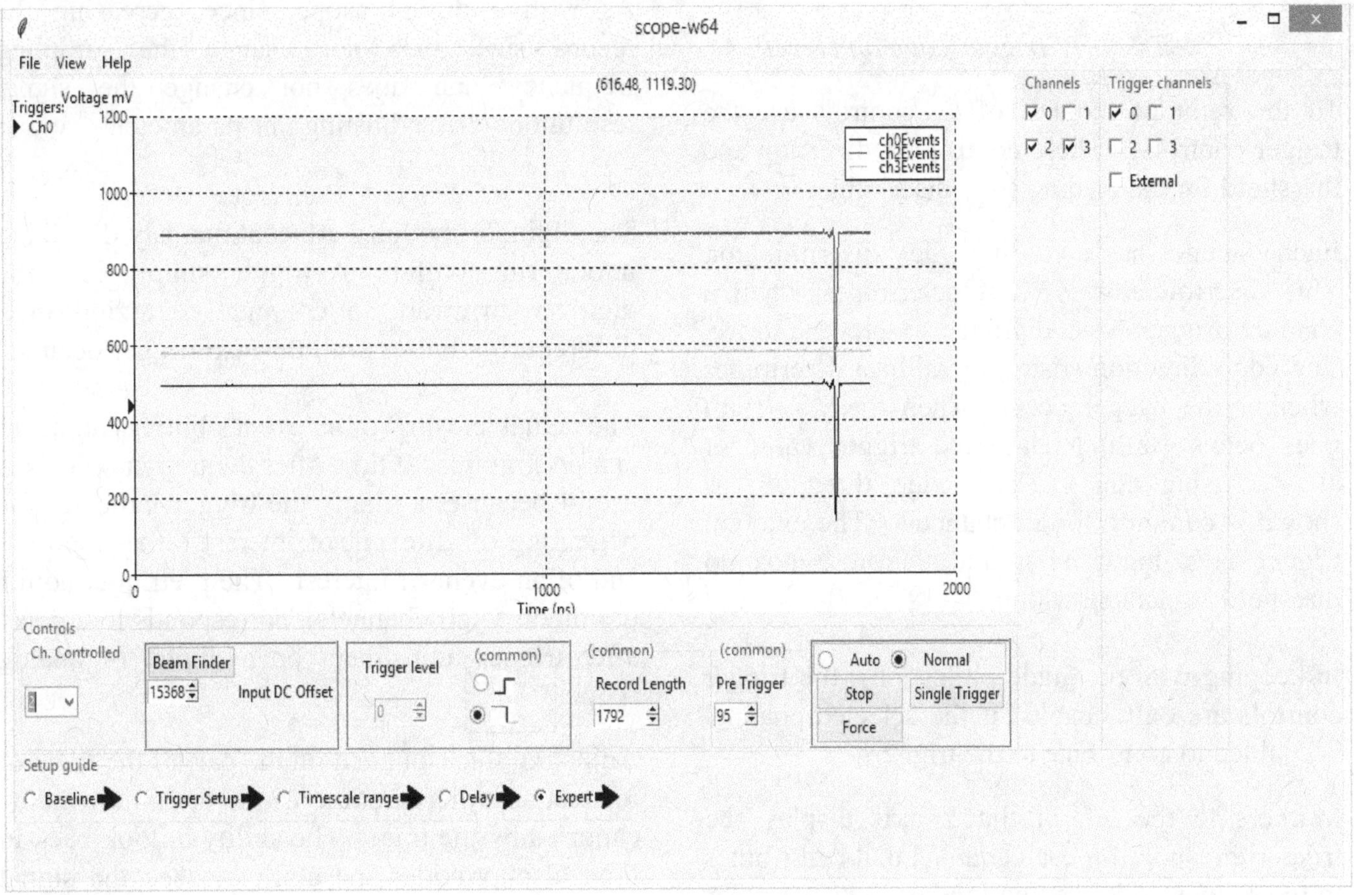

Figure 2

5.2 Scope controls

This section looks at the scope controls. For the most part, scope controls are laid out from left to right in the order in which they will be used. The procedure guide pane (see section 5.3) can further disable the set of controls that are not relevant to the operation being performed.

The left most control is a channel selection control. Most controls operate on a per-channel basis. Those that do not are labeled as common on the user interface. The selected channel determines which channel is selected for control.

5.2.1 DC Offset control

The left most box of controls is used to inject a DC offset on the signal. This is analogous to the vertical position knob on an analog/digital scope. By adjusting this value the signal can be raised or lowered within the voltage acceptance region of the digitizer. Note that each channel has an independent DC offset adjust.

Often when first plugging a signal into the scope, the user does not have a good idea where the baseline is in the window. This is due to DC offsets on the signal itself. The **Beam Finder** button attempts to automatically set the channel DC offset so that the signal baseline is located in the center of the acceptance window.

The beam finder operates by performing several software triggers. The idea is that these are asynchronous with the actual signal and are therefore likely to result in one or more traces that are largely baseline. The average value of several representative points is computed and, if there are significant outliers from this average they are discarded and the average repeated with the reduced data set. This average is again averaged over all software triggers and the DC offset required to center a trace point with that value is computed and programmed.

In practice this simplistic beam finder algorithm works quite well.

5.2.2 *Trigger edge and level*

To the right of the DC offset controls are the trigger controls. These control the direction and threshold for the leading edge discriminator.

Each channel has a leading edge discriminator. This discriminator is what determines when a channel triggers the digitizer to store a trace. The edge direction (rising or falling) determines whether the trigger occurs when the waveform goes below (falling edge) the trigger value or above (rising edge). The edge direction, as shown is common for all channels. The external trigger is a logic input and therefore has no threshold associated with it.

In keeping with the guide philosophy, the trigger controls are only enabled if the selected channel is enabled to contribute to the trigger.

Markers to the left of the Y axis display the trigger threshold for each channel that contributes to the trigger. A key at the top left links the color of each marker to the channel it controls. The marker color also matches the color of the corresponding channel's trace if that channel is enabled for display (it is legal to trigger on a channel without looking at it).

5.2.3 *Record Length Controls*

To right of the trigger level and edge adjustment is the record length control. This control is common across all channels of the digitizer.

Each digitizer module has a large memory dedicated to on-board event storage. The buffer organization of that memory is programmable. One can trade off the number of samples acquired per trace with the number of events the module can buffer before it is not able to respond to triggers.

On an oscilloscope adjusting the per event buffer size (record length) corresponds to adjusting the full scale time of the scope display.

As with a digital scope, since increasing the record size does not change the sampling frequency one does not change the signal resolution when adjusting this parameter.

5.2.4 *Pretrigger*

The digitizer modules are continuously digitizing into a ring buffer. A trigger simply tells the digitizer firmware to continue digitizing in a different ring buffer until the next trigger occurs.

The actual 'closing' of an event's buffer can occur at a programmable time after the trigger. This is useful because normally the trigger indicates the beginning of an event of interest rather than the end of an event of interest. The pretrigger adjust (common to all channels), corresponds to a delay after trigger adjustment on a digital or analog scope.

Adjusting this can position the part of the trace of interest anywhere in time within the time window captured by the trace. The ability to look back in time also provides the ability to see the signal prior to the actual trigger condition. This can be useful for signals with a slow rise-time that contain useful information on the leading edge of the signal.

One common use of this in nuclear physics is the use of fast/slow scintillator pairs to do particle identification. In that case one has a single photomultiplier on the back of a pair of detector crystals that react to ionizing radiation by emitting light. One crystal's properties may create a prompt signal while the other may create a much slower signal. Normally the slower signal provides something like the total energy while the prompt signal provides good timing (for the end of a time of flight leg for example). One can then use the discriminator to provide a low energy cut off but nonetheless look back to capture the timing of the prompt signal from the faster part of the detector.

5.2.5 *Data Acquisition Control*

The final control (rightmost) controls data acquisition. This section of the controls panel attempts to address several competing needs:

1. When first setting up it is normal to not really know what the trigger level should be or where the signal baseline will actually wind up (especially if you don't do a beam find.
2. Sometimes, when the trigger fails its good to see something even if it's not a meaningful signal.
3. When the trigger is set up properly it should be the only reason traces are saved by the module and read from the module.
4. There are times when you want to take exactly one trigger and then stop taking more data so that the trace that was acquired can be inspected closely.

These needs are addressed by the radio button pair and three buttons in the data acquisition control pane.

The push button just below the radio button pairs is labeled **Start** when data taking is in active, clicking it begins data taking and changes the label and function of that button to **Stop**. The radio button pair determines exactly how data is taken. In **Auto** mode, if a trigger has not been processed within a timeout, a software trigger is generated and the resulting trace is displayed. If there is an accidental coincidence with a trace that is not making the trigger condition that can be used to determine the correct trigger position. Otherwise a baseline trace will be displayed. When the **Normal** radio button is selected, the automatic software trigger described above is not performed, and only the trigger conditions describe by the GUI will result in a trace.

If **Single Trigger** is clicked, data taking halts when the next trigger occurs. Clicking **Single Trigger** again accepts exactly one more trigger. If **Force** is clicked a single software trigger is performed.

If data taking is halted (by clicking **Stop**), the most recent traces remain displayed.

5.3 The Procedure Guide

The set of radio buttons at the bottom of the window describes the normal flow of setting up the digitizer. When a radio button is selected, only the controls relevant to that step of the process are enabled. This provides a wizard like interface for setting up the digitizer but in a way where all steps are visible at all times, steps can easily be skipped if appropriate and arbitrary backtracking is possible. If the user believes they know what they are doing the can, at any time select the **Expert** radio button and all controls will be enabled.

This set of guide modes is a compromise between the need to help novice users set up a digitizer and the impatience a full wizard interface would create in more expert or experienced users. Furthermore, laying out the full process to the user provides a quick reference guide for users who *think* they know what they are doing but get stuck doing it.

5.4 Interacting with the plot

The scope program provides support for several simple but useful interactions with the trace. These interactions can be performed either when data taking is active or when data taking is halted (e.g. after a single trigger or when data taking is halted). Less frequently used operations are menu commands while operations that we believe will be frequently performed are implemented using a select : operate model.

The position of the cursor is continuously displayed. This allows the cursor to be used to extract simple information about the trace such as the time and height of trace features.

If the cursor is dragged over the trace (MB1 with motion), a rectangular region of interest is created and displayed. The region is stacked below the trace so that the trace is always visible. As the region of interest is changed its extent in both time and signal height are continuously displayed. When MB1 is released a pop up menu is displayed near the cursor.

- Doing nothing and eventually clicking **Cancel** provides a simple way to measure plot features. Most digital and analog scopes provide support for measuring voltage and time differences. This feature provides for simultaneous measurement of voltage and time differences.
- Clicking **Expand** expands the plot around the region of interest. Since Plotchart is allowed to choose the 'best' range and tick interval for a specified range of coordinate values, the actual expansion, in general will not be exactly the selected region of interest.
- Clicking **Info** provides the minimum and maximum values of the traces within the region of interest.

It is worth spending a bit more time describing the region of interest expansion. Multiple expansions are treated as a stack. Each expand operation pushes the previous plot limits to this expansion stack. The concept of an expansion stack was shamelessly stolen from BLT.

Whenver the scope display is expanded two buttons are displayed to the right of the guide pane. These buttons are labeled **Restore** and **Previous**. Clicking **Previous** pops the top of the zoom stack effectively going back one expansion level. Clicking **Restore** returns to the unexpanded display. Whenever the zoom stack is empty, these two buttons are removed from the user interface.

5.5 Menu commands

Less frequently used commands are relegated to the menu. The **View** menu provides the following functions:

- **Grid** toggles the visibility of a coordinate grid.
- **Real Coords** Toggles between axes labeled in ADC units (sample number and adc value) and physically meaningful coordinates (nanoseconds and millivolts).
- **Stab. Trigger** toggles on or off computations that stabilize the trigger position.

A few words about **Stab. Trigger.** There are two clocks in each module that run asynchronously. The sample clock is used to time the digitization of samples. The logic clock is used to clock the FPGA and other digital logic in the module. Triggers come a times that are related to the sampling clock but are determined by fpga firmware which is clocked by the logic clock. This means that left to itself, two completely identical signals may appear at different times in the traces. This can be distracting. Trigger stabilization is a software computation that locates the first trigger threshold crossing on the waveforms and shifts that to position it at exactly where it should be according to the value selected for the pretrigger. This stabilizes the position of the trigger in displayed time at the cost of moving the jitter to the points at the beginning and end of the waveform, which are normally uninteresting.

Turning on trigger stabilization while attempting to locate the baseline of the signal causes problems because traces acquired at that time may not have a discriminator crossing. Furthermore if the external trigger is used no meaningful shift can be computed because the discriminator may have had nothing to do with the trigger.

6. Packaging Concerns

From the very beginning, the goal was to package the software into a Starkit and bind that Starkit to platform dependent TclKits to form a set of Starpacks[7]. This would allow the application to be bound together with the CAEN Digitizer libraries providing for a nearly single file installation of the software on all supported platforms (currently 32 and 64 bit Linux and 32 and 64 bit Windows operating systems).

Fully single file installation is not possible because operating system device drivers for the USB and CONET interfaces are required. These not only have to be installed but, in the case of Linux loaded into the kernel and, in the case of Windows placed where the hotplug system can locate and dynamically install them when devices are detected.

Getting cross-platform StarPacks to work with compiled extensions that have dependencies loaded in the virtual filesystem is tricky and, without a number of searches of **http://wiki.tcl.tk** this would have taken quite a bit longer to get working. The wiki provided quite a few hints about what the pkgIndex.tcl file might need to look like but was somewhat vague on how to get dependent libraries loaded from the StarPack itself.

The original idea was to provide a thin wrapper around **Tcl_FSLoadFile** that could load the Digitizer libraries and its dependencies as part of the process of loading the digitizer wrapper package. This posed no problems under Windows. Under Linux, however even though the documentation of that function states that if the object cannot be loaded from the virtual file system..." Tcl will attempt to copy the file to a temporary directory and load that temporary file"...the load consistently failed.

This was eventually traced to the fact that while the file may have been copied, evidently Tcl_FSLoadFile did not supply sufficient information about the location of the temporary copy to allow the dynamic loader to find it, so the dynamic loader fell back to searching for the shared object in its standard set of directories.

The eventual work-around for this problem was to wrap the StarPack in a modified shell archive. The modifications unpacked the Starpack into ~/.caenscope, creating the directory if needed, defined the environment variable **LD_LIBRARY_PATH** to include ~/.caenscope and executed the StarPack.

The pkgIndex.tcl script, detecting a Linux platform copies the appropriate shared libraries to that directory and explicitly loads them from there. Experimentally it appeared that simply specifying the full path to the copied shared libraries was still insufficient to load them without the **LD_LIBRARY_PATH** definition.

7. Future work

The functionality of the scope application is sufficient to support setup of the CAEN family of digitizer modules. Future work is planned both to extend the functionality of the software and to clean up some loose ends:

1. Support will be added to export traces from the display to both text and binary files. A simple XML or JSON format will probably be used for the text format and SQLite is being considered as a binary format that would support the random access retrieval of an event from a collection of events.
2. The architecture of the software mostly follows the Model View Controller (MVC) software pattern. The breaks in that pattern must be removed as there is discussion that the Model and Controller components should be able to run as a headless server with well defined socket based communications providing the capability of using either the CAEN provided View or a custom user written view that might drive the digitizers in a real data acquisition system.
3. The need to copy the read only SQLite module capabilities database out into the file system can be removed using work done by Anton Kovalenko [8] that I became aware of after implementing the database copy out code. Since the module

capability database is read only, this should be safe.

4. While I think the implementation of the device capabilities database as an SQLite database was a good choice, it leaves begs the question of how to maintain deployed versions of the scope program as CAEN expands our digitizer product line. Specific issues are:
   a) How to update the capabilities database.
   b) How to provide updates to the CAENDigitizer libraries when new hardware and even digitizer firmware updates require it.

8. Conclusions

With the increased use of high frequency, high resolution flash ADC based digitization cards, tools are required to support both inexperienced and experienced users of these devices. Tcl and StarPacks provide a development environment that is a good balance between quick development and, simple deployment.

This papers has described CAEN Technologies work to provide a tool for the initial setup of its own product line of digitizers. The software is moving towards its first initial public releases. For the most part development has been smooth and trouble free.

9. References

[1] CAEN Digitizer Library is a freely available support library for the CAEN family of digitizers available at:
http://www.caen.it/csite/CaenProd.jsp?idmod=717&parent=38

[2] Tcl++ is a C++ encapsulation of the major features of libtcl. It has been recently encapsulated as a .deb package and is briefly descdribed in
http://www.tcl.tk/community/tcl2004/Papers/RonFox/fox.pdf

[3] G. Howlett Building Applications with BLT
http://www.ing.iac.es/~docs/external/tcl/BLT/handouts.pdf

[4] B. Techentin et al.
http://rbctoolkit.sourceforge.net/

[5] Plotchart was written by Arjen Markus and is part of Tklib one manpage source is:
http://docs.activestate.com/activetcl/8.5/tklib/plotchart/plotchart.html

[6] SNIT is W. Duquette's pure Tcl object oriented extension to Tcl/Tk. SNIT is part of TclLib and is described e.g. at
http://www.wjduquette.com/snit/snit.html

[7] S. Landers *Beyond TclKit - Starkits, Starpacks and other stuff* Presented Tcl 2002 Vancouver BC Sep. 16-20, 2002 Paper available online at
http://www.tcl.tk/community/tcl2002/archive/Tcl2002papers/landers-tclkit/tclkit.pdf

[8] A. Kovalenko Tcl VFS integration for Sqlite3
http://www.siftsoft.com/tclsqlitevfs.html

Cmdr

Andreas Kupries ActiveState Software Inc. 409 Granville Vancouver, BC CA
andreask@ActiveState.com

ABSTRACT

The `cmdr` framework is a set of 12 related Tcl packages for the easy specification of the interfaces of command line applications. This means the declaration of the set of commands provided by the application, and their parameters, be they options or positional inputs. At runtime the internals of the framework, guided by the chosen specification, handle the bulk of processing $::argv. This covers determining the requested command, mapping argument words to command parameters, and validating them. Additional features of the runtime are an integrated help system and interactive command line shells with basic command and argument completion.

1. INTRODUCTION

Following a short overview of the framework's history, the bulk of the paper describes its design and internal structure. The paper concludes with a dicussion of limitations, warts, and possible future directions to take.

Development of cmdr[3] (speak Commander) began as a rewrite of the `stackato` command line client's[1] because of various problems with the existing system, namely the use a global namespace for all options of all commands, and the hacks needed to support hierarchical commands.

Wanted was a system able to at least handle most of the tasks of command line processing automatically, like parsing the list of words, determining the requested command, separating named options from positional inputs, matching argument words to the parameter, etc.

Further wanted were facilities to ease the implementation of less common tasks, like validation of parameter values, transforming from external (string) to internal representations, performing checks across multiple parameters, etc.

Existing packages like getopt[10] and cmdline[8] were much too simple for all of the above, so development of a new package was begun. The TEPAM[8] package, which actually comes relatively near to the requirements, was not remembered at the time. It is also more geared towards the creation of procedures with more complex argument processing, and not the description of the entire command line syntax of applications.

A requirement going beyond the above, and initially more of a wish, was support for an interactive command line shell. This spawned the development of a CriTcl[4] binding[9] to the linenoise[2] C library which portably handles all the necessary low-level tasks regarding terminal access and control. Build on top of this `cmdr` not only supports command line shells in various places of the runtime, but also has command line completion.

This paper describes version 0.4 of the framework.

As a small motivating example see listing 1 which specifies a command line providing 3 commands for the management of command aliases. This is actually a slice of `stackato`'s interface, modified to fit.

While this example does not have the necessary backend procedures required to actually run the commands, it is enough to demonstrate the integrated help system. Listing 2 shows the output of `tclsh ./alias0.tcl help`.

The decoupling of command names from their implementations we see here makes it easy to re-arrange and re-label the user visible commands without having to touch any other part of the code.

Listing 3 for example shows how the specification would look like if a command hierarchy is prefered over a flat set of names.

The associated help is shown in listing 2, albeit in the shortest variant possible, the result of running the command `tclsh ./alias1.tcl help --list` [1].

[1] And a bit of manual breaking of lines normally done automatically, guided by the terminal width. The default of 80 did not fit here.

2. SPECIFICATION

The domain specific language demonstrated in the previous section is the first, and main, interface seen by a developer.

It actually consists of three separate languages, for the specification of the overall command hierarchy (see table 1), of the individual commands in that hierarchy (see table 2), and their parameters (see table 3).

2.1 General

The conceptual model underneath the command hierarchy is that of a tree.

The inner nodes of the tree represent command ensembles, here called "officer"s. Each officer knows one or more commands, and delegates actual execution to their respective specification, which may be another `officer`, or a `private`.

The leaf nodes of the tree represent the individual commands, here called "private"s. Each private is responsible for a single action, and knows how to perform it and the parameters used to configure that action at runtime.

The same model is graphically presented in the Entity-Relationship-Diagram 1 below.

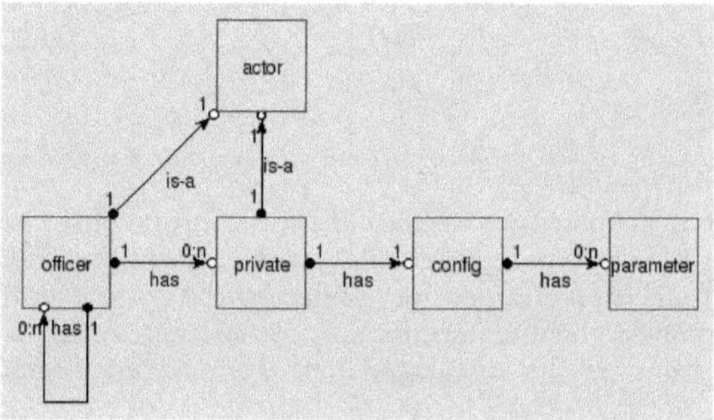

Figure 1: The Entities and their Relations

The not yet described "Actor" is the common base class for the ensembles and commands. The other, "Config", is the second interface seen by the developer, as the sole argument to the action callback argument of `private` (see 2nd-last row of table 1). This container holds all the declared parameters of the command the action is invoked for, and provides easy access to them through its methods at the time "Execution" (→ 3.4).

2.2 Officers

The three most common DSL commands used to specify officers (`officer`, `private`, and `description`, see table 1) have already been demonstrated in the examples (see listings 1 and 3).

alias *name* = *name'...*	Declare an alternate name for a command path.
alias *name*	Declare an alternate name for the previous command.
common *name script*	Declare shared code block.
default	Set last command as default.
description *text*	Set help text for the current ensemble.
ehandler *cmdprefix*	Execution Interposition.
officer *name script*	Declare a nested ensemble.
private *name script cmdprefix*	Declare a simple command. The script uses the commands found in table 2.
undocumented	Hide ensemble from help.

Table 1: Officer DSL

This leaves us with five commands not shown yet.

Of these `alias` is a structuring command, for the command hierarchy. It main uses are the creating of alternate command names, and of shortcuts through the command hierarchy. For example, `stackato`'s command specification for alias management is more like listing 3 and uses shortcuts similar to what is shown in listing 5 to provide the look of a flat namespace.

While `common` is a structuring command as well, its use is in structuring the specification itself. It creates named values, usually code blocks, which can be shared between specifications. Each block is visible in the current officer and its subordinates, but not to siblings. An example of such a block is shown in listing 6 (page), where it defines an option to access the subsystem for debug narative [8]. The example is actually special, as the code block named `*all*` is reserved by the framework. This code block, if defined, is automatically included at the front of all `private` specifications, i.e. shared across all specified commands. A very important trait for the option in the example, as it makes the debug setup available to all commands without having to explicitly include the block, and possibly forgetting such.

Use of the `undocumented` command influences the help generation, excluding all officers marked with it (and their subordinates) from the help. Note that subordinates reachable through aliases may be included, under the alias name, if not explicitly excluded themselves.

The last two commands influence the framework's behaviour at runtime

The `default` command sets up a default command to use at runtime if the currently processed word does not match any of the commands known to the officer. Without such a default an error would be thrown instead.

The `ehandler` command is possibly the most disruptive. It should normally only the specified at the top of the whole hierarchy. At runtime the framework will call the command prefix specified through it with a single argument, a script whose execution is equivalent to the phases "Parsing", "Comletion", and "Execution" of the framework, as described in section **??**. The handler must call this script, and can perform any application-specific actions before and after.

The handler's main uses are the capturing and handling of application-specific errors which should not abort the application, or shown as Tcl stacktrace, and for the cleanup of application-specific transient settings the parameter callbacks and/or command implementations may have set during their execution. This is especially important if the interactive command line shells of the framework are not disabled. Without such a handler and its bespoke cleanup code transient settings will leak between multiple commands run from such a shell, something which is definitely not wanted.

2.3 Privates

The specification of simple commands is relatively simple, with only seven commands (see table 2). The important parts are found in the parameter specifications, explained in the next section.

description *text*	Set help text for command.
interactive	Allow interactive shell.
undocumented	Hide command from help.
use *name*	Execute the named `common` block here.
input *name help script*	Declare a positional parameter. See table 3 for the available commands.
option *name help script*	Declare a named parameter. See table 3 for the available commands.
state *name help script*	Declare a hidden parameter. See table 3 for the available commands.

Table 2: Private DSL

The commands `description` and `undocumented` behave like the equivalents for officers.

`use` is the counterpart to `common` of officers, inserting the named code block it defines into the specification.

`interactive` influences the runtime. By default the only interactive command line shells are associated with the officers. Setting this marker activates such a shell for the command, to be invoked when required parameters do not have a value. The global command `cmdr::config interactive` can be used to globally activate this type of shell for all commands.

The remaining three commands all add one of the three kinds of parameters to the command.

2.4 Parameters

The parameters of `private` commands are the heart of the system, providing the space needed to transfer the command arguments to the implementations, and having the most attributes controlling their behaviour.

This complexity is mitigated strongly by the use of sensible defaults for each of the three possible kinds of parameter, i.e. positional `inputs`, named `options`, and `state` hidden from the command line. Each kind has its own construction command in the DSL for `private`, specifying the common information which cannot have defaults, i.e. the name identifying it to the system (→ 2.4.1, the help text describing it in informal speech, and, of course, the specification itself (see table 2).

The association between the specification commands, parameter attributes, and their defaults is found in table 3, with each group explained in the following sections.

2.4.1 Naming

We have two commands to influence the visible naming of all parameters.

As background, all parameters are named for proper identification within the framework and other Tcl code, i.e. the various calbacks, including a `private`'s action. This system name has to be unique within the `private` a parameter belongs to. Beyond that however the visible parameters have to be identified within help texts, and, in case of `options`, for detection during "Parsing" (→ 3.2). That is the visible naming, seen by a user of any application whose command line processing is based on the `cmdr` framework.

The `label` command handles this, using the system name as default. Note that in most cases this default is good enough. The only use case seen so far is when two semantically equivalent `input` and `option` parameters clash, requiring different internal names due to the requirement for uniqueness, yet also the same visible name and flag within the help to highight their connection and equivalence.

In case of `options` the `label` command and its default specifies the name of the primary flag recognized during "Parsing". If that is not enough for a specific `option` the command `alias` allows the specification of any number additional flags to be recognized. Note however that the framework automatically recognizes not only the specified flags, but also all unique prefixes, obviating the need for `alias` in many cases.

2.4.2 General control

The general handling of a parameter is influenced by three commands.

Like `officers` and `privates` parameters can be hidden from the generated help. The command for this is `undocumented`, the same as for the first two . This is mainly of use to hide `options` giving an application developer access to the internals of

Command	Attribute	Input	Option	State	Notes
–	name	–	–	–	Parameter name, unique within the `private`.
–	description	–	–	–	Help text.
–	visible	yes	yes	no	Parameter is (in)visible to "Parsing" (→ 3.2).
–	ordered	yes	no	n/a	Access during "Parsing" (→ 3.2) is ordered.
label *text*	label	`name`	`name`	n/a	Name to use in the help, and as primary flag (for an `option`).
alias *name*	aliases	n/a	none	n/a	Declare alternate flag for an `option` to be recognized by. Multiple aliases are allowed.
optional	optionality	no	n/a (yes)	n/a (no)	Declare `input` as optional.
test	acceptance	threshold	n/a	n/a	Control the matching of words to optional `inputs` (→ ??).
undocumented	undocumented	no	no	n/a (yes)	Declare as hidden from help.
list	listness	no	no	no	Declare as list-valued.
default *value*	default	*	*	*	Set constant default value. Details in section 2.4.3.
generate *cmdprefix*	generate	*	*	*	Set callback returning the default value. Details in section 2.4.3.
interact *?prompt?*	interact, prompt	*	*	*	Enable the interactive entry of the string value. Default prompt derives from the `label`. Details in section 2.4.3.
defered	defered	no	no	yes	Defer calculation of the internal representation until demanded.
immediate	defered	yes	yes	no	Complement of `defered`. Calculate the internal representation during "Completion" (→ 3.3).
presence	presence	no	no	n/a	Declare as boolean `option` without argument. Implies `default` and `validate` settings.
validate *cmdprefix*	validate	*	*	*	Declare validation type. Details in section 2.4.4.
when-complete *cmdprefix*	when-complete	none	none	none	Set callback executed when the value becomes known.
when-set *cmdprefix*	when-set	none	none	none	Set callback executed when the string value becomes known.

Table 3: Parameters: DSL, Attributes, and Defaults

their application, something a regular has no need of, and doesn't have to know about.

Next is the possibility of specific **inputs** not being required to be set by the user of the application, i.e. having sensible defaults (see also validation in section2.4.4). To mark such parameters use the command **optional**. During "Parsing" (→ 3.2) the system will then expend some effort to determine whether an argument word should be assigned to such a parameter, or not.

The **test** command is related to this, switching from the standard regime based on counting to a different one based on validation. The details are explained in section 3.2.

2.4.3 Representations

An important concept of parameters is something taken up from Tcl itself. The differentation between string and internal representations. Where Tcl uses internal representations to speed up its execution here this separation is that between the information delivered to the application by a user, and the application-specific data structures behind them.

All parameters will have an internal representation. This is usually derived from the string representation provided by the user. The details of that process are explained in section 2.4.4 about validation types. However we have cases where the user cannot specify a string representation (**states**), or is allowed to choose not to (optional **inputs**, **options**). For these cases three specification commands are made available enabling us to programmatically choose the internal representation. They are **default**, **generate**, and **interact**.

The first, **default**, provides a constant value for the internal representation. The second, **generate**, provides a callback to compute the internal representation at runtime. This is useful if the default is something which cannot be captured as a fixed value, for example a handle to some resource, or a dynamically created object. These two commands exclude each other, i.e. only of them can be specified.

If none of them are specified, and we need a default (see the cases above) a default is chosen per the two rules below:

1. Use the empty string for a **list** parameter.
2. Use the default value supplied by the chosen validation type (See section 2.4.4).

The third command, **interact**, actually does not specify an internal representation, but activates another method for the user to specify a string value for the parameter, outside of the command line. As such it has priority over either **default** and **generate**, and can be specified with either. A parameter marked with it will interactively ask the user for a value if none was specified on the command line.

To recapitulate:

1. A string representation specified on the command line has the highest priority and goes through the chosen validation type to get the associated internal representation.
2. If activated via **interact** a small shell is run asking the user for a value (or more, as per **list**). The result goes through the chosen validation type to get the associated internal representation.
3. After that the internal representation is either the declared **default**, or the result of invoking the **generate** callback. As internal representations they are **not** run through the chosen validation type.

A command just noted in the recapitulation is **list**. It is used to mark parameters whose string and thus internal value should be treated as a list. This affects the handling of the parameter during "Parsing" (→ 3.2), by **interact** above, and the use of the validation type. The last two ask for multiple values, and feed the elements of the string value separately through validation instead of just the string value in one. During "Parsing" treatment of **options** changes from keeping only the last assigned value to accumulation of all values. Similarly a list-**input** takes all remaining words on the command line for itself instead of just the current word. Because of this list-**inputs** are only allowed as the last parameter of a **private**.

The last two specification commands dealing with the representations control when the internal representation is created. A **defered** parameter will do it on-demand, on the first access to its value. A **immediate** parameter on the other hand will do this during "Completion" (→ 3.3).

2.4.4 Validation

The answer to the necessity of moving between the string and internal representations described in the previous section are the validation types. Given a string representation they either return the associated internal representation or raise an error, signaling that the input was illegal. This part of their work, the verification of the legality of the input string gave them their name.

Because of the same necessity all parameters must have a validation type assigned to them, and the system will choose which, if the user did not. This choice is made per the six rules below and always returns one of the standard types shown in table 4.

1. Use "identity" if a **generate** callback is specified.
2. Use "boolean" if no **default** is specified and the parameter is an **option**.
3. Use "identity" if no **default** is specified and the parameter is an **input**.

4. Use "boolean" if the specified `default` value is a Tcl boolean.

5. Use "integer" if the specified `default` value is a Tcl integer.

6. Use "identity" as fallback of last resort.

Name	Complete-able	Accepts
boolean	yes	A Tcl boolean
identity	no	All strings
≡ pass		
≡ str		
integer	no	A Tcl integer
rdirectory	yes	A readable directory name
rfile	yes	A readable file name
rpath	yes	A readable path
rwdirectory	yes	A read/writable directory name
rwfile	yes	A read/writable file name
rwpath	yes	A read/writable path

Table 4: Builtin Validation Types

The general concept of validation types was taken from `snit` [7], and modified to suit `cmdr`. Where `snit`'s types expect only a single method to validate the input `cmdr` expects all types to support an ensemble of four methods, one for the basic validation and transformation of the input, another for the release of any internal representation so generated, plus delivery of a default representation and support for command line completion. The details (method names, signatures, etc.) can be found in table 5.

{*}*vtype*...	Meaning
... complete p x	Return the list of legal string representations for the type and parameter p which have the incomplete word x as their prefix.
... default p	Return the default internal representation for the type and parameter p.
... release p x	Release the (resources associated with the) internal representation x of parameter p.
... validate p x	Verify that x is a legal string representation for p, and return the associated internal representation.

Table 5: Validation Type Methods

As an example the implementation of the standard boolean validation type is shown in listing 7. Note that while this example uses a `namespace ensemble` other methods are possible too, i.e. all the various object systems for Tcl would be suitable as well.

It should be noted that while `snit`'s validation types in principle allow for the transformation of input into a disparate internal representation, they never went so far as to allow complex representations which might require the release of resources after use.

Regarding the timing of a validation type's use of its methods see table 7 about the association of phases and callbacks.

The `validate` and `release` methods are primarily used during either "Completion" (→ 3.3) or "Execution" (→ 3.4), depending on the chosen deferal state. They may also be used during "Parsing" (→ 3.2), for optional `inputs` under the `test`-regime (→ 2.4.2).

The `complete` method will be used whereever the system activates an interactive command line shell where arguments may be assigned to parameters.

The `default` method on the other hand can expect to be invoked during "Dispatch" (→ 3.1), as part of the system's declaration processing, if not preempted by `default` and `generate` declarations for the parameter. Note here that the `default` method has the same signature as a `generate` callback and can be used as such. This is actually needed and useful when the default internal representation for a validation type cannot be expressed as a fixed value and its creation while parsing the specification itself is too early. We can still use the validation type for its generation, by hooking it explicitly into `generate` to change the timing of its invokation.

Not yet discussed so far is `presence`. This is best handled as part of the wider area of `options` with a `boolean` validation type assigned to them. These have associated special behaviours, both in the handling of the specification, and during "Parsing" (→ 3.2).

First, normal `boolean options`. They have automatic aliases declared for them, derived from their primary flag. An option named "foo" will have an alias of "no-foo", and the reverse. During parsing the "foo" and "no-foo" flags have inverse semantics, and both are allowed to occur without option argument following the flag. This is in contrast to all other options which must have such an argument. The parser essentially uses the validation type to decide if the word after the flag is a proper boolean value, or not, i.e. an argument to assign to the parameter, or not.

Now `presence` declares a variant of the above, a `boolean option` without the automatic aliases, and never taking an argument during "Parsing" (→ 3.2). Its mere presence on the command line will set its parameter. Their `default` is consequently fixed to "false" as well.

2.4.5 Signaling

Of the four callbacks supported by parameters the first two, `generate` and `validate` have been described already, in the sections 2.4.3 about representations and 2.4.4 about validation types, respectively.

This section explains the commonalities between the callbacks in general, and the last two, for notifications about state changes in detail.

All callbacks are treated as command prefixes, not scripts. There are no placeholder substitutions, only arguments added to each command prefix on invokation. This does not harm the generality of the system, as complex scripts can be used via procedures or equivalents (i.e. `apply`).

The signatures expected by the system are shown in the tables 6 and 5.

Callback	Signature
generate *cmd*	{*}$cmd *param*
validate *cmd*	See table 5
when-complete *cmd*	{*}$cmd *param intrep*
when-set *cmd*	{*}$cmd *param string*

Table 6: Callback signatures

The last two callbacks not yet described are the two state-change callbacks defined via `when-set` and `when-complete`. They are invoked when either the string representation of their parameter is set (`when-set`), or their internal representation (`when-complete`). Through them the framework can actively drive parts of the application while processing the command line, whereas normally the application drives access to parameters through their methods (see table 9).

	Dispatch	Parsing	Completion	Execution
validate (default)	*			
validate (complete)		*	`immediate`	`defered`
when-set		*		
generate			`immediate`	`defered`
validate (validate)		`test`	`immediate`	`defered`
validate (release)		`test`	`immediate`	`defered`
when-complete			`immediate`	`defered`

Table 7: Execution Phases and Callbacks

Due to their nature these callbacks are invoked at runtime during either "Parsing" (→ 3.2), "Completion" (→ 3.3), or "Execution" (→ 3.4). The details are shown in table 7. The specification commands influencing the timing, i.e. forcing the use in a specific phase are shown in the intersection of callback and phase.

3. EXECUTION

At runtime a command line is processed in four distinct phases, "Dispatch" (→ 3.1), "Parsing" (→ 3.2), "Completion" (→ 3.3), and "Execution" (→ 3.4), explained in more detail in the following sections.

3.1 Dispatch

The first phase determines the `private` to use. To this end it processes words from the command line and uses them to navigate the tree of `officers` until a `private` is reached.

Each word of the command line is treated as the name of the `officer` instance to descend into. An error will be thrown when encountering a name for which there is no known actor[2], and the current `officer` has no `default` declared for it.

On the converse, when reaching the end of the command line but not reaching a `private` the framework will not throw an error. It will start an interactive command line shell instead. This shell provides access to exactly the commands of the `officer` which was reached, plus two pseudo-commands to either exit this shell or gain help (`.exit`, and `.help`).

Execution of the command tree specification, i.e. generation of the associated internal `cmdr` data structures, is intertwined with this descend through the command tree. I.e. instead of processing the entire specification in full it is lazily unfolded on demand, ignoring all parts which are not needed. Note that the generated data structures are not destroyed after "Execution" (→ 3.4), but kept, avoiding the need to re-parse the parts of the specification already used at least once when an interactive command line shell is active.

[2] officer or private

3.2 Parsing

This is the most complex phase internally, having to assign the left-over words to the parameters of the chosen `private`, taking into account the kind of parameters, their requiredness, listness, and other attributes.

Generally processing the words from left to right `options` are detected in all positions, through their flags (primary, aliases, and all unique prefixes), followed by their (string) value to assign.

When a word cannot be the flag for an option the positional `inputs` are considered, in order of their declarations. For a mandatory `input` the word is simply assigned as its string value and processing continues with the next word, and the next `input`, if any. Operation becomes more complex when the `input` under consideration is `optional`. Now it is necessary to truly decide if the word should be assigned to this `input` or the following.

The standard method for this decision is to count words and compare to the count of mandatory `inputs` left. If there are more words available than required to satisfiy all mandatory `inputs`, then we can and do assign the current word to the optional input. Otherwise the current `input` is skipped and we consider the next. A set of condensed examples can be found in table 8, showing how a various numbers of argument words are assigned to a specific set of `inputs`, `optional` and non. This is called the "threshold" algorithm.

Parameter	A?	B	C?	D?	E
#Required	2		1	1	
2 arguments:		a			b
3 arguments:	a	b			c
4 arguments:	a	b	c		d
5 arguments:	a	b	c	d	e

Table 8: Example: Mapping arguments to optional inputs by threshold

The non-triviality in the above description is in the phrase to "count words". We cannot simply count all words left on the command line. To get a proper count we have discard/ignore all words belonging to options. At this point the processor essentially works ahead, processing and removing all flags/options and their arguments from the command line before performing the comparison and making its decision.

The whole behaviour however can be changed via `test` (→ 2.4.2). Instead of counting words the current word is run through the validation type of the current `input`. On acceptance the value is assigned to it, otherwise that `input` is skipped and the next one put under consideration.

After all of the above the system will process any options found after the last word assigned to the last `input` to consider.

Errors are thrown if we either find more words than `inputs` to assign to, or encountering an unknown option flag. Note that not having enough words for all required `inputs` is not an error unless the framework is not allowed to start an interactive shell. In this shell all parameters are mapped to shell commands taking a single argument, the string value of parameter to assign. Additional five pseudo commands are available to either abort, or commit to the action, or gain help (`.ok, .run, .exit, .cancel,` and `.help)`.

Parameters marked as `list`-valued also trigger special behaviours. For `options` the assigned values get accumulated instead of each new value overwriting the last. For `inputs` only one such parameter can exist, and will be the last of the `private`. The processor now takes all remaining words and assign them to this parameter. If the list is also optional then options may be processed ahead or not, depending on the chosen decision mode, as described for regular inputs above.

Then are the `boolean` and `presence options` modifying the handling of flags and flag arguments. The details of this were already explained in section 2.4.4.

3.3 Completion

This phase is reached when all words of the command line have been processed and no error was thrown by the preceding phases. At this point we know the `private` to use, and its parameters may have a string representation.

All `immediate`-mode parameters are now given their internal representation. The parameters marked as `defered` are ignored here and will get theirs on first access by the backend.

This completion of parameters is done in their order of declaration within the enclosing `private`. Note that when parameters have dependencies between them, i.e. the calculation of their internal representation requires the internal representation of another parameter then this order may be violated as the requesting parameter triggers completion in the requested one on access. If this is behaviour not wanted then it is the responsibility of the user specifying the `private` to place the parameters into an order where all parameters access only previously completed parameters during their completion.

3.4 Execution

The last phase is also the most simple.

It only invokes the Tcl command prefix associated with the chosen `private`, providing it with the `config` instance holding the parameter information extracted from the command line as its single argument.

Listing 8 is an example of very simple action implementations, matching to the initial example specifications in listings 1 and 3.

All parameters declared for the `private` are made accessible through individual methods associated with each. A parameter named P is mapped to the method "@P", with all methods provided by the parameter class accessible as sub-methods. This general access to all methods may be removed in the future, restricting actions and callbacks to a safe subset. A first approximation of such a set can be found in table 9.

cmdline	True if the parameter accessible on command line.
config ...	Access to the methods of the container the parameter belongs to, and thus all other parameters of the private.
default	Default value, if specified. See `hasdefault`.
defered	True if the internal representation is generated on demand.
description *?detail?*	Help text. May be generated.
documented	True if the parameter is not hidden from help.
forget	Squash the internal representation. See also `reset`.
generator	Command prefix to generate a default value (internal representation).
hasdefault	True if a default value was specified. See `default`.
help	Help structure describing the parameter.
interactive	True if the parameter allows interactive entry of its value.
is *type*	Check if the result of `type` matches the argument.
isbool	True if the parametr is a boolean option.
list	True if the parameter holds a list of values.
lock *reason*	For use in `when-set` callbacks. Allows parameters to exclude each other's use.
locker	The *reason* set by `lock`, if any.
name	The parameter's name.
options	List of option flags, if any.
ordered	True if the parameter is positional.
presence	True if the parameter is a boolean option not taking arguments.
primary *option*	True if the provided flag name is the primary option to be recognized (instead of an alias, or complement).
prompt	Text used as prompt during interactive entry.
required	True if the option is mandatory (`(input)` only).
reset	Squash internal and string representations. See also `forget`.
self	The parameter's instance command
set *value*	Programmatically set the string representation.
set?	True if the string representation was set.
string	Return the string representation, or error.
type	Parameter type. One of `input`, `option`, or `state`.
validator	Command prefix used to validate the string representation and transform it into the internal representation.
value	Return the internal representation. May calculate it now from the string representation.
when-complete	Command prefix invoked when the internal representation is set.
when-set	Command prefix invoked when the string representation is set.

Table 9: Parameter Methods

Calling "@P" without arguments is a shortcut for "@P value", i.e. the retrieval of the associated internal representation. Possibly calculating it if it is the first access and the parameter was in `defered` mode.

4. FUTURE DIRECTIONS

While I consider the framework to be quite mature, and it is already in use in a medium complex command line application, i.e. `stackato` [1], it is not without warts, nor opportunities for extension and improvement.

For example, the entire distinction between `immediate` and `defered` parameters is possibly not required.

The main use of `immediate` and "Completion" (→ 3.3) was to generate the internal representation of all parameters before invoking the action, validating all before use by the backend. Currently my thinking is beginning to doubt if that is as much of an advantage as I thought, over the converse, i.e. having everything `defered` and validating each parameter on first access. This would ignore all parameters not used by the chosen path through the code, leaving them unchecked. Which still offends my sensibilities somewhat.

Then there are the error messages currently generated for missing parameters, superfluous arguments, unknown options, etc. These are not as good as they could be, given the information available through the specification, i.e. all the help text. It might make sense to actually generate the help of the command and make it a part of the general error message.

Furthermore, currently all options are associated with specific commands. While the `common` and `use` commands allow the sharing of option definitions this is essentially duplication, even if hidden somewhat. Having actual global options not associated with any command, yet available to all is a request recently made for `stackato`. This would require some changes to "Dispatch" (→ 3.1), as it would have to recognize and process options as well, while navigating the command tree.

A wart I might have to live with is the hard-wired support for the special behaviours of `boolean` and `presence` options.

While I would like to replace that special code in "Parsing" (→ 3.2) with a general interface added to validation types and then moving them into the boolean type I currently do not see how this general interface should look like.

What is possible, would be to extend the validation types with optional methods to support type-specific interactive entry of values, to overide the simple shells currently used. These would then become fallbacks, used only for types without bespoke interaction. Related to that is the idea of adding a menu based interactor to the current set of general string and list entry interactors, to be used for validation types limited to a finite (and small) set of legal inputs. That is something which can be determined already, by inspecting the result of a type's `complete` method in response to an empty string.

A simple extension of the framework would the addition of more general validation types, i.e. useful to a broad class of applications. At least the builtin integer type could be extended to allow sub-typing, i.e. restriction to a range of integers instead of accepting all possible. Very application-specific validation types should be left out of the framework however.

On the side of the generated help the most important situations should be covered by the builtin formats, especially given that the `json` format provides access to essentially the entire specification in a portable format, convertible to any other format needed by a particular environment. Even so I am tempted to add direct support for at least doctools [8].

Structurally the help currently follows the hierarchy of commands and can show only either the single requested command, or all commands of a specific sub-tree. While this is ok for basic use a nicer help might have its own hierarchy, splitting the set of commands commands into logical sections which follow the use of the application instead. Support for this will require additional specification commands declaring the section(s) an application command is in.

APPENDIX

A. REFERENCES

[1] Various, Stackato Client https://github.com/ActiveState/stackato-cli
[2] Andreas Kupries, Linenoise. https://github.com/andreas-kupries/linenoise/, fork of Steve Bennet, https://github.com/msteveb/linenoise/, fork of Antirez, https://github.com/antirez/linenoise/
[3] Andreas Kupries, Cmdr. https://core.tcl.tk/akupries/cmdr/
[4] Andreas Kupries, Critcl https://github.com/andreas-kupries/critcl/
[5] Andreas Kupries, Kettle. https://core.tcl.tk/akupries/kettle/
[6] Andreas Kupries, Linenoise Utilities. https://core.tcl.tk/akupries/linenoise-utilities
[7] Will Duquette, Snit. https://core.tcl.tk/tcllib/doc/trunk/embedded/www/tcllib/files/modules/snit/snit.html#subsection11
[8] Various, Tcllib. https://core.tcl.tk/tcllib
[9] Andreas Kupries, Tcl Linenoise Binding. https://github.com/andreas-kupries/tcl-linenoise/
[10] Various, Tcl Core. https://core.tcl.tk/tcl/

B. LISTINGS

Listing 1: Simple alias management API

```
# -*- tcl -*
package require Tcl 8.5
package require cmdr
#package require foo-backend

cmdr create ::foo foo {
    private alias+ {
        description {
            Create a shortcut for a command (prefix).
        }
        input name {
            The name of the new shortcut.
        } {
            validate ::foo::backend::vt::notacommand
        }
        input command {
            The command (prefix) the name will map to.
        } {
            list
        }
    } ::foo::backend::alias::add

    private alias- {
        description {
            Remove a shortcut by name.
        }
        input name {
            The name of the shortcut to remove.
        } {
            validate ::foo::backend::vt::aliasname
        }
    } ::foo::backend::alias::remove

    private alias? {
        description {
            List the known aliases (shortcuts).
        }
    } ::foo::backend::alias::list
}

foo do {*}$argv
exit
```

Listing 2: Help for Listing 1

```
alias+ name command...
    Create a shortcut for a command (prefix).

    name    The name of the new shortcut.
    command The command (prefix) the name will map to.

alias- name
    Remove a shortcut by name.

    name The name of the shortcut to remove.

alias?
    List the known aliases (shortcuts).

help [OPTIONS] ?cmdname...?
    Retrieve help for a command or command set. Without
    arguments help for all commands is given. The default
    format is --full.

    --full  Activate full form of the help.
    --list  Activate list form of the help.
    --short Activate short form of the help.

    cmdname The entire command line, the name of the
            command to get help for. This can be several
            words.
```

Listing 3: Hierarchical commands

```
# -*- tcl -*
package require Tcl 8.5
package require cmdr
#package require foo-backend

cmdr create ::foo foo {
    officer alias {
        description {
            A collection of commands to manage
            user-specific shortcuts for command
            entry
        }

        private add {
            description {
                Create a shortcut for a command (prefix).
            }
            input name {
                The name of the new shortcut.
            } {
                validate ::foo::backend::vt::notacommand
            }
            input command {
                The command (prefix) the name will map to.
            } {
                list
            }
        } ::foo::backend::alias::add

        private remove {
            description {
                Remove a shortcut by name.
            }
            input name {
                The name of the shortcut to remove.
            } {
                validate ::foo::backend::vt::aliasname
            }
        } ::foo::backend::alias::remove

        private list {
            description {
                List the known aliases (shortcuts).
            }
        } ::foo::backend::alias::list
    }
}

foo do {*}$argv
exit
```

Listing 4: Help for Listing 3 (–list format)

```
alias add name command...
alias help [OPTIONS] ?cmdname...?
alias list
alias remove name
help [OPTIONS] ?cmdname...?
```

Listing 5: Specifying alternate names

```
alias alias+ = alias add
alias alias- = alias remove
alias alias? = alias list
```

Listing 6: Option shared by all commands

```
common *all* {
    option debug {
        Activate client internal tracing.
    } {
        undocumented
        list
        when-complete [lambda {p tags} {
            foreach t $tags { debug on $t }
        }]
    }
}
```

Listing 7: Validation type: Boolean

```
package require cmdr::validate::common

namespace eval ::cmdr::validate::boolean {
    namespace export default validate complete release
    namespace ensemble create

    namespace import ::cmdr::validate::common::fail
    namespace import ::cmdr::validate::common::complete-enum
}

proc ::cmdr::validate::boolean::release {p x} {
    # Simple internal representation. Nothing to release.
    return
}

proc ::cmdr::validate::boolean::default {p}  {
    return no
}

proc ::cmdr::validate::boolean::complete {p x} {
    # x is string representation. Result as well.
    return [complete-enum {
        yes no false true on off 0 1
    } 1 $x]
}

proc ::cmdr::validate::boolean::validate {p x} {
    # x is string representation. Result is internal representation.
    if {[string is boolean -strict $x]} {
        return $x
    }
    fail $p BOOLEAN "a boolean" $x
}
```

Listing 8: Simple alias management backend

```
# -*- tcl -*-
# # ## ### ##### ######## ############# #####################

namespace eval ::foo::backend::alias {
    namespace export list add remove
    namespace ensemble create
}

# # ## ### ##### ######## ############# #####################
## Command implementations.

proc ::foo::backend::alias::list {config} {
    set aliases [manager known]

    if {[$config @json]} {
        puts [jmap aliases $aliases]
        return
    }

    [table::do t {Alias Command} {
        foreach {name command} $aliases {
            $t add $name $command
        }
    } show display
    return
}

proc ::foo::backend::alias::add {config} {
    set name    [$config @name]
    set command [$config @command]

    manager add $name $command
    say [color green "Successfully aliased '$name' to '$command'"]
    return
}

proc ::foo::backend::alias::remove {config} {
    set name [$config @name]

    if {![manager has $name]} {
        err [color red "Unknown alias '$name'"]
    } else {
        manager remove $name
        say [color green "Successfully unaliased '$name'"]
    }
    return
}

# # ## ### ##### ######## ############# #####################
package provide foo::backend::alias 0
```

Public Key Infrastructure and the Tool Command Language

Roy S. Keene
Jemimah Ruhala

September 23rd, 2013

Abstract

Public key cryptography, also known as asymmetric cryptography, is a mechanism by which messages can be transformed (either encrypted or decrypted) with a private key and then reassembled with a related, but separate public key. The public key infrastructure (PKI) that supports the trust model by which two parties that have no previous knowledge of each other can verify each others identity through trust anchors is implemented using digital signatures made possible by public key cryptography. Being able to participate in PKI directly with Tcl scripts makes many interesting and useful applications possible. The PKI module in Tcllib implements the various PKI related standards and algorithms for Tcl scripts to accomplish this goal including PKCS#1, X.509, and RSA. This paper aims to explain the high-level concepts related to PKI, describe the scope of the various standards and algorithms implemented, and explore the possibilities of PKI in Tcl.

1 PKI

The purpose of Public Key Infrastructure (PKI) is to provide a mechanism to establish the authenticity of an unknown party. Most people assume PKI is a complex system with a lot of moving parts. However, this is not the case. A simple PKI implementation is fairly straight-forward.

PKI establishes authenticity using certificates, which certify that some external entity has verified that an unknown party is who it claims to be. This certificate is presented by the unknown party as a means of identifying itself to you.

1.1 Public Key Cryptography

Public key cryptography, or asymmetric cryptography uses *key pairs* to perform cryptographic operations on values. This is in contrast to symmetric cryptography which uses a single key to perform cryptographic operations. In public key cryptography there are two related, but distinct, keys:

- A public key
- A private key

The relationship between these two keys differs depending on the public key cryptography algorithm, but in all cases it is impossible[1] to derive the private key from the public key.

Public key cryptography uses mathematical operations to perform operations on numerical values that can only be reversed or verified with the opposite key. That is, if something is encrypted with the private key it can only be decrypted or verified with the public key. Conversely, if something is encrypted with the public key it can only be decrypted or verified with the private key.

Given that there are two different keys (public and private) involved with public key encryption, refering to encryption in a general sense can be ambiguous. Which key do we use to encrypt something with ? For reasons that should be made clear later, when we talk about encryption within the context of public key cryptography, we are usually talking about encrypting a plain text value with the public key. This results in a cipher text that can only be decoded by an entity possessing the private key.

In the context of public key cryptography, encrypting a value with the private key is generally used for digital signatures. Because messages encrypted with the private key can only be decrypted (or verified)

[1]Theoretically infeasable given sufficiently large and correctly generated keys

with the public key part of the key pair we can assert that if the message is meaningful when decrypted with the public key then it could have only been encrypted by an entity possessing the private key.

1.2 RSA

The most common public key cryptography algorithm in use today is RSA[2]. RSA is named for Ron Rivest, Adi Shamir, and Leonard Adleman who made the algorithm public and are thus widely credited as the inventors of the algorithm.

1.2.1 Description of RSA Key Pairs

The RSA algorithm defines the following pairs of keys in the following way:

- RSA Public Key, made up of
  - The public exponent (commonly called e), often just called the exponent
  - The public modulus (commonly called n), often just called the modulus
- RSA Private Key, made up of
  - The private exponent (commonly called d), often just called the private key since it's the only part of it

In the remainder of this document whenever RSA is used a simple 16-bit RSA key pair will be used:

- Public Key
  - Public Exponent: 65537
  - Public Modulus: 37837
- Private Key
  - Private Exponent: 40193

In practice RSA keys are much larger, as of this writing the recommended minimum size of RSA keys is 2048-bits.

[2] According to RSA

1.2.2 RSA Algorithm

The RSA algorithm is a relatively easy to demonstrate public key cryptography algorithm. A simple definition of applying RSA is "modular exponentiation". Modular arithmetic (denoted by the "$\mathbb{Z}$" symbol and a modulo value) is applied to values that have had the the exponentiation operator applied to them. A simple example of modular exponentiation is:

$$3^4(\mathbb{Z}5) = 1$$

which is 3 raised to the power of 4 all modulo 5. Since $3^4 = 81$ and $81(\mathbb{Z}5) = 1$ (modulus is the remainder of a division operation and $\frac{81}{5}$ results in 16 even divisions and 1 remainder), the result is 1.

Another way to think of modular arithmetic is to think of it in the same way we think of numeric bases (such as binary, octal, decimal, hexadecimal) and using only the least significant digit of that base. The value 81 in base 5 is 311, the least significant digit of which is 1 and therefore $81(\mathbb{Z}5) = 1$.

1.2.3 RSA Encryption

RSA encryption is a form of public key encryption and therefore uses the public key. The RSA encryption function is defined as:

$$plain^{publicExponent}(\mathbb{Z}publicModulus) = cipher$$

For example:

$$26729^{65537}(\mathbb{Z}37837) = 36784$$

is modular exponentiation of the plain text 26729 raised the power of 65537, which is the public exponent, all modulo the public modulus of 37837, which results in the cipher text 36784. The above example is also an example of encrypting the value 26729 (which is 0x6869 in hexadecimal, or "hi" in ASCII) with an RSA key whose public exponent is 65537 and whose public modulus is 37837 resulting in the encrypted value of 36784.

This can only be reversed using the private key as the exponent instead of the public exponent. That is:

$$cipher^{privateExponent}(\mathbb{Z}publicModulus) = plain$$

For example:

$$30784^{40193}(\mathbb{Z}37837) = 26729$$

1.2.4 RSA Digital Signatures

Looking closer at the RSA encryption example of modular exponentiation, we can see some of the public key cryptography properties that we need starting to emerge. Specifically we cannot take the cipher text value and convert it back to the plain text with just the public information. We must know the private exponent (or be able to derive it by factoring the public modulus, but given a complex and correctly generated key pair this should be impossible) to reverse the operation.

However RSA encryption is not very useful for digital signatures because it requires the private key to do anything meaningful. With a digital signature, we want to perform an operation on some plain text using our private exponent that can be verified using only the public key. Fortunately RSA allows us to do that by simply swapping the values around. That is:

$$plain^{privateExponent}(\mathbb{Z}publicModulus) = cipher$$

For example:

$$12345^{40193}(\mathbb{Z}37837) = 3293$$

which CAN be reversed using only public information, as in:

$$cipher^{publicExponent}(\mathbb{Z}publicModulus) = plain$$

For example:

$$3293^{65537}(\mathbb{Z}37837) = 12345$$

RSA guarantees that the chance of there being another private key which generates the same cipher text for a given plain text is extremely low relative to the size of the key. Therefore we can assume that if a given cipher text can be decrypted to a plain text using a given public key then it must have been encrypted with the secretly held private key and thus as long as the private key is protected as a secret, only the holder could have generated this message.

1.3 Digital Signatures

Directly encrypting a message with a private key is a workable solution for short messages but not in the general case. RSA and most other public key cryptography systems cannot encrypt (with either the public key or the private key) messages larger than the size of the key. That is, if the key is 16 bits then the plain text message can be no larger than 16 bits. For RSA the specific limit is that the value can be no larger than the public modulus due to the fact that all operations are modulo the public modulus.

Instead of directly encrypting the plain text a cryptographically secure message digest algorithm such as MD5[3], SHA1[4], or SHA256[5] is used to compute a cryptographically secure digest of the message which is typically much smaller than the message itself. This digest is then encrypted with the private key and verified with the public key. In this way, arbitrarily long messages can be digitally signed.

1.4 Encryption

The same limitation that exists for message length with respect to digital signatures also applies to encryption. The message encrypted with RSA must be no larger than the public key. Again, for RSA this is due the fact that the public modulo is applied to all operations.

Thus for the general case of encryption of an arbitrarily long message using a public key cryptography system two different cryptographic algorithms are typically used:

- A public key (asymmetric) cryptography key
- A symmetric key

Instead of directly encrypting the plain text a symmetric cipher such as AES[6], ARCFOUR/RC4, or 3DES[7] is used with a secure randomly generated symmetric cipher's key. This symmetric key is then encrypted with the asymmetric cipher's public key. The plain text is then encrypted with the selected symmetric cipher and the generated symmetric cipher's key.

1.5 Certificates

As previously mentioned in section 1, certificates are used to certify that one entity (the issuer of the certificate) says that another entity (the subject of the certificate) is a given identity under certain conditions.

So what makes up a certificate ? Certificates are specified by the ITU-T standard X.509 and contain the following information:

[3] MD5 is defined in RFC 1321
[4] SHA1 is defined in RFC 3174
[5] SHA256 is defined in RFC 4634
[6] AES is defined in FIPS PUB 197
[7] 3DES is defined in FIPS PUB 46-3

- X.509 Standard version number (optional) which identifies the revision of X.509 that this certificate complies with
- Issuer, which is the "distinguished name" of the entity who issued (that is, signed) the certificate
- Serial Number, which is a unique number per issuer to uniquely identify this certificate from the issuer
- Subject, which is the "distinguished name" of the entity who is being certified (and also who holds the private key)
- Issue date and expiration date, which define the time frame in which the certificate is valid
- The public key, including the algorithm and algorithm-specific public key data – for RSA this is the public modulus and public-exponent
- If this is X.509 version number 3 then X.509 extensions may be specified which restrict the uses of this certificate
- The digital signature of all of the previous data encoded in ASN.1 Distinguished Encoding Rules (DER) as specified by ITU-T standard X.690, which for RSA is the cryptographic message digest of the previous data, which is then padded (per PKCS#1), and finally encrypted with the private key of the issuer

So now we have a system where an unknown and untrusted party can assert to you a fully-qualified (also known as "distinguished") name and also provide a reference to who is certifying that this assertion is true within the parameters specified in the certificate.

What is to stop someone from taking a certificate from an existing entity, which must be publicly accessible otherwise there would be no way to identify the entity, and using it? Once again, public key cryptography is the answer here. A certificate only proves that the Issuer signed a request for the Subject. A certificate does not prove that you you are talking to is legitimately the subject specified in the certificate but it *does* provide a mechanism to do that. The public key being certified is in the certificate so all that is needed is for you to issue some sort of challenge for the party presenting the certificate to prove that it has the private key that corresponds with the certified public key. How this challenge is done depends on the protocol and is outside the scope of this document.

1.6 Finally... PKI

At this point we have described all of the vital components to a simple PKI system:

- A method to identify an entity
- A method for one entity to assert the identity of another entity

With these simple tools we can construct a system where we trust few entities to act as authoritative sources of identity information for unknown entities. Entities which act as authoritative sources of trust are known as Certificate Authorities and are identified by certificates with the X.509v3 extension known as "Basic Constraints" set to the value of "true". Certificate authority certificates may be signed by other certificate authorities or they may be self-signed. A self-signed certificate authority certificate is known as a "root certificate authority certificate" while a certificate authority certificate signed by another certificate authority is known as an "intermediate certificate authority certificate".

The result of such a system is a hierarchy of certificate authorities which can issue certificates. If trust is given to one of the certificate authorities then any certificates issued by that certificate authority (directly, or indirectly through a chain of subordinate or intermediate certificate authorities) can also be trusted as having met the requirements of that certificate authority.

1.7 More Complete PKI

While a simple PKI system is straight-forward to describe, a more complete (and secure) PKI system is more complex due to things such as revocation lists (CRLs) and the many X.509v3 extensions which can be used to limit the utility of X.509 certificates. This document will not cover those items due to their complexity and scope.

2 PKI with Tcl

Tcl version 8.5 and newer transparently support arithmetic on arbitrarily big integers which enables us to write a pure Tcl implementation of RSA using the [expr] command. Versions prior to 8.5 could use the *bigmath* package within TCLLIB at a considerable cost for speed.

2.1 The pki Package

The *pki* package is a module within TCLLIB, a collection of popular TCL-based packages. It requires Tcl version 8.5 for its big integer support.

The *pki* package provides an interface for most things related to PKI. It originally started as just an RSA package but as additional needs for interoperability arose more and more PKI support was added.

Currently it only supports the RSA public key cryptography system but is extensible to support additional algorithms (and indeed this is how PKCS#11 support is implemented).

The rest of this section briefly describes the interface to the *pki* package.

2.1.1 pki::encrypt

The [pki::encrypt] command encrypts a message with a key from a public key cryptography algorithm, such as RSA. Either the public key or the private key may be used to encrypt the message. It is worth noting that not every public key cryptography algorithm supports encryption and decryption. Notable the Digital Signature Algorithm[8] (DSA) only supports creating and verifying signatures.

The encrypted message is returned on success and an error is raised upon failure. In general, assuming a valid key has been supplied, the most common error returned is that the message is larger than the key and the algorithm does not support that.

The [pki::encrypt], [pki::decrypt], [pki::sign], and [pki::verify] commands each examine the key to determine what backend to call to handle the specific operation. The RSA backend is always registered as it is a part of the "pki" package. Additional backends may be registered at run-time.

2.1.2 pki::decrypt

The [pki::decrypt] command decrypts a previously encrypted message with a key from a public key cryptography algorithm, such as RSA. Either the public key or the private key may be used to decrypt the encrypted message.

The decrypted message is returned on success and an error is raised upon failure. It is worth noting that the decrypted message returned may be invalid if the key is not valid, however this is usually caught due to RSA PKCS#1 v1.5 padding on encrypted messages.

[8]DSA is specified in FIPS 186-4

2.1.3 pki::sign

The [pki::sign] command creates the digital signature of a message with a key from a public key cryptography algorithm, such as RSA. This will require the key supplied to include the private key.

The signature is returned on success and an error is raised upon failure.

2.1.4 pki::verify

The [pki::verify] command verifies that a digital signature is valid for a given message, signature, and key.

If the message can successfully be verified then "true" is returned otherwise "false" is returned.

2.1.5 pki::pkcs::parse_key

The [pki::pkcs::parse_key] command loads the supplied PKCS#1 key pair (or just the public key, if requested) into a key structure used internally by the "pki" package. If the key is encrypted a password may be supplied to decrypt it. If the key is encrypted and no password is supplied an error is raised.

The key is returned on success and an error is raised upon failure.

2.1.6 pki::pkcs::create_csr

The [pki::pkcs::create_csr] command creates the supplied PKCS#1 certificate signing request (CSR) with a specified key and the request subject given. A certificate signing request is the standardized message format handled by certificate authorities to create a certificate. It includes the public key, the requested name, and a signature of the entire request.

2.1.7 pki::pkcs::parse_csr

The [pki::pkcs::parse_csr] command reads the supplied PKCS#1 certificate signing request (CSR) and returns the public key information as well as the requested name as a single key object.

2.1.8 pki::x509::parse_cert

The [pki::pkcs::parse_cert] command reads the supplied X.509 certificate and returns the public key information as well as the other information in the certificate in a single certificate object, which may also be used as a public key object. At this point is worth nothing that the key object used internally by the "pki" package is just a Tcl dictionary (dict) and may freely be accessed as such.

2.1.9 pki::x509::verify_cert

The [pki::x509::verify_cert] command verifies that a certificate is properly signed by a trusted certificate authority, which may either be a root certificate authority or an intermediate certificate authority. It is worth noting that this does not verify that the certificate may be used for any particular purpose or even that it may be used at this time, but only that it was legitimately issued by a trusted certificate authority.

If the certificate can be verified to have been issued by a trusted certificate authority then "true" is returned otherwise "false" is returned.

2.1.10 pki::x509::validate_cert

The [pki::x509::validate_cert] command verifies that a certificate may be used for some purpose, such as SSL/TLS, being a certificate authority responsible for signing a subject. It checks the parameters of the X.509v3 certificate such as validity period (issue date and expiration date), the subject distinguished name, the "Basic Constraints" extension, and other attributes based on how it is invoked.

If the certificate can be determined to be valid for the specified purpose then "true" is returned otherwise "false" is returned.

2.1.11 pki::x509::create_cert

The [pki::x509::create_cert] command creates an X.509 certificate from a certificate signing request using a specified certificate authority key to sign it, a specified serial number, and with the given additional X.509 parameters. The process of creating a certificate is sometimes called "signing a certificate" which is a misnomer since there is no such thing as an unsigned certificate[9] in X.509.

The parameters to [pki::x509::create_cert] are rather unwieldy at this point due to the number of required parameters and newer versions will likely replace the positional parameters with named parameters.

Upon success the certificate is returned in either PEM or DER format which are suitable for exchange with other PKI systems. It must be parsed with [pki::x509::parse_cert] before it can be used internally with the "pki" package.

[9] Indeed, an unsigned certificate would certify nothing

2.1.12 pki::rsa::generate

The [pki::x509::generate] command generates an RSA key of a given size. You can also optionally specify the public key exponent to use rather than the default of 65537, but it is not advisable to actually do so since it may decrease the security of the generated key.

2.2 The "pki::pkcs11" Package

The "pki::pkcs11" package uses and extends the "pki" package with support for RSA PKCS#11 hardware security modules (HSMs) such as cryptographic accelerators or smart-cards. Unlike the "pki" module it is not written in Tcl, but is written in C. This is due to the fact that the RSA PKCS#11 standard specifies a C API for "cryptoki modules".

The "pki::pkcs11" module has a relatively simple interface thanks to re-using most of the "pki" package for operations and supporting only the most basic RSA PKCS#11 functionality.

2.2.1 pki::pkcs11::loadmodule

The [pki::pkcs11::loadmodule] command loads a "cryptoki module", which is an RSA PKCS#11 compliant library (DLL or shared object, for example) that will be used for accessing a specific hardware device.

If the specified module can be successly loaded an opaque handle is returned otherwise an error is raised.

2.2.2 pki::pkcs11::unloadmodule

The [pki::pkcs11::unloadmodule] command unloads and frees allocated structures for an RSA PKCS#11 cryptoki module specified by the opaque handle. After the specified module is unloaded the opaque handle may no longer be used.

Upon success "true" is returned otherwise "false" is returned.

2.2.3 pki::pkcs11::listslots

The [pki::pkcs11::listslots] command lists the slots that are available for a given opaque cryptoki module handle. In RSA PKCS#11 a slots contain at most one token which can contain objects such as certificates, public keys, private keys, etc.

Upon successful operation a list is returned. The returned list contains one element per slot. Each item of the returned list is itself a sub-list containing the following items:

1. The slot identification number for the slot
2. The label of the slot
3. Flags set for the slot

If there is an error in processing the request then an error is raised. If there are no slots available then an empty list is returned.

2.2.4 pki::pkcs11::listcerts

The [pki::pkcs11::listcerts] command lists the certificate objects available for a given handle and slot identification number.

Upon successful operation a list is returned. Each item of the returned list contains a certificate/key object (as would be returned by [pki::x509::parse_cert]). If there is an error in processing the request then an error is raised. If there are no certificate objects for a given slot identification number associated with a given opaque handle then an empty list is returned.

2.2.5 pki::pkcs11::encrypt

The [pki::pkcs11::encrypt] command is not intended to be called directly by end-user applications. It calls the C_Encrypt() function within the loaded RSA PKCS#11 cryptoki module. Instead of calling this command end-user applications should call the [pki::encrypt], [pki::decrypt], or [pki::sign] command which will invoke this command if the key supplied indicates it is a PKCS#11 module.

Because RSA PKCS#11 cryptoki modules expose functions to perform public key cryptography they do not need to export the private key in order for applications to perform cryptographic operations that use the private key. For example a user using a smart-card can prove that he has access to his private key and thus legitimately is associated with the certificates presented without being able read to the private key at all. Instead the smart-card performs the cryptographic operation and returns a cryptographic result. This means that there is no way for an adversary to acquire the private key for a smart-card[10] user since the user themselves cannot read the private key.

2.2.6 pki::pkcs11::decrypt

The [pki::pkcs11::decrypt] command, like the [pki::pkcs11::decrypt] command, is not intended to be called directly by end-user applications.

[10]Except for the possibility of physically acquiring the device

2.2.7 pki::pkcs11::login

The [pki::pkcs11::login] command logs into a device by calling the RSA PKCS#11 cryptoki module's C_Login() function. Because cryptographic modules perform cryptographic operations using the private key they will often be require the user to verify to the hardware security module or smart-card that they legitimately should be able to perform that operation by supplying a password. If a login is required to use a particular hardware token then the LOGIN_REQUIRED flag will be set in the result from [pki::pkcs11::listslots] for the slot that the token is in.

If the password successfully logs into the device then "true" is returned. If the password is incorrect then "false" is returned. If some other error condition is asserted then an error is raised.

2.2.8 pki::pkcs11::logout

The [pki::pkcs11::logout] command logs out of a device by calling the RSA PKCS#11 crytptoki module's C_Logout() function. Once you are logged out, token attempts to perform cryptographic operations will probably fail.

2.3 Doing Something Useful

2.3.1 Establishing a Simple Certificate Authority

The very first thing we need to be concerned with when establishing a public key infrastructure system is the establishment of an authority to certify identities. This is our certificate authority. All we need for a minimal certificate authority is certificate authority certificate and some way to ensure that we do not issue certificates with duplicate serial numbers. We can do this from within Tcl using the "pki" module easily.

First we must load the "pki" package, which can be obtained from TCLLIB or from http://rkeene.org/devel/pki/.

```
% package require pki 0.3
```

Then we need to generate our private key. Since RSA is the only public key cryptography algorithm currently implemented we should use that:

```
% set ca_key [pki::rsa::generate 2048]
```

Next we need to "sign our key" which will necessarily be stored as a certificate (a key that was simply signed would not include any identifying information and would be generally useless). Since this key will be our first certificate authority certificate it must be signed by its own key and is therefore self-signed and also therefore a root certificate authority. The "pki" package does not provide a nice way to handle certificate authorities. To accomplish that we just add a "subject" key to the "ca_key" dictionary:

```
% set ca_key_subject \
    "CN=Example Root CA"
% dict set ca_key subject \
    $ca_key_subject
```

After we have updated this object we can use sign it using the [pki::x509::create_cert] command:

```
% set issue_date [clock seconds]
% set expire_date [clock add \
    $issue_date 1 year]
% set ca_cert
    [pki::x509::create_cert \
    $ca_key $ca_key 1 $issue_date \
    $expire_date 1 [list] 1]
```

At this point we have successfully established our certificate authority by creating a private key and a signed certificate which identifies us. We should save our private key, which is stored in the dictionary named "ca_key", and our certificate which is represented by the value stored in the variable "ca_cert" somewhere to prevent losing them and also in such a way that others may not access them.

2.3.2 Provisioning User Certificates

Now that we have a certificate authority, our users may start using it. The first thing they will want to do is obtain a copy of our certificate authority certificate through a secure and trusted channel in order to establish trust with it. After that they will also want to generate their own RSA private key:

```
% package require pki 0.3
% set user_key [pki::rsa::generate 2048]
```

Next the user should generate a certificate signing request (CSR) so that the certificate authority will know the public key as well as what identity the user is claiming to be. This is done with the [pki::pkcs::create_csr] command:

```
% set user_csr [pki::pkcs::create_csr \
    $user_key [list "CN" "Joe User"] 1]
```

Then the user can distribute the CSR to the certificate authority over a trusted channel (although all of the information in the CSR is public if the channel is compromised, a malicious man-in-the-middle could alter the request so that his or her public key be used instead) and the certificate authority can generate a certificate:

```
# (On Certificate Authority)
% set user_csr {//From User//}
% set user_csr_list \
    [pki::pkcs::parse_csr $user_csr]
% set issue_date [clock seconds]
% set expire_date [clock add \
    $issue_date 1 year]
% set user_cert \
    [pki::x509::create_cert \
    $user_csr_list $ca_key 2 \
    $issue_date $expire_date 0 [list] \
    1]
```

The certificate authority can then give the user his or her certificate over any channel since it's public.

2.3.3 Securely Exchanging Messages

Once several users have certificates issued by our certificate authority they can use the trust they have established with the certificate authority and the certificate authority certificate to validate messages between them, creating a secure and trusted channel between two users who may have never previously communicated.

This can be done by creating a simple ad-hoc protocol for the users to communicate where users:

1. Initially exchange certificates with the peer
2. Each side performs some action to verify that the Subject of the certificate is who they are talking to
3. Each side validates that the certificate is valid using [pki::x509::validate_cert]
4. Each side securely generates a 128-bit key for AES using the "aes" package (from TCLLIB)
5. Each side encrypts the 128-bit key as well as the initialization vector (IV) with the peer's public key, which can only be successfully decrypted by the peer
6. Each side decrypts the received 128-bit key and IV using his or her private key

7. Each side initializes an AES chain block cipher mode stream for sending encrypted blocks to its peer and another AES chain block cipher mode stream for receiving encrypted blocks

3 Legal Information

Since the *pki* package implements RSA, which is strong cryptography, it must be registered with the United States Department of Commerce. Currently the *pki* module is registered with Export Registration Number (ERN) R103416 and is authorized for export and re-export from the United States. No effort has been made to ensure that it can be imported to- or exported from other countries.

Tcl 2013

New Orleans, LA

September 23-27, 2013

Session V

September 26 1:30-3:00pm

Optimizing Tcl Bytecode

Donal Fellows
The University of Manchester / Tcl Core Team
donal.k.fellows@manchester.ac.uk

1. Abstract

The Tcl interpreter has an evaluation strategy of parsing a script into a sequence of commands, and compiling each of those commands into a sequence of bytecodes that will produce the result of the command. I have made a number of extensions to the scope of commands that are handled this way over the years, but in 2012 I started looking at a new way to do the compilation, with an aim to eventually creating an "interpreter" suitable for Tcl 9. This paper looks at the changes made (some of which are present in 8.6.0, and the rest of which will appear in 8.6.1) and the prospects for future directions.

1. Introduction

During the development of Tcl 8.6, Kevin Kenny and Ozgur Dogan Ugurlu demonstrated[1] (through the implementation of the command ::tcl::unsupported::assemble) that it was possible to create an assembler for Tcl bytecodes that was sufficiently safe that it was suitable for exposure in a Safe Interpreter. In particular, it became clear that there were a set of constraints that could be applied that would ensure that a Tcl assembler would never generate code that could crash; access to parts of the stack not "owned" by the code was prohibited. Though infinite loops were still possible — excluding infinite loops requires either totally emasculating the capabilities of Tcl or the possibility of proving exceptionally complex mathematical theorems — those loops would never exceed properly calculable stack bounds.

I found this absolutely fascinating, as it showed that the bytecode that we had been generating was not nearly as unruly as I had previously feared; my problems with writing compilation commands such as for switch and dict had been more due to my not being aware of those implicit constraints, rather than their absence. It also allowed us to quantify exactly what was wrong with the compilation of break and continue, both of which had long been known to be problematic in cases previously only known in an operational sense.

When we considered the implications of this, we realized that it also made it substantially easier to consider compilation of Tcl to actual native code. Previous attempts[2] had focused on a simplistic transformation of the existing bytecodes to their machine-code equivalents, but that is a strategy that is unlikely to yield significant benefits for several reasons:

1. The bytecode that they are starting from is significantly non-optimal in the first place.
2. Tcl commands are potentially highly dynamic, with the option for their implementations to be changed substantially as a script executes.
3. The value-model of Tcl is very strongly rooted in the concept of an immutable reference with typed views, which is substantially different to that of machine code (mutable references to machine words) or languages like C (mutable references to typed variables).

The combination of these issues means that compilation of Tcl to machine code is a significant challenge. This paper will be primarily looking at dealing with the first part of this problem, so that the bytecode that the compilation starts from is at least a stronger foundation. The advantage of working on this part is that the results of doing this can be made available to the community more rapidly than the other parts; full compilation will require a lot more work to support than tweaking things to work better within current constraints.

In this paper, I present a summary of Tcl's bytecode system in Section 2. In Section 3, I describe how I have been improving the coverage of commands that bytecode is generated for. In Section 4, I describe the improvements I have made to the bytecode generated for a number of existing Tcl commands. In Section 5, I talk about an improvement to the introspection tools for Tcl bytecode so as to more simply expose the information that is there to scripts. In Section 6, I describe the simple optimizer that I have created for Tcl bytecode, and in Section 7 I present some performance measurements to examine whether I am making any progress on the performance front. Finally, I examine possible future directions in Section 8.

2. About Bytecode

Tcl's current system of compilation uses a custom target called Bytecode[3], designed primarily to be an in-memory and on-disk data structure[1] that has minimal space consumption as a primary goal.

The fundamental model of bytecode execution is that there is a stack of values that represent intermediate working values, arguments and results. Every command becomes a sequence of instructions that ends up with the result of the command being pushed on the stack; in the simplest case, a command is compiled into a push of all the argument words and an invoke via Tcl's basic command dispatch, which will in turn replace those argument words with the single result value. The pushing of the argument words may be non-trivial if the words are complex compounds of various substitutions, but the overall model is comparatively simple.

When this simple universal execution strategy is used, the command in question is referred to as *uncompiled*. This is obviously not actually true — we have just discussed what the compilation is! — but the key is that the actual embodiment of the semantics of the command is still the standard implementation function; all that is bytecode-compiled is the assembly of the arguments and the lookup and invocation of that function. With a "compiled" command, the semantics of the command are embodied by a direct sequence of bytecode instructions. Those instructions will produce the result of the command without (typically) going through command dispatch.

Command compilation

Each compiled command has its own strategy for producing instructions, the command compiler, which is asked to consider how to do the compilation in a particular case. Any failure of the command compiler will cause the standard compilation to be used, which is also used when the command name itself is dynamically generated (*e.g.*, the value of a variable or the result of a command), as at that point Tcl is unable to statically determine the command compiler to use.[2]

---

[1] Support for what became the TclPro compiler and the tbcload extension was part of the original mandate, though it is not part that is officially supported for general free use. However, the consequences of that support are subtly scattered through the code.

[2] It is a consequence of this that TclOO instance dispatch is unlikely to ever be compiled; a key usage pattern of TclOO is to hold the name of the instance to invoke in a variable, clearly a case that cannot ever be compiled to anything substantially better than the current dispatch mechanism.

Command compilers can fail for many reasons. One of the main reasons is if one of their arguments is not a literal despite the compiler requiring it to be; this is what happens when any of the arguments to `while` is not a literal. The other two common reasons for failure are if there is a lack of a local variable table (LVT) in the compilation context, or if given the wrong number of arguments, though this is very much not an exhaustive set.

The lack of an LVT case requires some explanation. The local variable table is a *numerically indexed* collection of variables that is used to hold the formal arguments to a procedure, the local variables inside that procedure, and whatever extra information is necessary (local temporary variables that hold values in patterns that would interfere with the stack). Some instructions for compiling commands only exist in a form that accesses the local variable table, so compilations that necessarily use those instructions cannot be done without an LVT present: this is exactly why `foreach` is not efficient except when used in a procedure (or other procedure-like entity, such as a lambda term or TclOO method).

Exposure of bytecode in Tcl scripts

There has been a disassembler for Tcl bytecodes since they were introduced in Tcl 8.0, but up to 8.4, this was one of the most hidden features (it required setting a magic variable and then reading standard output, itself tricky on Windows). In 8.5, this disassembler was exposed more cleanly via the `disassemble` command in the `tcl::unsupported` namespace.

In 8.6 this was joined by `assemble`, though the two commands shared very little in terms of actual syntax beyond the names of the instructions. In addition, the supported instruction sets were also subtly different, mainly due to it being hard to correctly and safely issue some instructions.

3. Improving Coverage

In order to improve the overall generation of bytecode by Tcl, it is necessary to increase the fraction of Tcl code that can be compiled to pure bytecode. That is, an instruction sequence is pure bytecode if it does not contain any of the instructions `invokeStk1`, `invokeStk4` (commonly just referred to as `invokeStk`, as they are a linked pair) or `invokeExpanded`[3]. Script fragments that have their instruction sequences entirely free of those instructions are entirely predictable in their behaviour, at least at an operational/type-theoretic level.

But what was the status of Tcl's compilation of commands back in mid-2012? Well, there had been some adjustments done during the development of 8.6, but they had been rather piecemeal. After the introduction of compilation strategies for `subst` (in 2009), `unset` (in 2010) and `dict with` (in 2011), not much had really changed; the set of scripts that would be likely to become pure bytecode was indeed very small.

Improving key loop types

To change this, I instead took a different tack and looked at scripts where I wanted them to *become* pure bytecode. An example of the sort of script that I wanted to be pure was an inner loop of a simple value-generating coroutine. Such a coroutine is this one, which yields first its own name (often a useful thing to do), then each of its arguments, and finally it causes the receiving loop to break.

```
proc all args {
    yield [info coroutine]
    foreach item $args {
        yield $item
    }
    return -code break
}
```

[3] The other instruction that should not be present is `invokeReplace`, which I will discuss later in this paper.

This coroutine body procedure would be created and its values consumed something like this:

```
set c [coroutine X all "foo" "bar"]
while 1 {
    puts "X\[[incr i]\] = [$c]"
}
```

As you can see, all the commands in all are part of Tcl itself, and ones that are reasonably likely to occur in an inner loop. Furthermore, all the operations involve data that is available locally; it is all either immediately present on the stack, in the stack frame, or in the interpreter.

An alternative mechanism for doing such a simple yielding loop is this one:

```
proc all args {
    yield [info coroutine]
    foreach x [lrange $args 0 end-1] {
        yield $x
    }
    return [lindex $args end]
}
```

This has a different pattern of usage, or rather two slightly different patterns, one of which is done with info commands:

```
set c [coroutine X all "foo" "bar"]
while {[llength [info commands $c]]} {
    puts "X\[[incr i]\] = [$c]"
}
```

And the other with namespace which (equivalent to having the -command option specified):

```
set c [coroutine X all "foo" "bar"]
while {[namespace which $c] ne ""} {
    puts "X\[[incr i]\] = [$c]"
}
```

Making these as pure as practical (*i.e.*, the generating and receiving loops except for the necessary call to the coroutine itself, and — in this illustrative example — the call to puts to print the values) required being able to bytecode-compile both a way to actually produce values, yield, and a way to detect whether the coroutine had terminated from both within and outside the coroutine. Within the coroutine, it was a matter of making info coroutine be a compiled operation (interior termination detection is really just a matter of whether a non-yielding exit from the coroutine is performed, such as a return) and from outside the coroutine it was a matter of allowing for a way to query whether a particular command existed, which was done in different ways by different people: some used info commands with a literal non-pattern argument, and others used namespace which -command.

Similar concerns with determining whether a procedure call actually provided a value for some optional argument encouraged me to add info level to the compilation list. I also did namespace current and self object, as these are very common in some coding styles, while representing information that is readily available.

The compilations of all of these introspection commands are to straightforward instructions that implement the functionality; thus, the coroName instruction implements the functionality of info coroutine, resolveCmd implements namespace which, the yield instruction (unsurprisingly) implements the core of the yield command, etc.

Examining the Teapot

Yet for all that, I did not feel that I had made much of an impact in the coverage. I needed a different technique for selecting what commands would attract improvements. So I turned to the Tcl packages that I had installed in my local Teapot repository.

The vast majority of packages in the Teapot are either wholly or partially scripts, so this forms a substantial body of Tcl code that is in current use. By looking at this and finding what commands were common but uncompiled, I would at least establish a set of commands that *should* be compiled if possible and reasonable. Not all of them actually ought to be compiled (for example, there is no real benefit to compiling commands that do I/O) but it would at least establish some priority; very rarely used commands clearly need not attract significant effort.

In particular, I studied the core ensemble commands array, dict, namespace and string. (The vast majority of info and interp is only used on code that does not need to be fast, and chan is almost entirely focused on OS access.)

As can be seen in Table 1 and in more depth in Appendix 1 (the frequency counts date from October 2012), just how frequent the various subcommands are varies widely; array set is nearly 70 times more common than array size. In addition, some of the subcommands are largely impractical to implement: the operations that *read* the state of an array (size, get and names) have really rather strange trace behaviour, using privileged access to the implementation of the arrays to operate (the existence of elements has to be checked during the processing of those subcommands). But it does indicate that array set is a strong candidate for compilation.

Command	Incidence	Practical
array size	37	No
array exists	56	Yes
array unset	191	Yes
array get	479	No
array names	1085	No
array set	2511	Yes

Table 1: Incidence of array subcommands

Similarly, I have identified that the first, last, map, and range operations of string are practical, as are the code, qualifiers and tail operations of namespace, and the merge operation of dict. (Strictly, string last is not actually sufficiently frequent to be worthwhile, but its functionality is required to implement the more frequent namespace qualifiers operation.) Some of the *impractical* operations were namespace eval (very common, but crosses stack frame boundaries) and string is (potentially very relevant, but very complex).

Generating values

In addition, I looked for commands that could be used to produce literals. With the introduction of lmap and dict map in 8.6, we have increased the need to be able to produce a literal value as the result of evaluating a Tcl script. A few techniques were in common use:

- expr *123* — Fine for numbers, but poor where the value is non-numeric or (even worse) looks like a number but isn't.
- subst *abc* — A reasonable way of producing a simple value, but not actually commonly chosen.
- format *abc* — A way that works provided the literal being produced has no %-substitutions in it, but otherwise problematic. Also slow.
- format "%s" *abc* — Lacks the formal problems of the option immediately above, but still very slow.
- list *abc* — Not correct at all except for literal lists! This is particularly obvious when the literal being produced contains spaces.
- return -level 0 *abc* — The "official" method, hardly used by anyone due to it being so thoroughly unobvious.

It was clear that it was desirable to make more of these operations efficient. In particular, wherever these commands produce a constant value or a value determined entirely by arguments, there is an excellent opportunity for generating the operation via efficient bytecodes. Since some of these were already bytecoded (expr, subst, list and that complex return form) what I was seeking to do was to ensure that the other potential common forms were efficient: in particular, where format has constant arguments or is only using simple string concatenation (literal pieces plus exactly %s) then it is entirely practical to bytecode them. The other forms of format remain uncompiled.

4. Improving Generation

But it is not just that the set of commands for which instructions are issued has been extended; I have also looked at improving the generation of bytecode for existing commands.

In particular, the very complex commands switch, try and dict with have had a lot of attention from me, as have the built-in ensembles *as generic features*. I have also worked on changing the break and continue compilers so that they jump to their target instruction locations (after doing appropriate clean-up) rather going to the expense of throwing exceptions.

Improving ensembles

One of the key features of Tcl's ensembles is that they can be bytecode compiled into. This is a key feature that distinguishes them from objects; they are command groupings, but the name of the command and its subcommand are expected to normally be literals in scripts. This is particularly true for those ensembles defined by Tcl itself. (Enabling compilation for all ensembles would have the unfortunate side effect of making the Snit extension enormously more expensive.)

The ensemble dispatch mechanism in Tcl 8.5 normally uses a cache in the subcommand's Tcl_Obj to hold a reference to the implementation command to dispatch to (building that cache from the ensemble's internal table if it does not exist or has been modified) and dispatches via Tcl_EvalObjv. This mechanism is fairly quick, but has some overhead relative to directly invoking the command. Where the ensemble is marked for compilation (via an internal flag not exposed to third-party code, used for string, info, etc.), the subcommand is a known literal, and the implementation command has a compilation implementation of its own, the compiler for that implementation is called with the rewritten argument list so that bytecode is generated. This means that we can use this mechanism for well known core Tcl ensembles with no degradation in performance.

However, the mechanism is not *that* fast where specialist bytecode compilers are not available. In particular, there are a number of steps that are relatively costly, such as the rewrite of the argument lists and the double dispatch (once to process the overall ensemble command, and a second time for the dispatch to the implementation), and a fair number of the subcommands that it is used with are relevant for use in high-performance code (*e.g.*, the string tolower command is really rather common when cleaning up external data).

To improve this situation, I have done two things. The first is to embed a new mechanism in Tcl (via the new bytecode instruction invokeReplace) to perform the efficient dispatch of ensemble subcommands. This embeds part of the mechanism described above; it reduces the overhead of the dispatch mechanism to the minimum (*i.e.*, a single call to Tcl_EvalObjv) while preserving the exact externally visible semantics that already existed. The second improvement is to add very simple command compilers to many (but not all) of the existing subcommand implementations; these simple compilers just check if the correct number of arguments is supplied (*i.e.*, that there will be no call to Tcl_WrongNumArgs at runtime, as that is one of the few functions that can observe the differences due to ensemble dispatch) and if the right number of arguments is present, issues a direct invokeStk instruction to call the relevant implementation command.

Following this change, we can now observe four different ways that ensemble subcommands can be dispatched:

1. Directly compiled subcommands just generate normal bytecode:

```
string range foo 2 3
```

Compiles to:

```
push "foo"
strrangeImm 2 3
```

2. Simple subcommands become invocations of the underlying implementation:

```
string tolower foo
```

Compiles to:

```
push "::tcl::string::tolower"
push "foo"
invokeStk1 2
```

3. Complex subcommands become the *replacing* invoke of the subcommand:

```
namespace eval ::foo { bar }
```

Compiles to:

```
push "namespace"
push "eval"
push "::foo"
push " bar "
push "::tcl::namespace::eval"
invokeReplace 4 2
```

4. Invocations of uncompiled ensembles use the old mechanism:

```
userEnsembleExample x y
```

Compiles to:

```
push "userEnsembleExample"
push "x"
push "y"
invokeStk1 3
```

The criteria for whether a subcommand is deemed to be "complex" are whether it evaluates a script during it's processing (as those scripts can contain a call to `info level` or `info frame`, both of which can observe the difference), or whether the subcommand has a non-trivial mechanism for determining if the correct number of arguments has been supplied (the `chan copy` command is one of these).

As previously noted, this mechanism is not enabled for ensembles created outside the core of Tcl. This is because the cost of deleting or doing an update of a compiled ensemble is substantial: it triggers the re-compilation of all bytecode in the interpreter. The impact on Snit in particular would be enormous, given that it is constructing an object system on top of the ensemble mechanism.

Improving switch

The **switch** command has a number of main modes of operation from the perspective of bytecode generation. There are three principal ones:

- *Jump table.* This is generated when doing exact matching of the argument, and is fast especially when the number of things to compare against is large (such as in the implementation of the `clock` command's format parser). This was already substantially correct, as it did not need to retain a copy of the value to test against for any length of time.

- *Sequence of conditions.* This is what is normally generated, and is what is used for case-insensitive exact matches, glob matches and simple regular expression matches. This is the area that had a substantive amount of work applied to it, mainly to ensure that the computed stack depth used during the compilation of the body scripts was actually correct so that any break or continue across the `switch` command would function correctly instead of causing one of a whole variety of crashes.

  Note that this did not substantially change the actual code generated; this is much more about getting correct metadata about the generated code, so that *other* code could be generated correctly.

- *Uncompiled.* This represents the degenerate case, and is used in awkward situations such as when a script is not a literal, or when a particularly complex regular expression match is used (particularly with capturing of the subexpressions). This case remains in need of substantial work in the future in order to reduce the number of variations of switch that are not compiled.

Improving try

For the try command, the key to understanding its fundamental complexity is that there are two major conditions to consider when doing code generation: the correct way to create code depends strongly on whether or not there are any on or trap clauses[4], and whether or not there is a finally clause. If there are neither, the try is little more than an eval variant (without the concatenation).

The aim of any code generation plan for a construct like try has to be to keep the amount of overhead down. Additionally, care has to be taken when an error occurs during the processing of any on, trap or finally clauses, as the original exception state has to be embedded in the option dictionary's -during option. The major opportunity for optimization is when there is *no* finally clause and *no* trapping of a TCL_OK result, when it is possible to allow the exiting of the context without having to do a full trap and reissue of all exceptions; only the actual exceptional cases need special extra processing.

If we look at this code:

```
try {
    puts "foo bar"
} on error msg {
    puts "bad stuff: $msg"
}
```

[4] The only difference between a trap clause and an on error clause is that the former also checks whether the given words match a prefix of the -errorcode list.

This is only compiled when placed in a context with a local variable table (*i.e.*, in a procedure, lambda term or method) and it produces this rather long bytecode sequence in Tcl 8.6.0 (for clarity, the parts that are *not* actually executed normally are indented, and the parts that *are* normally executed are in bold):

```
beginCatch4 0
push "puts"
push "foo bar"
invokeStk1 2
push "0"
reverse 2
jump1 +4                          # → pc 22
 pushReturnCode
 pushResult
pushReturnOpts                    # = pc 22
endCatch
storeScalar1 %2
pop
storeScalar1 %1
pop
dup
push "1"
eq
jumpFalse4 +26                    # → pc 60
 pop
 loadScalar1 %1
 storeScalar1 %msg
 pop
 push "puts"
 push "bad stuff: "
 loadScalar1 %msg
 concat1 2
 invokeStk1 2
 jump4 +11                        # → pc 66
pop                               # = pc 60
loadScalar1 %2
loadScalar1 %1
returnStk
done                              # = pc 66
```

With the changes, this is now rather longer (alas) because of the need to handle the -during exception logging, but also correct and faster when no errors occur:

```
beginCatch4 0
push "puts"
push "foo bar"
invokeStk1 2
endCatch
jump4 +103                        # → pc 115
 pushReturnCode
```

```
pushResult
pushReturnOpts
endCatch
storeScalar1 %2
pop
storeScalar1 %1
pop
dup
push "1"
eq
jumpFalse4 +78                  # → pc 109
pop
loadScalar1 %1
storeScalar1 %msg
pop
beginCatch4 1
push "puts"
push "bad stuff: "
loadScalar1 %msg
concat1 2
invokeStk1 2
endCatch
jump4 +57                       # → pc 115
pushResult
pushReturnOpts
pushReturnCode
endCatch
push "1"
eq
jumpFalse1 +28                  # → pc 98
loadScalar1 %2
reverse 2
storeScalar1 %2
pop
push "-during"
reverse 2
dictSet 1 %2
reverse 2                       # = pc 98
returnStk
jump4 +11                       # → pc 115
pop                             # = pc 109
loadScalar1 %2
loadScalar1 %1
returnStk
done                            # = pc 115
```

In particular, I have highlighted in bold the instructions taken when no error occurs in the body; as can be seen, the number of instructions processed in this, the expected case, is now far smaller; the *execution overhead* of the try command is demonstrably reduced despite the increase in length of bytecode created. This difference is only exacerbated when the try command has a sequence of trap clauses instead of a single simple on error clause.

Improving dict with

Sometimes, the Tcl community find things to do with Tcl commands that I never anticipated. So it was with dict with, where one of the key use-cases has turned out to be converting a dictionary into a group of local variables *without* maintaining the binding to the mapping in the dictionary. The common idiom for this technique is to use an empty body script, and that has the advantage that it is a case that can be simply detected during compilation.

When I detect this case, I am able to determine precisely that there can be no exceptions arising from the evaluation of the body of the dict with — no commands, no substitutions, therefore no errors — so I can omit the (complex!) code stanza to manage exceptions arising from the body script. Indeed, I can actually omit virtually everything from the implementation of the command other than the operation to expand the dictionary into variables and the operation to write the values back. The latter has to remain as I cannot prove at the time of issuing the code that none of the variables have a trace set on them that modifies the values.

Improving break and continue

Traditionally, the break and continue commands are implemented as commands that produce the specialized result codes TCL_BREAK (defined to be 3 in tcl.h) and TCL_CONTINUE (4) respectively. In the bytecode-compiled era, these have been translated into instructions (with the same names as the commands) that generate the relevant exception conditions. However, this is actually not very efficient, as it requires the code processing these conditions to jump outside the main bytecode evaluation loop to the separate code that finds the exception target in the two cases.

Instead, I track exactly what exception trapping ranges are present at the point where the break/continue is issued. By finding the innermost active range, I can directly determine where the exception would end up branching to, and directly use a jump instruction instead. This is a significantly more optimal instruction sequence.

However, there are some *significant* wrinkles to this. In particular, it is possible for the stack depth to be different between the place where the break/continue command is being compiled and the place where we want to jump to; this is actually a bug in Tcl's bytecode generation of long standing. The problem is not (usually) the nesting of commands that you see with most Tcl scripts, but rather more esoteric scripts such as:

```
while 1 {
   puts "foo,[continue]"
}
```

This is problematic because words for the inner invocation of puts are being placed on the evaluation stack when the continue is processed, and a skip back to the start of the loop without resetting (whether done via an exception or via a direct jump) results in the overall stack depth growing without reasonable bound. Preventing this requires additional pop instructions to be done before the jump so that the stack depth is correct for the target instruction. This does somewhat decrease the efficiency in this case, but since it is rare and previously a critical error, the cost is entirely justifiable. (The complexity of tracking the stack depths and jump targets is only borne during compilation, not execution.)

A variation on this (also handled) is where there are expansions being processed on the stack at the same time, because expansions have their own tracking stack.

Improving expanding list

The final major improvement to code generation that I have made was to the list command when some of its arguments are derived from expansion. While it is not generally possible to handle expansion which produces the first word of a command, as it easily becomes impractical to figure out what command is being compiled, when that command is capable of processing any number of arguments and producing a result, it should be possible to make a compiled version of that command. The only command for which I have done this is list, where an all expanding arguments version:

```
list {*}$foo {*}$bar
```

is actually semantically equivalent to this:

```
concat [lrange $foo 0 end] \
       [lrange $bar 0 end]
```

However, it can be implemented in a considerably more efficient manner, as there is no need to consider what is going on with string interpretations; it can be a pure list operation.

In terms of how the code generated changes, this:

```
list {*}$foo {*}$bar
```

used to compile to this[5]:

```
expandStart
push "list"
loadScalar %foo
expandStkTop 2
loadScalar %bar
expandStkTop 3
invokeExpanded
```

Following this change, we instead generate this sequence of instructions:

```
loadScalar %foo
loadScalar %bar
listConcat
```

This sequence with three arguments to list, one of which is expanded:

```
list $foo $bar {*}$grill
```

Used to compile to this:

[5] It turns out that the numeric parameter to expandStkTop is not actually necessary for the instruction to function correctly, not now that stack depth calculations are correct.

```
expandStart
push "list"
loadScalar %foo
loadScalar %bar
loadScalar %grill
expandStkTop 4
invokeExpanded
```

But now becomes this:

```
loadScalar %foo
loadScalar %bar
list 2
loadScalar %grill
listConcat
```

The listConcat instruction used is a simple binary operation to concatenate two lists.

It should be noted that the mechanism for allowing a command to take charge of what instructions it is compiled when expansion is present is generic. The potential exists to increase the number of commands that produce efficient code, but most commands have the issue that they support additional options or fixed-position arguments, so compilers have to be relatively careful; the list command is a special case in that it is a simple command that treats all arguments (after the initial command name) exactly the same.

5. Improving Inspection

As part of this work, and with a little minor prodding from Colin McCormack, I found that there were some fairly severe limitations on the built-in disassembler that needed to be addressed.

Disassembler history

The disassembler in Tcl 8.5 was originally a part of Tcl 8.0 as a debugging tool. It was enabled by setting the variable tcl_traceCompile to 2 and causing the code in question to be compiled, when it would print the disassembled bytecode directly to standard out. (In situations without a real C-level stdout, such as in *wish* or *tkcon* on Windows, no output would be produced at all.) As you can no doubt guess, this was highly tricky to use; you had to wrap it in something like this, assuming an argument to the procedure was required for it to work:

```
proc disasProc {procedureName} {
    global tcl_traceCompile
    rename set SET
    rename SET set
    set tcl_traceCompile 2
    catch {$procedureName}
    set tcl_traceCompile 0
    return
}
```

This was horrible (especially the need to flush the bytecode cache by bumping the compilation epoch) so in Tcl 8.5 I altered the code to do the direct printing to instead dump its results out to a string buffer instead of printing directly, and wrapped this into the disassemble command (which was put in the tcl::unsupported namespace to signify that we were not guaranteeing the interface) together with a bit of code to allow the control of exactly what was being printed. This allowed the equivalent of the above to be done with:

```
proc disasProc {procedureName} {
    puts [disassemble proc \
            $procedureName]
}
```

This is an enormous improvement in usability, and works correctly on all platforms. (The parameter passed as proc above is used to disambiguate between procedures, scripts, lambda/apply terms, etc.)

However, the results of the disassembly (used in abbreviated form earlier in this paper) are difficult to consume in a script, as they are designed purely to be a basic debugging tool. In particular, they intermix metadata and the disassembly information. There is also quite a bit of information in the bytecode itself that is not exposed in the disassembled code, mostly relating to the parsed script's commands.

The new disassembler

To address this, I have created an additional disassembler[6] that takes the same arguments as the existing disassembler, but instead of producing its results as a complex string, it generates a dictionary that describes the bytecode. The description dictionary contains these keys:

- `literals` — contains a list of all literal values used in `push` instructions in the bytecode.
- `variables` — contains a list of information about all variables defined in the bytecode. Each variable is represented by a list where the first word is a set of flags (*e.g.*, "`scalar`" to indicate that the variable is a simple variable) and the second word is the name of the variable; temporary variables don't have the second word as they are unnamed.
- `exception` — contains a list of dictionaries that describe the *exception ranges* in the bytecode. Each of these dictionaries states what type it is (`catch` ranges trap all non-`TCL_OK` exceptions, `loop` ranges only trap `TCL_BREAK` and `TCL_CONTINUE`), what range of instructions are covered, and where to jump to when an exception occurs.
- `instructions` — contains a *dictionary* of the disassembled code, with the keys of the (inner) dictionary being the numeric addresses of the instructions in order and the values of the dictionary each being a list that is the disassembly of the instruction. The first value in each list is the instruction name, and the subsequent values are the arguments. Each argument may be an integer, a reference to a literal (an index into the `literals` list preceded by "@"), a jump target (an address preceded by "`pc` "), a variable index (a "%" followed by the index into the `variables` list), an immediate index literal (starts with a period, ".", followed by a list index which may be either start- or end-relative), or an auxiliary index (a "?" followed by an index into the `auxiliary` list).
- `auxiliary` — contains a list of auxiliary information descriptors. This is used to encode three key things: the description of what variables are used by the `foreach`-related instructions, the description of relative jumps to use in a `jumpTable` instruction, and the description of how to map variables in the instructions used to compile `dict update`. Each descriptor is a dictionary where the only guaranteed key is `name`, which holds the name of the type of auxiliary information encoded in the particular record.
- `commands` — contains a list of dictionaries that describe what commands were detected in the code that was compiled to produce the bytecode. The order of the list of dictionaries is the order in which the commands start within the script. For each command, the dictionary contains the range of instructions generated from that command (as addresses, in the `codefrom` and `codeto` members), the range of the source code that the command occupied (as offsets from the beginning of the script, in the `scriptfrom` and `scripto` members), and in the `script` element, the full text of the command that was compiled (which can include subcommands).

[6] This is `::tcl::unsupported::getbytecode` at the time of writing. This is not a name that I consider to be a long-term name, as it is not *getting* the bytecode so much as *describing* it.

- script — contains the full text of the script that was actually compiled to produce the bytecode.
- namespace — contains the fully qualified name of the namespace used as context to resolve commands in the bytecode.
- stackdepth — contains the maximum stack depth (approximately the maximum number of arguments that need to be on the stack at once, plus the space for evaluating expressions).
- exceptdepth — contains the maximum depth of nested exception ranges.

The general principle of how the information is encoded in the result of getbytecode is to ensure that the maximum amount of information from the low-level bytecode is present *without* exposing any of the complex encodings that are used there or requiring consumers of the result to know how each of the instructions actually treats its result. In fact, this isn't *quite* all the information in the bytecode, but it is exceptionally difficult to make use of the rest (such as the interpreter reference and the compilation epoch) from scripts.

Using the disassembly

Though the output of getbytecode is not easy to read as a person, for scripts it is exceptionally easy to process. This makes it easy to do things like analysing the flow of control in the program, detecting automatically where loops are and allowing the visualization of how exception ranges are used.

An example of what can be done with this is shown in Appendix 2, where the controlflow command (based on a heavily-modified version of a x86 instruction renderer[4] originally written in Python) prints out the address of each instruction followed by the instruction itself, with arguments converted to an easier-to-read form (*e.g.*, variable references are converted to %*name*, or %%%*index* if they are nameless temporaries). Arrows are added as a prefix to indicate jumps, the different colour applied to the instructions in the middle of the output indicates that a (loop) exception range is in force, and the two coloured addresses are the targets for the exception range, one for TCL_CONTINUE (being where to go to start the next loop iteration) and the other for TCL_BREAK (for finishing the loop). The output part of the code renders to a normal Unix terminal.

It should be noted that the technique I used is not infallible when it comes to display. When asked to display a moderately complex procedure, such as those present in the implementation of Tcl's clock command (*e.g.*, ParseClockFormatFormat2), that has a number of substantial switch statements that compile into jump tables, the number of indents becomes larger than any reasonable width of terminal.

6. Optimization

Given all the work described above, it has become clear that it is necessary to generate improved bytecode. There are a number of places where simply generating better code *within* the implementation of a command was not generating good code within the wider stream of bytecode.

For example, it is the fundamental structure of Tcl command compilation that they overall push a single word onto the bytecode execution engine's stack. Then, in the common case where the result of the command is not needed, that word is then immediately popped off the stack again. It is therefore closer to optimal to not push the value in the first place, if it is possible to avoid doing so. Some cases are particularly easy to determine, such as where the commands being compiled always produce an empty (or other constant) value as their results; the last step of the compilation of both for and foreach is the push of an empty value, and it is very rare to actually use the results of those commands precisely because it is always the empty string.

Yet to *safely* avoid doing that extra work at runtime, you have to be cautious during compilation. In particular, suppose the generation of the pointless result is followed by a pop of the value, but the pop can also be jumped to from elsewhere (a pattern easily generated when using the if command) then might well be wrong to just remove the push/pop sequence as that will cause other code paths to create an unbalanced stack.

The simplest way of preventing such problems with code removal is to determine if there are any jumps (of any kind, including conditionals, result-branch operations, jump tables, exception targets, etc.) and to only do the removal when the pop can only be reached by that one push. This safety requirement reduces the number of optimizations done, but ensures that those that are done are correct.

Optimizations performed

There are a number of optimizations that are done now that were not part of Tcl 8.6.0. These are:

- Removal of push/pop sequences, as described earlier.
- Folding logical not into a following branch by inverting the branch instruction's condition.
- Removing tryCvtNumeric (part of the compilation of expressions) when the subsequent instruction will perform the numeric conversion anyway.
- Advancing jumps to their ultimate target, instead of having them pass through a chain of jumps and nops to get there. This was a relatively common pattern, especially given that jumps are now being generated from break and continue commands.
- Removing startCommand instructions[7] where the code is found to be suitably "well-behaved", such as compiling to bytecode without any invoking of external commands or being located within the implementation of Tcl. Unlike the other optimizations described here, this one is done by rerunning the compiler in a special mode where it simply does not issue the instruction we want to exclude.
- Removing outright unreachable code at the end of a bytecode compilation. Where there is code after a done instruction that is not jumped to, it is possible to determine exactly that the following code cannot possibly be executed, and so makes it a good candidate for removal. However, this is an exceptionally minor optimization, as unreachable code is not executed by virtue of its very unreachability.

These optimizations are supported by a new peephole optimization within the execution engine. I added a special case to the processing of pop instructions so that a sequence of pops would be handled more efficiently. The optimizer generates such sequences at this point because it does not move any pointers into the bytecode other than those held by simple jump and branch instructions. In particular, command boundaries are not modified; they have a singularly complex encoding that it is non-trivial to work with.

[7] The startCommand instruction is used to skip the rest of the bytecode of a command when the compilation epoch of the interpreter has been updated since the start of processing of the bytecode in question, typically in response to a rename or deletion of a command with a bytecode compiler attached to it. It is a common instruction to deal with a rare case so as to ensure official semantic correctness, and unfortunately is relatively expensive to process.

7. Performance Measurements

In order to compare the performance of Tcl between different versions, it is necessary to be very specific about what is actually being tested. In particular, it is easy to measure something completely different to what you *expected* to measure. To that end, the code used to perform the performance measurements is included in Appendix 3; the timings in Table 2 are rounded to 4 significant figures and are in microseconds.

Program	8.5.14	8.6b1	8.6b2	8.6.0+
ListConcat	0.418	1.564	0.544	0.493
Fibonacci	1.266	1.722	1.441	1.441
ListIterate	3.077	3.315	2.091	2.176
ProcCall	0.863	1.449	1.310	1.264
LoopCB	1.074	1.714	1.404	1.617
EnsDispatch1	0.975	1.944	1.400	0.888
EnsDispatch2	0.489	1.385	0.990	0.393
EnsDispatch3	0.520	1.598	1.261	1.112
EnsDispatch4	0.448	1.311	0.803	0.804
DictWith	2.634	4.072	1.895	1.289
TryNormal	*N/A*	26.221	1.385	0.522
TryError	*N/A*	39.313	3.804	3.931
TryNested	*N/A*	57.236	7.727	11.788
TryOver	*N/A*	39.230	4.120	4.290

Table 2: Times to execute key programs

The *ListConcat* program tests the performance of the new way of handling expansion in the `list` command. The *Fibonacci* program tests general bytecode and integer operation handling, the *ListIterate* program tests general bytecode and list operation handling, and the *ProcCall* program tests the costs of calling a procedure. The *LoopCB* program tests the costs of the `break` and `continue` commands. The *EnsDispatch** programs test the performance of ensembles: *EnsDispatch1* tests the costs of doing ensemble dispatch for two cases where we can convert to a direct invocation of the implementation command, *EnsDispatch2* tests the costs where we can fully compile to bytecode, *EnsDispatch3* tests a case that still has to use the full ensemble dispatch mechanism, and *EnsDispatch4* tests the costs for user-defined ensembles, verifying that no unreasonable costs have been introduced inadvertently. The *DictWith* program illustrates the handling of the empty-body special case in `dict with`. The *Try** programs illustrate the change of profile of costs associated with `try`: *TryNormal* shows what happens when no error is trapped, *TryError* shows a trapped error, *TryNested* shows the relative costs of throwing an error in a handler script (note that none of these execute on Tcl 8.5; the `try` command was new in 8.6, and was not compiled fully in 8.6b1), and *TryOver* shows the overhead associated with the evidence collection technique used in *TryNested* (using the interior workload associated with *TryNormal*).

Performance tests were done on a MacBook Pro with a 2.7GHz Intel Core i7 processor running OS X 10.8.4. The tests were deliberately not disk intensive, and the amount of memory used was much smaller than the free memory available. The executables used for these performance tests were compiled from clean checkouts of the source tree for the release versions associated with each tag from fossil, except for 8.6.0+, which corresponds to the commit labelled `bc57d06610b7`. All were compiled with exactly the same version of the compiler, and using the default, optimizing configuration. The benchmark driver script forces compilation of the code being benchmarked by running it once, then runs it for 100k iterations each of 20 times, taking the minimum (so as to try to avoid any potential problems with jitter due to the OS).

The overall evidence[8] is that some of the optimizations are definitely valuable; for example, the optimizations to core ensemble dispatch restore or even improve on the speed that was in Tcl 8.5 for the majority of ensem-

[8] It makes no sense to combine the performance figures, as the benchmarks are not chosen at all to represent realistic code or to give equal weight to all operations. They are best regarded as *samplings* of the performance of *small parts* of the implementation of Tcl.

ble subcommands. Similarly, some other operations (e.g., `dict with`, `try` in the non-error case) are clearly much cheaper now.

However, not everything is faster; command dispatch is definitely slower in 8.6 than in 8.5 and that has an impact on many of these benchmarks (most notably *ProcCall* and *EnsDispatch4*) and I have no idea why *ListIterate* is so much faster in 8.6 and *LoopCB* so much slower; further examination of the situation will be required. The increase in execution time of *TryNested* is expected due to the change of semantics of option dictionary handling in the error-in-handler case; *TryOver* confirms that this is the cause, and not the additional overhead of the error trapping used in our little benchmarking framework.

8. Future Considerations

This document represents on-going work; many things remain to be done in each of the areas described. For example, in the area of language coverage, we still need to analyse what is the actual set of commands required to allow the majority of Tcl scripts to be virtually entirely compiled to bytecode without the use of the generic dispatch sequence. There are a number of commands that are fairly common, relatively simple, but which are not compiled (*e.g.*, `string trim`). Which ones can we change that status on? This remains to be determined.

On the other hand, we also know that the large majority of Tcl scripts are going to be continuing to call commands even after conversion to bytecode. This is because there is an on-going need to invoke user-defined commands, whether they are procedures, objects or functionality defined in an extension written in a foreign language. What can we do to make that step more efficient? Can we support anything like inlining of procedures? (It is my theory that the last question can be definitely answered affirmatively with relative ease provided the local variable table has no named entries in it, but that's an incredibly restrictive condition; the real question is whether it is possible to do so with fewer restrictions, and to what extent the results change the visible semantics.)

When it comes to the quality of the generated code, more can be done. In particular, the current mechanisms for exception handling are especially complex, and have a far-reaching impact on code generation. Perhaps adding a mechanism such as perhaps internal subroutines *à la* classic BASIC would enable at least some reduction in complexity.

There is also the fact that we currently need to explicitly push exception depths on the stack; it would be far nicer (from the perspective of code *generation* at least) if the target stack depth information were encoded in the exception range record. After all, we now have that information accurately during code generation.

For the disassembly side of things, the obvious thing to do now would be to move to allowing the assembler to be able to handle what the disassembler produces in some way, possibly with syntactic changes, so that we can perform a full round-trip from Tcl code to bytecode to disassembled bytecode to code that is executable again. Currently there are a few key things missing, most notably including the ability to issue the `foreach`-related instructions. The aim would be to enable the writing of more of the optimizer in Tcl itself (ignoring for now the problems associated with optimizing the optimizer's own code).

However, for all the above, the major challenge for the future of bytecodes has to be to improve the optimizer. The next step has to be to actually remove irrelevant and unreachable code and other miscellaneous related structures (*e.g.*, exception ranges). This would let the code issued be made quite a bit more compact. This might in turn require substantial reconfiguration of the in-memory representation of bytecode.

Longer term

The real goal is meeting the Lehenbauer Challenges and achieving speedups of between 2× (*i.e.*, code that executes in half the time) and 10× (*i.e.*, code that executes in a tenth of the time) as these will improve a great many Tcl scripts instead of specific code. The optimization strategies described within this document may go some way towards addressing the lower end of that range of improvements depending on the exact profile of code to be improved (indeed, the *DictWith* micro-benchmark in Section 7 already achieves a better-than-double speedup), but the higher end will definitely require native code generation.

The aim of this work is therefore to provide an improved basis for generating code where it is possible to more easily analyse the code to be native-compiled and determine its real type behaviour. Proving micro-theorems about the types of variables is the key to determining how to generate *good* native code from Tcl programs, and it is conjectured that bytecode has a key advantage over straight Tcl code as a starting point in that the type logic of bytecode is more static. It remains to be seen if this conjecture is actually a true one.

9. References

[1] Ugurlu, O.D., Kenny K., *A bytecode assembler for Tcl*, in Proceedings of the 17th Annual Tcl/Tk Conference (Tcl'2010), Tcl Community Association, Whitmore Lake, MI, 2010.

[2] Vitale, B., Abdelrahman, T.S., *Catenation and specialization for Tcl virtual machine performance*, in Proceedings of the 2004 Workshop on Interpreters, Virtual Machines and Emulators (IVME'04), pages 42–50, ACM, Washington, DC, 2004. doi:10.1145/1059579.1059591

[3] Lewis, B., *An on-the-fly bytecode compiler for Tcl*, in Proceedings of the 4th Annual USENIX Tcl/Tk Workshop, USENIX, Berkeley, CA, 1996.

[4] Fairchild, D., *Automagical ASM Control Flow Arrow-Annotation*, weblog entry at http://blog.fairchild.dk/2013/06/automagical-asm-control-flow-arrow-annotation/, June 11, 2013, accessed June 19, 2013.

Appendix 1: Teapot Ensemble Subcommand Frequency Tables

In the tables below, the assessment of whether a command is practical to bytecode depends mainly on the internal complexity of the command; commands that create or destroy commands are *always* considered to be impractical as they potentially modify the interpreter epoch. The final column states whether the subcommand was bytecode-compiled in Tcl 8.6b2, *i.e.*, prior to the work in this paper.

The shell script used to extract the information was (with the environment variables `$TEAPOT_REPOSITORY` and `$TCL_CMD` supplying the place to look for the sources and the command to look for respectively):

```
find $TEAPOT_REPOSITORY -name "*.tm" -print0 | xargs -0 grep -lw $TCL_CMD \
    | xargs cat | grep -w $TCL_CMD | sed -nE "
        /$TCL_CMD +\[a-z\]/ {
            s/^.*$TCL_CMD (\[a-z\]*).*\$/\\1/
            p
        }
    " | sort | uniq -c | sort -n
```

The result of that script was then hand-filtered to remove irrelevant values (such as words in free-text that just happen to mention the major command) and to coalesce abbreviations onto their main subcommand.

For the `string` command (subcommands not mentioned did not occur):

Command	# Uses	Practical to Bytecode	Bytecoded in 8.6b2
string totitle	1	Possibly	No
string replace	2	Possibly	No
string trimleft	8	Yes	No
string last	28	Yes	No
string trimright	33	Yes	No
string repeat	34	Possibly	No
string toupper	145	Possibly	No
string trim	147	Yes	No
string index	245	Yes	Yes
string tolower	248	Possibly	No
string is	424	Possibly	No
string map	569	Possibly	No
string first	674	Yes	No
string range	892	Yes	No
string match	898	Yes	Yes
string length	1100	Yes	Yes
string equal	2129	Yes	Yes
string compare	5971	Yes	Yes

For the `dict` command (subcommands not mentioned did not occur; note that `dict map` was only introduced after this survey was done):

Command	# Uses	Practical to Bytecode	Bytecoded in 8.6b2
dict keys	1	Yes	No
dict with	1	Yes	Yes
dict unset	2	Yes	No
dict lappend	3	Yes	Yes
dict values	8	Yes	No
dict for	8	Yes	Yes
dict merge	15	Yes	No
dict incr	18	Yes	Yes
dict create	22	Yes	No
dict append	28	Yes	Yes
dict exists	34	Yes	No
dict get	297	Yes	Yes
dict set	347	Yes	Yes

For the namespace command (subcommands not mentioned did not occur):

Command	# Uses	Practical to Bytecode	Bytecoded in 8.6b2
namespace forget	3	No	No
namespace inscope	6	Possibly	No
namespace parent	7	Yes	No
namespace children	17	Possibly	No
namespace qualifiers	30	Yes	No
namespace exists	50	Yes	No
namespace which	56	Yes	No
namespace delete	77	No	No
namespace code	116	Yes	No
namespace import	130	No	No
namespace upvar	132	Yes	Yes
namespace origin	153	Possibly	No
namespace tail	206	Yes	No
namespace ensemble	269	No	No
namespace current	272	Yes	No
namespace export	757	Possibly	No
namespace eval	2681	No	No

For the array command (subcommands not mentioned did not occur):

Command	# Uses	Practical to Bytecode	Bytecoded in 8.6b2
array size	37	Possibly	No
array exists	56	Yes	No
array unset	191	Yes	No
array get	479	Possibly	No
array names	1085	Possibly	No
array set	2511	Yes	No

For the info command (subcommands not mentioned did not occur; note that info class and info object are themselves ensembles, and that info patchlevel is impractical due to the "interesting" failure mode behaviour):

Command	#Uses	Practical To Bytecode	Bytecoded in 8.6b2
info class	1	Yes (parts)	No
info default	1	No	No
info loaded	1	No	No
info frame	2	Possibly	No
info sharedlibextension	4	No	No
info nameofexecutable	8	No	No
info object	8	Yes (parts)	No
info patchlevel	11	No	No
info complete	12	Possibly	No
info body	29	No	No
info vars	33	Possibly	No
info args	42	No	No
info procs	50	No	No
info hostname	54	No	No
info script	67	Possibly	No
info commands	274	Possibly	No
info level	587	Yes	No
info exists	3822	Yes	Yes

For other ensembles, they are typically wholly impractical to bytecode other than through generic mechanisms (*e.g.*, the chan ensemble, which is thoroughly entangled with the I/O subsystem and so likely to encounter dominating OS-related delays, but which still benefits from the generic improvements to the ensemble mechanism).

Appendix 2: Example of controlflow Output

Sample code used to create the output:

```
controlflow lambda {{a b c} {
    set sum 0
    foreach x [list $a $b $c] {
        incr sum [expr {$x**2}]
    }
    puts "sum of squares: $sum"
}}
```

Output from the above code:

```
 0 push1 "0"
 2 storeScalar1 %sum
 4 pop
 5 startCommand ➡ 61 2
14 loadScalar1 %a
16 loadScalar1 %b
18 loadScalar1 %c
20 list 3
25 storeScalar1 %%%4
27 pop
28 foreach_start4 {data %%%4 loop %%%5 assign %x}
33   foreach_step4 {data %%%4 loop %%%5 assign %x}
38   jumpFalse1 ➡ 59
40   startCommand ➡ 56 2
49   loadScalar1 %x
51   push1 "2"
53   expon
54   incrScalar1 %sum
56   pop
57 jump1 ➡ 33
59 push1 ""
61 pop
62 push1 "puts"
64 push1 "sum\ of\ squares:\ "
66 loadScalar1 %sum
68 concat1 2
70 invokeStk1 2
72 done
```

As you can see, the implementation of the loop body has been indented, and the (loop) exception range — the range of instructions where a TCL_BREAK or TCL_CONTINUE instruction will trigger a jump to a nominated target instruction — has been highlighted in red. The break-target for the exception range has its address highlighted in blue, the continue-target has its address highlighted in red.

The source to the controlflow command is too long to include in this document. It can be downloaded from DropBox: https://dl.dropboxusercontent.com/u/19238925/Tcl/2013/controlflow.tcl

Appendix 3: Performance Measurement Script

The performance measurements of Section 7 were done with this consolidated script.

```
package require Tcl 8.5

proc listConcat {a b c} {
    list $a $b {*}$c
}

proc Fibonacci {n} {
```

```
    set a 0
    set b 1
    for {set i 2} {$i <= $n} {incr i} {
        set b [expr {$a + [set a $b]}]
    }
    return $b
}

proc iter {param} {
    set result {}
    foreach x $param {
        lappend result [string length $param]
    }
    return $result
}

proc inner {} {
    return "ok"
}
proc outer {} {
    inner; inner; inner; inner; inner
}

proc loopcb {x} {
    for {set i 0} {$i < 10000} {incr i} {
        if {$i == $x} break
        continue
    }
    return "ok"
}

proc ensDispatch1 {} {
    info tclversion
    info patchlevel
}

proc ensDispatch2 {} {
    namespace current
    info level
}

proc ensDispatch3 {} {
    namespace inscope :: {return -level 0 "ok"}
    namespace inscope :: {return -level 0 "ok"}
}

proc ensDispatch4 {} {
    ens4 foo bar
```

```
}
namespace ensemble create -command ens4 -map {
    foo {::ens4core}
}
proc ens4core {msg} {
    return $msg
}

proc dictWithAdd {d} {
    dict with d {}
    return [expr {$a + $b}]
}

proc tryNormal {} {
    set d 1.875
    try {
        set x [expr {$d / $d}]
    } on error {} {
        set x "error happened"
    }
    return $x
}

proc tryError {} {
    # Zero divided by zero is an error (no NaN please!)
    set d 0.0
    try {
        set x [expr {$d / $d}]
    } on error {} {
        set x "error happened"
    }
    return $x
}

proc tryNested {} {
    set d 0.0
    catch {
        try {
            set x [expr {$d / $d}]
        } on error {} {
            error "error happened"
        }
    } msg opt
    return $opt
}

proc tryNestedOver {} {
    set d 0.0
```

```
    catch {
        try {
            set x [expr {$d / $d}]
        } on error {} {
            set x "error happened"
        }
    } msg opt
    return $opt
}

proc benchmark {title script {version 8.5}} {
    if {[package vsatisfies [info patchlevel] $version]} {
        eval $script
        for {set i 0} {$i < 20} {incr i} {
            lappend t [lindex [time $script 100000] 0]
        }
        puts [format "%s: %4f" $title [tcl::mathfunc::min {*}$t]]
    } else {
        puts [format "%s: N/A" $title]
    }
}

benchmark "ListConcat"    { listConcat {a b c} {d e f} {g h i} }
benchmark "Fibonacci"     { Fibonacci 10 }
benchmark "ListIterate"   { iter {a aaa aaaaa} }
benchmark "ProcCall"      { outer }
benchmark "LoopCB"        { loopcb 10}
benchmark "EnsDispatch1"  { ensDispatch1 }
benchmark "EnsDispatch2"  { ensDispatch2 }
benchmark "EnsDispatch3"  { ensDispatch3 }
benchmark "EnsDispatch4"  { ensDispatch4 }
benchmark "DictWith"      { dictWithAdd {a 1 b 2 c 4} }
benchmark "TryNormal"     { tryNormal }      8.6
benchmark "TryError"      { tryError }       8.6
benchmark "TryNested"     { tryNested }      8.6
benchmark "TryNestedOver" { tryNestedOver }  8.6
```

This script can be downloaded from DropBox:
https://dl.dropboxusercontent.com/u/19238925/Tcl/2013/optbench.tcl

Tcl 2013
New Orleans, LA
September 23-27, 2013

Session VI

September 26 3:15-4:15pm

Tcl, The Glue for a New Generation of Nuclear Physics Experiments

Ronald Fox
National Superconducting Cyclotron Laboratory, Michigan State University
640 S Shaw Lane
East Lansing, MI 48824-1321
fox@nscl.msu.edu

CAEN Technologies
1140 Bay Street Suite 2C
Staten Island, NY 10305
ron@caentech.com

ABSTRACT

This paper will describe two case studies in which Tcl components played a key role integrating diverse detector data acquisition systems together into a coherent integrated data acquisition system. At the NSCL Tcl and NSCLDAQ were used to integrate the recently upgraded S800 Spectrograph Data acquisition system with that of GRETINA, a large segmented Germanium gamma-ray tracking detector. At Argonne National Laboratories, the CHICO2 detector system, using a tailored version of NSCLDAQ, was integrated with the Digital Gammasphere detector system. The work done to perform these integrations will be described as well as the experience gained from campaigns with these integrated systems.

1. INTRODUCTION

The detector systems used in experimental nuclear physics have been steadily growing in complexity. As a result, some detectors are required to have integrated data acquisition systems built with data flow architectures designed to meet the specific, specialized needs of those detectors. This is in marked contrast to the prior generation of detector systems which would often allow a laboratory like the NSCL to use a single general purpose data acquisition system to instrument all detectors in use at that institution.

In many cases, however these complex, large channel count detector systems are single purpose specialized detectors and, in order to get useful science, they must be run in conjunction with one or more other detectors. The integration of these diverse detector systems, each with their own, data acquisition system, each system with its own design goals, is one of the new and recurring challenges software development for nuclear experimental physics.

In this paper I will first describe the basics of a nuclear physics experiment. I will then describe a pair of case studies where the NSCLDAQ general purpose data acquisition, through its prominent use of Tcl/Tk was used to 'glue' pairs of diverse detector systems together to present an integrated system to the users performing experiments with them.

The first case study will describe CAEN Technologies work to integrate the CHICO II detector system with Digital Gammasphere. The two detector systems will be described along with their data acquisition systems. The integration will be described as well. The second case study will describe the NSCL's integration of the data acquisition system for its S800 charged particle Spectrometer with the GRETINA segmented germanium gamma-ray tracking detector.

The detectors will be described along with the data acquisition systems each uses as well as the integration effort and the role Tcl played in this work.

Finally, experiences with the integrated systems will be described as well as future work and what this implies for the data acquisition systems for the Facility for Rare Isotope Beams under construction at the NSCL.

2. BACKGROUND

This section describes how experiments in nuclear physics are performed. The NSCL Data Acquisition System (NSCLDAQ) is also briefly described along with some of the roles Tcl/Tk plays in that system.

2.1 Nuclear Physics Experiments

Since in general, atomic nuclei are much smaller than the wavelengths of visible light, microscopy is not an effective tool to explore the structure of and the forces that bind the nucleus together. Experiments on nuclei are performed by colliding nuclei with other particles whose quantum wavelengths are of the same order of magnitude as the nucleus itself.

The protons and neutrons within a nucleus are bound together by what is known as the *nuclear strong force.* For elements heavier than hydrogen, the nucleus is a positively charged electromagnetic compound particle, and therefore affects the trajectories of other charged particles.

The charge distribution of nuclei can therefore be probed by the way electrons scatter off the nucleus because electrons will only feel the Coulomb force due to the nuclear charge. Other nuclei with energies that allow the repulsive Coulomb barrier to be crossed can map the strong force and hence the structure and energy levels of the target nucleus.

Producing projectiles with sufficient energies to interact with nuclei in a useful way for experiments is why nuclear experimental physicists require accelerator laboratories in which to perform their experiments.

When nuclei collide, they interpenetrate, and, depending on the total energy of the resulting system, and the impact parameter (a measure of how far apart the center of masses of the colliding nuclei are) they may break up (fission), glue together (fusion), or some combination of the two processes.

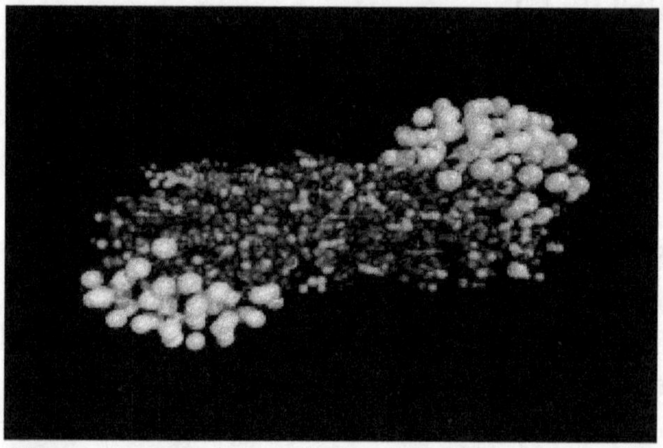

Illustration 1: A collision between two lead nuclei

Given high enough energies and sufficient numbers of protons and neutrons, the results of these collisions can be very complicated as shown in Illustrations 1 above and 2 below:

Illustration 2: The same lead-lead collision as seen by the ALICE detector at CERN/LHC

The showers of particles that are emitted by these collisions are also not directly visible. Complex detector systems are required to "see" them and determine important physical characteristics such as their kinetic energies, the time of detection their masses and flight direction.

The signals from these detectors are digitized, read out and transmitted to computer systems which perform online analysis and record the data for further study offline. The number of computer nodes that are involved in an experiment can be as few as one, and as many as 100 or more. The CMS detector system at CERN's LHC requires 100's of nodes running 1000's of programs and produces 1.5Mbytesof data for each recorded collision[1]. With collisions being detected many 1000's of times per second complex *trigger systems* are used to filter out data that is not of interest, lowering the rate of CMS events recorded to fewer than 100/second.

The increasingly lower cost of computing and innovations in detector instrumentation are rapidly pushing low and intermediate energy nuclear physics experiments such as those performed at the National Superconducting Cyclotron Laboratory at Michigan State University and ATLAS at Argonne National Laboratories to use larger and larger detector systems. These larger detector systems produce data flow problems that are difficult to solve in the general purpose data acquisition systems that have been used by these labs in the past. This in turn pushes detector designers to include special purpose data acquisition systems as part of their detector designs.

Special purpose data acquisition systems solve the data flow and data handling problems of specific detector systems, but do not address how to take data when there is a need to use more than one detector system in an experiment. For example the Gammasphere detector is, as the name implies capable of detecting γ-rays but without the addition of a charged particle detector such as CHICO[3], is unable to perform important particle-γ coincidence experiments.

An increasingly important problem, therefore, is the knitting of detector specific data acquisition systems into an integrated *meta data acquisition* system that can be used in a practical manner to perform useful experiments.

2.2 NSCLDAQ

The NSCL Data Acquisition system (NSCLDAQ) is a general purpose data acquisition system. This system has been described partially at past Tcl conferences, most recently at Tcl 2011[4]. This section provides a very brief overview of the system as it is today.

NSCLDAQ's core is a ring buffer data distribution system. Each ring buffer can have a single producer and a number of consumers. Access to consumer get pointers and the single producer put pointer is mediated by a pure Tcl server called the **Ringmaster**. Ringmaster maintains a persistent TCP/IP connection with all resource holders allowing it to release resources on client exit regardless of the cleanliness of that exit.

Distribution of data to remote systems is handled by setting up a proxy ring buffer in the remote system and an ordinary client in the local system. The local client sends data from the ring over a simple TCP/IP socket to the producer for the proxy ring. As ring buffers are identified to the system via a URI name space, remote ring access requests can be automatically detected and the set up of the proxy ring is transparent to the consumer.

A ring naming convention ensures that only one proxy ring is created for a given remote proxy ring in a local system.

Several loosely coupled and even uncoupled components as well as application frameworks provide support for various data sources and useful data consumers (for example event recording, status display and support for supplying data to non NSCLDAQ aware clients). Tcl/Tk figures prominently in all user interface applications and, in many cases also provides an extension and scripting language for these components.

One of the integrating components is a user interface that controls data source programs. This **ReadoutShell** provides an integrated start up of the event recording software as requested by the user. The ReadoutShell user interface is shown in illustration 3 below:

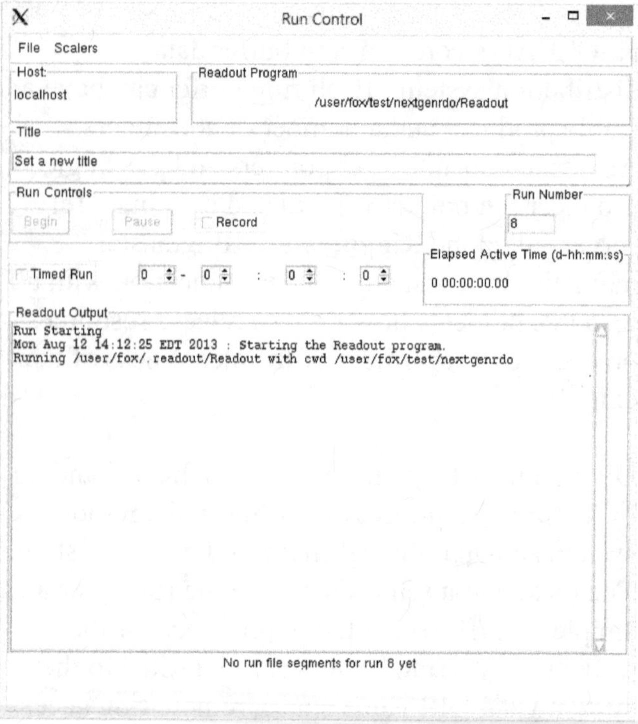

Illustration 3: ReadoutShell's user interface.

An important feature are the extension points provided by the ReadoutShell. It turns out that these will play a key role in the knitting together or diverse data acquisition systems.

When ReadoutShell starts it looks for a user extension script named **ReadoutCallouts.tcl**. If found that script is sourced at the global level and can provide several **procs** that are called at well defined points of ReadoutShell's operation. ReadoutShell itself exports an API these extensions can use. The extension points are:

- **OnStart** – Invoked when the Readout program is started by the ReadoutShell.
- **OnBegin** – Invoked just prior to beginning a data taking run.
- **OnEnd** – Invoked just prior to ending a data taking run.
- **OnPause** – Invoked just prior to pausing a data taking run.
- **OnResume** – Invoked just prior to resuming a data taking run.

Another important, however non-Tcl difference we will come across is implicit in the nature of the ring-buffer implementation:

- Ring buffers are named entities
- An arbitrary number of ring buffers can be instantiated.
- There is not really any preferred set of clients (producers or consumers) to any ring buffer. A ring buffer client is just a program that uses the Ring buffer API
- The ring buffer software provides a pair of clients that make the production of ring buffer to ring buffer pipelines easy to construct. These clients are used by the ring buffer API set up data transmission from host ring to remote proxy ring:
    - *ringtostdout* – copies data from a ring buffer to stdout
    - *stdintoring* – puts data on stdin into a ring.

It turns out that *ringtostdout* and *stdintoring* can be used as the source sink of data from UNIX pipelines of programs.

3. CHICO2 AND GAMMASPHERE

The CHICO2 detector is a charged particle position sensitive detector. It has been optimized to work with both the GRETINA and GAMMASPHERE γ-ray detectors. We will see more of GRETINA in the next section.

CHICO2's geometry allows the GAMASPHERE detector to fully close around CHICO2. CHICO2 also fits within the GRETINA detector frame. Furthermore the CHICO2 position resolution has been optimized to work well with both GAMMASPHERE and GRETINA's position resolutions. [5] provides a summary of CHICO2 and its design goals. Illustration 4 below shows the Chico2 detector with GAMMASPHERE.

GAMMASPHERE is best known in the popular press as the nuclear physics detector that made a cameo appearance in the Universal Studios movie *The Incredible Hulk.* The scale model of GAMMASPHERE created in that movie is

Illustration 4: Chico2 and one hemisphere of GAMMASPHERE

on display at the time this paper is being written at Universal Studios in Orlando, FL.

GAMMASPHERE (the real one) is located in an ATLAS beam line at Argonne National Laboratories (ANL). Prior to using CHICO2 with GRETINA, the detector had several physics runs scheduled for Spring/Summer 2013 with GAMMASPHERE.

Illustration 5: Gammasphere to the right of its best known user; Dr. Bruce Banner.

CHICO2 has a data acquisition system based on NSCLDAQ. This author provided that system under direct contract to Lawrence Livermore National Laboratories (LLNL) which, together with Rochester University, built the CHICO2 detector. NSCLDAQ system allowed CHICO2 to be tested at Rochester University prior to its shipment and installation with GAMMASPHERE at ANL.

GAMMASPHERE recently upgraded its own data acquisition system to a fully Flash ADC continuously Digitizing System. The name of this system is "Digital Gammasphere" (DGS). This system is described in [6]. A block diagram from the talk slides for that reference, which focuses on the electronics is shown as Illustration 5 below:

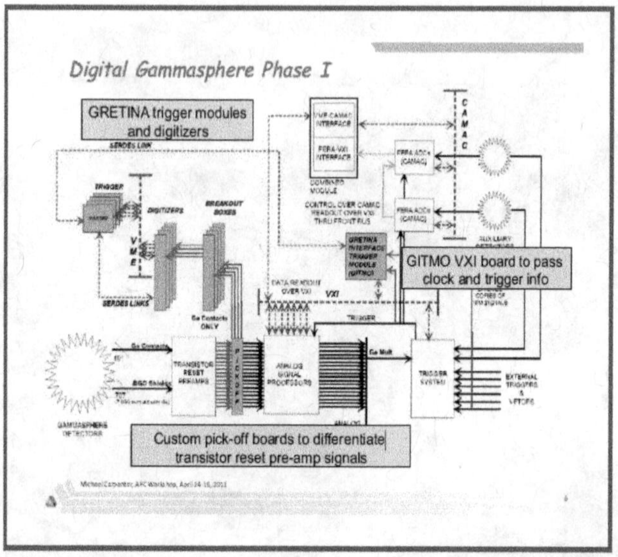

Illustration 6: Block diagram of digital gammasphere

Only features important to the integration with CHICO2 will be described below.

3.1 GAMMASPHERE Run Control

DGS's run control is managed via an EPICS[7] process variable. A second EPICS process variable reports the run state. The DGS run state machine only provides Running and Halted states while the NSCL run state machine provides an additional Paused state.

Unlike many data acquisition systems, of its sort, DGS does not build events online but accumulates event segments in a set of files (one per contributing computer). Offline analysis software (which may be run as soon as a data taking run completes), builds events and produces initial check spectra. The NSCLDAQ on the other hand interfaces with the NSCLSpectTcl[8] analysis software to provide online spectra.

3.2 The CHICO2 Data acquisition System

CHICO2's data acquisition system is an implementation of the NSCLDAQ using the VM-USB readout and SpecTcl described in [10]. As such it uses the ReadoutShell software described previously.

A block diagram of the CHICO2 electronics is shown below in Illustration 7

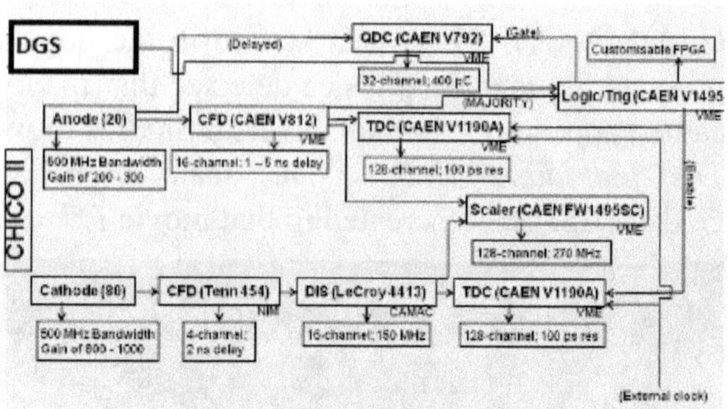

Illustration 7: The CHICO2 electronics diagram.

With the exception of the CAEN V1495SC Scaler module and the CAEN V1495 logic module all modules were already well supported by that software.

A Driver module was written to support adding the V1495SC module to the Readout configuration file making it available to the NSCL Scaler display (a pure Tcl application as well). We will come back to the role and support provided for the V1495 logic modules in the section below.

3.3 Integrating the two systems

Integration therefore involved finding and implementing answers to the following questions

- Who controls the run and how?
- Where is event data recorded and how does it get there?
- How is the event trigger determined and passed between the detectors?
- How are timestamps produced in CHICO2 such that they are meaningful to DGS data and can be used to build events in offline analysis.

The simplest problem to solve turned out to be that of timestamps. While the Gammasphere time stamp and trigger distribution system module was a VXI format module[9] (VME with an extra connector making for a 9-U format), the module designer J.T. Anderson had just completed a VME (6-U) format module. A driver module for this device was incorporated in the NSCL VM-USB readout software to provide the capability of adding this module to the Tcl configuration file that drives the readout. The SpecTcl 'unpacker' for this module simply ignored the data packet produced by that module.

At a very early stage it was determined that it would be much simpler to use the NSCLDAQ ReadoutShell's extension to control DGS than it would be to modify the DGS run control panel to control NSCLDAQ; since the NSCLDAQ ReadoutShell is a pure Tcl application it was a relatively simple matter to use the EpicsTcl[11] package to set the DGS run control PV and monitor the state of the DGS PV in a text widget. These were all implemented via the ReadoutShell's ReadoutCallouts.tcl extension script. The ReadoutShell's API directly supported the addition of a DGS status strip with the run state.

The actual event trigger was a bit more interesting. Due to the timing considerations. Chico2 trigger decisions was a hardware discriminator and quite fast relative to the GAMMASPHERE trigger decision. This was because the GAMMASPHERE trigger decision is the result of FPGA based analysis of the digitized waveforms (note this is done in parallel with digitization but nonetheless sufficient information must be digitized to provide for a digital constant fraction discrimination).

Furthermore, DGS required a DGS trigger accept to be received in one or more of its GITMO or Myriad modules to accept the digitized data as an event. The necessary logic and delays were encapsulated in firmware programmed by Carlo Tintori of CAEN Technologies. This firmware was embedded in a CAEN V1495 FPGA module.

A pure Tcl control panel was written that interfaced with the slow controls server of the VMUSB Readout program. The control panel controlled internal delays that lined up GAMMASPHERE's trigger with CHICO2 triggers. Output trigger widths were also controlled, and most importantly, the control panel allowed internal test points of the FPGA firmware to be gated to module outputs where they could be monitored. Without this it would have been much harder to set the internal module timing.

As we have previously written, DGS does not actually do online data monitoring. Data from each of its I/O controllers (IOCs), are recorded in a separate file. Once data taking is complete for a run (an experiment in general consists of many runs), offline analysis is done immediately to build both events and spectra from the events fragments in these files.

We decided that, while the CHICO2 DAQ system could locally record data, it would be advantageous to also provide the the ability to send CHICO2 data to DGS as if CHICO2 were an IOC. Unfortunately, the protocol used to send data from IOCS to DGS is quite complex. We decided instead to use a simple push protocol.

A ring buffer consumer for CHICO2 event data was started whenever a run began. After connecting to a very simple Tcl catching program, the data consumer wrapped each CHICO2 event inside a DGS header and sent them to the catcher. The catcher opened an event file with the appropriate name and saved data to disk without interpretation. The sender was written in C++ and the catcher was a pure Tcl program.

A small library of functions was provided to DGS (in C) that decoded the CHICO2 events and supplied them to the caller. This made the integration of CHICO2 event fragments with DGS event fragments a straightforward bit of programming. That work was done by the DGS collaboration.

3.4 Experimental experience

After completing the integration, a set of commissioning test runs and physics runs were performed using the ATLAS[12] accelerator at ANL. The commissioning with stable beams went smoothly. Analysis performed were able to demonstrate particle γ coincidences between Chico2 and DGS without any difficulty.

The physics runs using unstable beams from the CARIBU[13] ion source were also smooth from the data acquisition standpoint. Unfortunately the beam intensities on target were much lower than originally predicted, and unforeseen analog contaminants were present in the desired beams. As a result, the physics runs did not get the hoped for statistics.

ANL Atlas is currently down while a power transformer damaged in a lightning strike is replaced. When scheduled running resumes, GRETINA will have been installed at ANL and the CHICO2 DAQ system will be integrated with that system in a manner similar to that described in the next section.

4. S800 AND GRETINA

GRETINA[14] consists of a number of segmented high purity germanium detectors. The signals from each crystal's central contact and each segment are continuously digitized at 100MHz. FPGA based digital signal processing of these waveforms coupled with complex deconvolution algorithms allow the detector to achieve position and energy resolutions that are better than achievable by a single segment in isolation. Compton tracking allows suppression of γ-rays that either did not originate in the detector or that scattered out prior to depositing full energy in the detector. This detector was constructed by a large collaboration largely based at LBNL.

In the Fall of 2011, after commissioning runs at LBNL, GRETINA was transported to the NSCL to begin a year long experimental campaign. The experiments performed required looking at coincidences between radioactive isotope projectile-like fragments and the γ-rays emitted by those fragments as the decay from the excited states they populate on collision with the nuclei in fixed targets.

The NSCL device used to identify and detect the projectile fragments was the S800 spectrometer[15] and its associated detector package.

This section will describe the GRETINA data acquisition system, the S800 data acquisition system and the work done to fuse those two very different systems into a coherent whole.

4.1 The GRETINA Data Acquisition System

GRETINA is an example of a new breed of waveform digitizing data acquisition systems. A block diagram of the data acquisition system is shown below in Illustration 7 below.

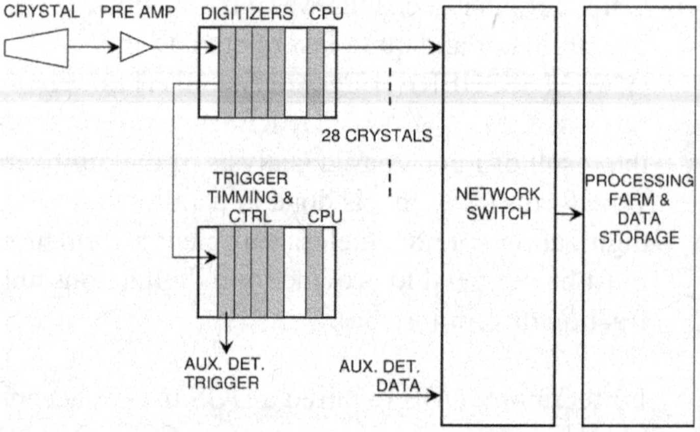

Illustration 8: Block diagram of GRETINA DAQ

The processing farm to the right side of the picture contains several hundred server level compute nodes that:

- Determine the interaction points in the detector crystals from waveform information.
- Put event fragments from the crystals into a time ordered list
- Save this ordered list online to a modest Network file appliance.

The entire system is controlled by a number of EPICS[16] process variables. The event reorderer (which GRETINA calls the Global Event builder), provides a tap that allows computers external to the GRETINA cluster to obtain sets of consecutive samples from the Global Event Builder.

The GEB is more properly an event fragment orderer. The samples it provides have the form of event fragments that are wrapped in headers that contain time-stamps from the GRETINA digitizer 100MHz timebase and payload sizes as well as fragment type descriptors that allow analysis software to know roughly what to expect in the fragment payloads. These event fragments have monotonically increasing timestamps within a data taking run.

4.2 The S800 Data acquisition system

The data acquisition system for the S800 spectrograph at the NSCL is shown below in illustration 9 below.

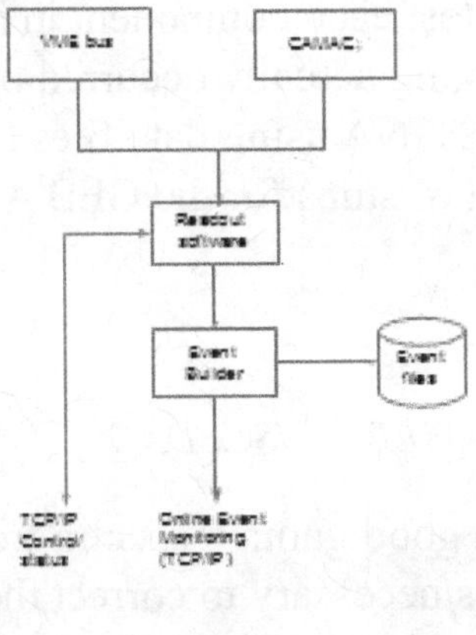

Illustration 9: S800 Data Acquisition system block diagram

In this illustration, the Readout programs and event builder are co-resident in a single computer system. There is nothing in that architecture that requires that. The Readout software makes use of a VM-USB[16] (VME/USB list mode bus adapter) to interface with the VME based electronics and a CC-USB[17] (CAMAC/USB list mode adapter) to interface with the CAMAC based electronics.

Some of the modules in both the VME and CAMAC buses are field programmable gate array modules (FPGA) with custom firmware to autonomously readout external digitization hardware. One of these FPGA modules includes an externally clocked counter to produce an event time stamp and logic to support synchronization of the initialization of that counter with other timestamped systems.

The S800 system does not use any NSCL DAQ software. One of the monitoring programs used by the S800 support group is, however NSCLSpecTcl.

4.3 Merging the two systems.

A successful merger of the S800 and GRETINA data acquisition systems requires that:

- Coordination of the time-stamp synchronization between the S800 and GRETINA be properly managed.
- Data from the S800 be provided to the GRETINA GEB in a format acceptable to that software.

This is sufficient to allow GRETINA to produce ordered fragment files which can then be analyzed offline. In order to try to get some physics information online during the run, we need the following as well:

- The ability to get data from the GRETINA GEB sampling output tap.

- The ability to merge fragments that occur within a predefined coincidence time window into single events.
- The ability to provide those built events to analysis software.

Since the appropriate analysis software existed within the context of the NSCL Data acquisition system, making the built events from GRETINA a data source for NSCLDAQ is sufficient to meet these needs.

Additionally it was deemed highly useful to provide a coherent run control for the detectors as would later be done for the Chico2/Gammasphere case study already described.

4.3.1 Event Data from S800 to the GEB

In order to send data from the S800 to the GRETINA GEB, we must:

- Accept data from a connection to the S800 TCP/IP monitor port.
- Extract events from the block structured data provided by the S800 monitor port
- Extract the time stamp from each event
- Wrap the event in a GRETINA GEB header and lastly
- Use the GRETINA GEB API to post each event to the GRETINA GEB.

We also wanted to be able to monitor the S800 events in isolation prior to submitting them to the GRETINA GEB. This suggested performing the first two steps of the process above, inserting the results in an NSCLDAQ ring buffer and performing the last two steps in an NSCLDAQ ring buffer client.

The serial nature of the operations described above along with the existence of the *stdintoring* and *ringtostdout* components of NSCLDAQ suggested the use of UNIX command pipelines for both of these processes. We could imagine the insertion pipeline would be something like:

```
netcat | evtextract | stdintoring
```

Initially a structure like this was tried. What we found, however was that UNIX netcat was too heavily and intelligently buffered to support the low data rates of secondary beam experiments. Furthermore, netcat did not guarantee the pipeline received the end of run indicator block before the start of the next run pushed it through.

Therefore this structure was used but with the netcat like functionality we needed re-written in the Tcl script shown below:

```
while {![eof $fd]} {
    chan copy $fd stdout -size 8192
    flush stdout
}
```

where the fd variable above was the socket connected to the S800 monitor TCP/IP port.

Similarly the ring client is a pipeline of ringtostdout, a program that extract timestamps from events, wraps them and pushes them to the GRETINA GEB. In order to make the time stamp extraction generic, this is actually done in a shared object that is specified on the command line that starts the program. This allows the output pipeline to send data from any NSCLDAQ data source to the GRETINA GEB.

The pipeline structure described above also allowed us to test each component in isolation. Integration testing actually occurred prior to the arrival of GRETINA using data files from the S800 and a set of stubs for the GEB API.

4.3.2 Data from GEB to NSCLDAQ

In order to get good gamma spectra from GRETINA it is necessary to correct the gamma-ray energies for the Doppler effect that arises from the fact that they are emitted from the remainder of the projectile which is moving forward from the target. To do this we need to know the velocity of that projectile-like fragment, and that requires building events from the S800 and GRETINA to detect particle-gamma coincidences.

In the context of the SeGA (segmented Germanium array at NSCL), Doppler correction code already has been written for S800/SeGA particle gamma coincidences. If we can provide S800/GRETINA built events, that code can also be used to Doppler correct the gamma rays GRETINA sees.

The GRETINA GEB includes an interface that allows clients to selectively receive a sample of the data it has ordered. The sample fills a buffer with a time-contiguous set of fragments.

Unfortunately, what we get from the GEB are not built events, but ordered fragments. To determine if there is a particle-gamma coincidence in the per-existing NSCLSpecTcl code we need to:

- Accept data from the GEB sample tap.
- Glue together fragments that occur within the specified coincidence window of the first fragment of a sequence
- Format the result as NSCL ring buffer event items.
- Insert those items in a ring buffer where NSCLSpecTcl can retrieve them for online analysis.

This again suggests a Unix pipeline of the form:

```
tapcat | glom | stdintoring
```

Where

- *tapcat* is a command that reads data from the GEB sample tap and sends it to stdout.
- *glom* is a program that accepts GEB data on its stdin, glues (gloms) together fragments into built events which are emitted in NSCLDAQ ring buffer format on its stdout.
- *stdintoring* is a component of NSCLDAQ that takes ring items on stdin and drops them into an NSCLDAQ ring buffer..

This pipe structure allowed the building program (*glom*) to be tested on event file data. Furthermore, with GRETINA moving to Argonne National Laboratory to continue its experimental program at ATLAS, *tapcat* will be used by them as input to their own GRETINA online analysis software.

4.3.3 Consolidated control

Consolidated run control was done essentially in the same way as Chico2, using the call out script facility of the NSCLDAQ run control software. In this, case, however neither detector system uses an NSCLDAQ readout program.

Therefore what we had to provide was:

- A call out extension that knows how to manage GRETINA runs.
- A call out extension that knows how to manage S800 runs.
- A call out extension that knows in which order the S800 and GRETINA must be started and stopped and is able to tell GRETINA when to start the S800/GRETINA time stamp synchronization process.
- A dummy NSCLDAQ readout program that ignores all run control commands sent to it.

The three call out extensions are all pure Tcl components, with the GRETINA script relying on EpicsTcl, since EPICS is used to control GRETINA's runs. The dummy NSCLDAQ readout program is really just

```
cat >/dev/null
```

5. RESULTS

CHICO2's integration was successful but unfortunately satisfactory beams from CARIBU could not be achieved before ANL/ATLAS suffered its power transformer. The next projected CHICO2 runs will actually involve a planned integration of CHICO2 and GRETINA which is being installed at ANL/ATLAS.

The GRETINA/S800 integration resulted in a year of successful physics runs. The on-line Doppler corrected gamma spectra made possible by this integration, provided invaluable information about the detector and experimental resolution.

During the year of running the code which wed the two detectors together did not express any defects. Furthermore the adoption of the *tapcat* program by ANL/ATLAS for its installation of GRETINA demonstrated the value of breaking up the data flow into a set of simple filter elements. While this concept is well known to Unix shell programs I am not aware of other uses of it in the main data flow path of a nuclear physics data acquisition system.

The generic data flow architecture of NSCLDAQ proved more than equal to the task of handling the data flows required of the GRETINA and S800 detectors.

The use of a Tcl based Run control program made it quite easy to extend the software to control detectors with control paths that were not originally planned for.

Future planned work includes the coupling of the CHICO2 detector with GRETINA for physics runs scheduled at ANL ATLAS in 2014.

In 2022, Michigan State University under a grant from the Department of Energy will be commissioning the Facility for Rare Isotope Research (FRIB). During the construction period, discussions are already underway about what detector systems would be useful for experiments performed at this facility.

In parallel with detector discussion groups, a committee including the author is discussing what we believe will be the high level requirements of a data acquisition system at the FRIB. We believe that the trend towards larger, more complex detectors will continue. We also believe that these detectors will, for the most part, have their own continuously digitizing data acquisitions systems, such as DGS and GRETINA do now.

We are therefore firming up the specifications of what might best be called a *meta-data acuisition system* one that is designed from the start to couple together two or more detector systems to build integrated experiments. The case studies described in this paper demonstrate that the NSCLDAQ systems has many of the attributes an FRIB metaDAQ system needs.

7. REFERENCES

[1] G. Bauer et al. *Monitoring the CMS Data Acquisition System* presented at the 17th International Conference on Computing in High Energy and Nuclear Physics (CHEP09), published in **Journal of Physics: Conference Series** 219 (2010) 022042

[2] M.P. Carpenter *How far from stability can we go using Gammasphere and the ANL Fragment Mass Analyzer?* Presented at CAPTURE GAMMA-RAY SPECTROSCOPY AND RELATED TOPICS: 10th International Symposium 30 Aug-3 Sep 1999 Sante Fe, New Mexico (USA) published in **AIP Conf. Proc.** 529, pp. 175-183.

[3] M.W. Simon*, D. Cline, C.Y. Wu, R.W. Gray, R. Teng, C. Long *CHICO, a heavy ion detector*

for Gammasphere **Nuclear Instruments and Methods in Physics Research A** 452 (2000) 205-222

[4] R. Fox et al. *Tcl at the NSCL: a 30 (15?) year retrospective* presented at Tcl 2011 October 24-28 Manassas, VA available online at: http://www.tclcommunityassociation.org/wub/proceedings/Proceedings-2011/RonFox/nscltcl.pdf

[5] CHICO2 is described at: http://www.pas.rochester.edu/~cline/Research/Chico2.html

[6] M.P. Carpenter et al. *Digital Data Acquisition System for Gammasphere* Presented at the 2011 Fall Meeting of the APS Division of Nuclear Physics East Lansing, MI October 26-29, 2011 published in the **BAPS** Volume 56, Number 12

[7] S.A. Lewis *Overview of the Experimental Physics and Industrial Control System: EPICS* Online at: http://csg.lbl.gov/EPICS/OverView.pdf

[8] R. Fox, C. Bolen, K. Orji, J. Venema *NSCLSpecTcl Meeting the Needs of Preliminary Nuclear Physics Data Analysis* Presented at Tcl 2004 available online at: http://www.tcl.tk/community/tcl2004/Papers/RonFox/fox.pdf

[9] J.T. Anderson *FPGA and VHDL Developments for DGS and DSSD* internal presentation to the ANL GAMMASPHERE Group September 20, 2012 online at

[10] R. Fox, K. Paräjärvi, J. Turunen, H. Toivonen *A Domain Specific Language for defining Nuclear Physics Experiments.* Presented at Tcl 2008 Manassas, VA October 20-24, 2008 available online at: http://www.tclcommunityassociation.org/wub/proceedings/Proceedings-2008/proceedings/nuclearDSL/stukdsl.pdf

[11] R. Fox *Tcl/Tk Tools for EPICS Control Systems.* Presented at Tcl 2007 New Orleans, LA September 24-38, 2007 Available online at: http://www.tclcommunityassociation.org/wub/proceedings/Proceedings-2007/proceedings/Gui/epics.pdf

[12] For a description of ATLAS and its capabilities see: http://www.phy.anl.gov/atlas/

[13] For information about CARIBU see: http://www.phy.anl.gov/atlas/caribu/ATLAS_Cf_upgrade.pdf

[14] GRETINA proposal A. Machiavelli et al. At http://radware.phy.ornl.gov/greta/Gretina_prop_partial.pdf

[15] *The S800 spectrograph* D. Bazin et al. **Interactions with Materials and Atoms** B V204 May 2003 pg 629-633.

[16] http://www.wiener-d.com/sc/modules/vme--modules/vm-usb.html

[17] http://www.wiener-d.com/sc/modules/camac--modules/cc-usb.html

A Plague of Gofers:

Generalized Rule-Based Data Entry With Lazy Data Retrieval

William H. Duquette
Jet Propulsion Laboratory, California Institute of Technology
William.H.Duquette@jpl.nasa.gov

Abstract

A gofer value is a data value that tells the application how to retrieve a desired piece of data on demand, according to some rule, and a gofer type is the code that validates gofer values and retrieves the data on demand. The advantage of using a gofer is that the value returned can change over the lifetime of the gofer value as state of the application changes. The gofer infrastructure allows the definition of gofer types consisting of many different rules, with support for GUI creation and editing of gofer values.

For example, the user may desire that a particular simulation input affect all civilian groups residing in a particular set of neighborhoods. Instead of listing the groups explicitly, the user chooses the relevant rule and the neighborhoods of interest; at each time step, the simulation can determine the groups that currently reside in the chosen neighborhoods.

1. Background

The Athena Regional Stability Simulation is a model of political actors and the effects of their actions in a particular region of the world. The region is divided into neighborhoods, in which reside various civilian groups. The actors have a variety of assets, including money, military and police forces, and means of communication, which they use to achieve their political ends. The user of Athena models the behavior of the actors in the simulation by defining their strategies, which consist of a prioritized list of tactics; then, the actor's behavior is determined by the tactics the actor executes.

2. The Problem

Consider a tactic that performs a particular bit of behavior: for example, paying money to fund social services for particular groups in the civilian population. The tactic has several parameters, of which these are the most important:

- The list of groups for which services are to be funded

- The amount of money to spend during the current week

Now, there are any number of ways the user might select the list of groups and the sum of money. He might want the groups that reside in a particular neighborhood, or the groups that support the actor who will execute the tactic. He might want the actor to spend a specific amount of money, or the amount of money required to achieve a particular result, or 40% of the actor's available cash. From a software point of view, however, we have always required that the user enter the precise list of groups and the precise sum of money.

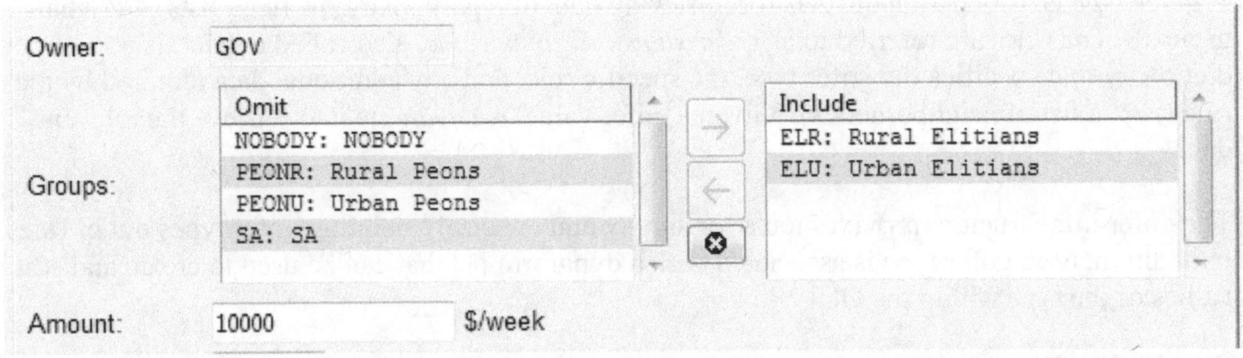

Now suppose the user wants to select all civilian groups that support a particular actor. He has to go through the output data to figure out which groups those are, and enter them in the tactic's dialog. If there are many of them, this is tedious and error-prone. And worse than that, tactics are defined before the simulation begins to run, but the list of groups that support an actor can change as the simulation is running. If he enters a specific list of groups, it may become incorrect over the course of the run. In short, there is really no way to do what the Athena user wants to do.

3. The Solution: Rule-based Data Retrieval

The solution is to redefine the tactic parameters. Instead of entering the desired data values, the user enters rules for retrieving the desired data values. That is, instead of

- The list of groups for which services are to be funded
- The amount of money to spend during the current week

the user enters

- A rule for selecting a list of civilian groups
- A rule for choosing a sum of money

When it is time to execute the tactic, the tactic code evaluates the rules to retrieve the desired data values.

This solves the problem nicely, but it poses two further challenges. First, we need to be able to edit these rule descriptions in the GUI in a user-friendly way. Second, there is likely to be a large number of these data-retrieval rules for any given data type (i.e., "list of civilian groups"). The code related to any particular rule needs to be both concise and maintainable. Athena's "gofer" concept handles both of these challenges.

A *gofer type* is a collection of rules for retrieving data of a particular type (e.g., lists of civilian groups). The rules are referred to as *gofer rules*. A *gofer value*, also called a *gdict*, is a dictionary that specifies the gofer type, the specific rule, and any additional data required by the rule (e.g., a list of neighborhoods). Given a gofer value, we *evaluate* it to retrieve the relevant data.

The gofer infrastructure provides tools for simply and concisely building gofer types out of rules. In addition, each gofer type is associated with a dynaform [1] that can be used to create and edit values of the type within the GUI.

4. Gofer Types

A gofer type is a type-definition object [2] that collects together a set of related gofer rules. That is, it is an ensemble whose subcommands operate on gofer values that belonging to the type. Like all type-definition objects it includes a `validate` method, of which more later; but more importantly it includes an `eval` method, which is used to evaluate gofer values and retrieve the desired data.

4.1 Evaluating Gofer Values

For example, suppose the user wants to select all civilian groups resident in neighborhoods N1 and N2. This is an application of the `gofer::CIVGROUPS` gofer type, which returns lists of civilian groups. The corresponding gdict looks like this:

```
% set gdict {_type CIVGROUPS _rule RESIDENT_IN nlist {N1 N2}}
```

Every gdict has a `_type` key and a `_rule` key, along with keys for any rule-specific parameters. In this case, the `nlist` parameter is a list of neighborhoods. Evaluating this value will return a list of the names of groups resident in the two neighborhoods:

```
% gofer::CIVGROUPS eval $gdict
G1 G2 G3 G4
%
```

4.2 Validating Gofer Values

The gofer type's `validate` method takes a gdict and validates it, throwing an error with error code INVALID if any problem is found and returning the gdict in canonical form otherwise.

Gofer values derive from user input, and Athena tends to be forgiving of user input. Group names, for example, are canonically in upper case, but Athena allows group names to be entered in lower case as well. Thus, a validate method is responsible not only for finding errors, but for putting values into the form the application expects.

In the case of a gdict, the `_type` and `_rule` keys are canonically the first two keys, and their values are canonically in upper case. The canonical form of other keys is naturally rule-dependent.

For example:

```
% set gdict {_type civgroups _rule resident_in nlist {n1 n2}}
% gofer::CIVGROUPS validate $gdict
_type CIVGROUPS _rule RESIDENT_IN nlist {N1 N2}
```

4.3 Generating Narrative Strings

It is often desirable to display a gofer value in the GUI, but the standard gdict isn't terribly readable for the average user. The gofer type's `narrative` method takes a gdict and produces a human-readable narrative string, suitable for embedding in a longer sentence. For example,

```
% set gdict {_type CIVGROUPS _rule RESIDENT_IN nlist {N1 N2}}
% gofer::CIVGROUPS narrative $gdict
all civilian groups resident in neighborhoods N1 and N2
```

4.4 Representing Raw Inputs

Of course, sometimes one will want to choose the list of groups by hand, in the old-fashioned way. Consequently, every gofer type has a `BY_VALUE` rule with one parameter, `raw_value`, that is used to represent a value chosen by hand. For example,

```
% set gdict {_type CIVGROUPS _rule BY_VALUE raw_value {G1 G4}}
```

This gdict simply evaluates to its raw value:

```
% gofer::CIVGROUPS eval $gdict
G1 G4
```

4.5 Auto-Translation of Raw Inputs

To ease the integration of gofers and the import of older Athena scenarios after gofers have been added, we allow for the following special case. On validation, if a gofer value does not begin with the `_type` key we assume that it is simply a raw value, and translate it into a gdict with the `BY_VALUE` rule. For example,

```
% gofer::CIVGROUPS validate {G1 G2 G3}
_type CIVGROUPS _rule BY_VALUE raw_value {G1 G2 G3}
```

Of course, the `raw_value` must also be a valid value for the gofer type's `BY_VALUE` rule.

5. Defining a Gofer Type

At base, a gofer type is simply an ensemble command with the right subcommands and semantics; it could be implemented as a namespace ensemble, or as a Snit type ensemble [3], and we started with the latter. It developed that distinct gofer types have a great deal of mechanism in common, and so the type ensembles evolved into instances of a Snit type called `goferType`. Even then, there was a boilerplate code that needed to be written over and over for each type.

Consequently, gofer types are created using the `gofer define` command, which creates the instance of goferType and also performs a number of other housekeeping chores. Then, once the type object exists, rules are added to it.

5.1 Creating the Gofer Type

For example, the `gofer::CIVGROUPS` type is created as follows:

```
gofer define CIVGROUPS {
    rc "" -width 3in -span 3
    label {
        Enter a rule for selecting a set of civilian groups:
    }
    rc

    rc
    selector _rule {
        case BY_VALUE "By name" {
            rc "Select groups from the following list:"
            rc
            enumlist raw_value -dictcmd {::civgroup names} \
                -width 30 -height 10
        }
        . . .
    }
}
```

First, this command creates an instance of `goferType` called `::gofer::CIVGROUPS`, and registers it with the `gofer` command.

Next, it specifies a dynaform to use for editing values of the gofer type. The first field in the dynaform script must be a `selector` field called `_rule`, with one case for each of the type's rules. The `case` names must match the rule names.

Every gofer value includes a `_type` key, and yet no `_type` field appears in the script. This is because `_type` has to appear at the beginning of every gofer type's dynaform script as an invisible context field, and so `gofer define` adds it in automatically.

5.2 Adding a Rule to a Gofer Type

Initially, the new type will have no rules associated with it; they must be implemented individually. Each rule is represented in the code as a type-definition object for the rule's own parameters in the gdict. Again, this rule object could be implemented as a namespace ensemble or a Snit type ensemble; but as before we discovered that distinct rule objects had a certain amount of boilerplate code in common. For convenience, then, rule objects are defined using the `gofer rule` command, which takes a partial Snit type definition script, adds boilerplate, and registers the rule with its gofer type object.

For example, here is the definition of the BY_VALUE rule:

```
gofer rule CIVGROUPS BY_VALUE {raw_value} {
    typemethod validate {gdict} {
        dict with gdict {}
        dict create raw_value \
            [listval "groups" {civgroup validate} $raw_value]
    }

    typemethod narrative {gdict {opt ""}} {
        dict with gdict {}
        return [listnar "group" "these groups" $raw_value $opt]
    }

    typemethod eval {gdict} {
        dict get $gdict raw_value
    }
}
```

The `gofer rule` command takes four arguments:

- The type name, e.g., `CIVGROUPS`
- The rule name, e.g., `BY_VALUE`
- A list of the names of the rule's parameters, e.g., `{raw_value}`
- A Snit type body with type methods for the essential rule operations: `validate`, `narrative`, and `eval`.

It creates a rule object, a Snit type ensemble, called `::gofer::CIVGROUPS::BY_VALUE`, and registers it with the `CIVGROUPS` type.

5.3 Semantics of Gofer Rule Operations

The rule operations differ slightly from the similarly named gofer operations.

- The `validate` operation takes a gdict and validates only the keys that are associated with this particular rule. Any other keys are ignored. It returns a dictionary containing only keys associated with this particular rule, with the values in canonical form.

- The `narrative` operation returns a narrative string given a valid gdict for this rule. As with `validate`, it ignores any keys but those associated with this rule, e.g., it ignores the `_type` and `_rule` keys.

- The `eval` operation evaluates the gdict; again, it ignores any keys but those associated with this rule.

5.4 Helper Commands

One of the goals of the gofer system is that rule definitions should be as concise as possible; consequently, shared code has been ruthlessly abstracted. For example, the `validate` and `narrative` methods shown above for the `BY_VALUE` rule make use of the helper routines `listval` and `listnar`. The precise semantics of these commands doesn't matter for the purposes of this discussion; the main point is that they perform part of the job in a standard way.

To make adding helpers easier, the `gofer rule` command adds a namespace path containing `::gofer` and `::gofer::`*`typename`* to the rule object's namespace. Thus, the `::gofer` module can provide helpers for use by any rule, and a given gofer type can provide helpers for use by its own rules, simply by defining procs within their namespaces.

5.5 Sharing Rules

It is not uncommon for a rule to be used by more than one gofer type. For example, Athena has three kinds of group, and so in addition to `gofer::CIVGROUPS` we have also defined `gofer::GROUPS`, which returns a list of any kind of group. But a list of civilian groups is also simply a list of groups, and so almost all of the rules in `gofer::CIVGROUPS` can shared with `gofer::GROUPS`. This is done using the `gofer rulefrom` command.

For example, the following command is part of the definition of gofer::GROUPS:

```
gofer rulefrom GROUPS CIV_RESIDENT_IN \
    ::gofer::CIVGROUPS::RESIDENT_IN
```

The `gofer::GROUPS`' `CIV_RESIDENT_IN` rule is simply mapped to the given rule object.

5.6 Gofer Rules and Dynaform Cases

As noted in Section 5.1, a gofer type has a dynaform that has a selector case for each of the type's rules. It might seem like each rule's case script could be defined by the rule object, and the full dynaform built up from the pieces. The difficulty is that the descriptive text in the dynaform case often needs to be slightly different for each use of the rule, depending on the type with which it is associated. Rather than imposing an unpleasant consistency across the GUI for all types that use a rule, we chose to leave the dynaform script in one piece.

5.7 Invoking a Gofer Operation

The gofer type and its rule objects work together to implement the three primary gofer operations: `validate`, `narrative`, and `eval`. When the operation is passed a gdict, the gofer type determines the rule from the `_rule` key, and passes the gdict along to the rule object, returning the result.

Only the `validate` operation involves any additional complexity. The rule object's `validate` method only validates and canonicalizes the rule-specific parameters. The gofer type's validate method appends the result to a stub containing the `_type` and `_rule` keys, and returns that.

5.8 Sanity Checking

A gofer type is built out of many small pieces, all of which need to hook together just right. In particular, each of a gofer type's rules has to have a case in the type's dynaform (and vice versa), and the case has to contain a field for each of the rule's parameters.

One could wait for the user to discover any mismatches; instead, we wrote a routine, the `gofer check` command, which does a complete sweep of all defined gofer types and throws an error if any problems are found. This routine is called by the application's test suite, ensuring that all potential problems are found as part of the build process.

6. The `gofer` Convenience Command and the `_type` Key

As noted frequently above, each valid gdict begins with the `_type` key, which names the specific gofer type. One might think that since gofer types are distinct in use—if you need a list of civilian groups, you don't use a gofer type that retrieves quantities of money—that this piece of information is extraneous. And in fact, our initial implementation omitted it.

However, Athena is scriptable; and since there are user commands for creating tactics, we also need user commands for constructing and evaluating gofer values. For convenience, then, we added the `_type` key to support `gofer` subcommands that operate on gdicts of arbitrary type.

For example,

```
% set gdict [gofer construct civgroups resident_in {n1 n2}]
_type CIVGROUPS _rule RESIDENT_IN nlist {N1 N2}
% gofer narrative $gdict
all civilian groups resident in neighborhoods N1 and N2
% gofer eval $gdict
G1 G2 G3 G4
%
```

7. Status and Future Work

Gofers are a new feature in Athena. At present, we have defined four gopher types, for lists of actors, lists of civilian groups, lists of force groups, and lists of groups in general. The total number of rule objects is currently around 40, with `gofer::GROUPS` defining a number of rules of its own and reusing most of the `gofer::CIVGROUPS` and `gofer::FRCGROUPS` rules. These gofers are currently used by only two of Athena's eighteen tactics.

Clearly there is much work left to be done. We need to update the existing tactics to use gofer parameters as appropriate. As we do so, we will discover additional gofers that we need to define. And then, the sets of rules included in the four existing gofers are only preliminary; as the users become more familiar with gofers and what they can do, they will have their own ideas as to what would be useful. It's early days yet.

Nevertheless, the gofer architecture appears to be up to the job. New gofer types can be added without disturbing existing gofer types, and new rules can be added to any existing gofer type without disturbing other rules, or breaking any existing scenario data that uses the existing rules. In that sense, the gofer system is complete; it now simply remains to exploit it ruthlessly.

8. References

[1] Duquette, William H., "Dynaforms and Dynaviews", 20th Tcl/Tk Conference, Proceedings.

[2] Duquette, William H., "Type-Definition Objects", 12th Tcl/Tk Conference, http://trs-new.jpl.nasa.gov/dspace/bitstream/2014/37573/1/05-2409.pdf.

[3] Duquette, William, Snit Object Framework, found in Tcllib, http://tcllib.sourceforge.net/doc/snit.html.

9. Acknowledgements

This research was carried out at the Jet Propulsion Laboratory, California Institute of Technology, under a contract with the National Aeronautics and Space Administration, during the development of the Athena Stability & Recovery Operations Simulation (Athena) for the TRADOC G2 Intelligence Support Activity (TRISA) at Fort Leavenworth, Kansas.

Tcl 2013
New Orleans, LA
September 23-27, 2013

Session VII
September

Tcl Fast Track: From a Novel Concept to Global Launch in Eleven Months

Clif Flynt
Noumena Corporation
Whitmore Lake, MI

Bruce Ross
The ROMaN Project, Inc
Cary, NC

September 6, 2013

Abstract

The LORACIS™ Remote Monitoring software was developed for the clinical trials industry to allow the rapid verification of reported data from human studies while markedly reducing unproductive time and travel expenses. The successful completion of this unique and complex software was achieved in just eleven months due to our selection of Tcl as the programming language.

1 Introduction

1.1 Clinical Trials and the Monitoring of Study Data

Every prescription drug on the global market, and all diagnostic and therapeutic devices, must first undergo a long process of scientific evaluation and clinical testing (clinical trials) to find out if they are effective and safe for use. In the U.S. the Food and Drug Administration (FDA) controls this approval process; other nations have similar regulatory agencies.

These clinical trials are necessary and scientifically important, but are also very expensive to conduct. In 2012, the global cost for all clinical trials exceeded $42 billion. Approximately 25% of the total cost for conducting a clinical trial is spent on the verification and validation of the study data reported by the investigating physicians. This process is called monitoring and involves frequent travel to their clinics and hospitals for comparing the study medical records versus the study data.

In the end, it is the consumers of health care who must pay these costs every time our doctors write a prescription or orders a diagnostic test. In 2011, the FDA issued a draft guidance document that encouraged the clinical trials industry to develop new ways of monitoring clinical trials, including the adoption of new technologies and implementation of risk-based methods. While only a draft document, the FDA was giving study sponsors (e.g. pharmaceutical companies), consulting firms (CROs, clinical research organizations), and investigators the green light to develop new systems and processes to improve the quality and lower the overall cost for each study.

LORACIS^{TM} Remote Monitoring (LORACIS) was conceived in early 2011, prior to the FDAs publication of the draft guidance document; however, following that event our development time-line had to be compressed since it was likely that other companies would create similar products.

1.2 Regulatory Background

Every clinical trial must comply with hundreds of international, Federal, state, and local regulations or else risk being hit with fines, lawsuits, investigations, and rejection of their study results. The full regulatory background is far beyond the scope of this paper, but the two most relevant categories of regulations must be reviewed to place the rest of the story into its proper context.

Patient Privacy and Data Protections: The clinical trials industry is arguably one of the most heavily regulated industries in the world. Each country has one or more government agencies dedicated to creating regulations for the research, manufacturing, packaging, and sales of drugs, medical devices, and diagnostic tests in response to laws passed by their respective legislative or judicial branches.

These agencies include the U.S. Food and Drug Administration (FDA) the Health Canada Agency (HCA), and the European Medicines Agency (EMA). In the U.S., there are additional government agencies with regulations that must be complied with during the the conduct of clinical studies, including the Department of Health and Human Services (DHHS) and the Department Homeland Security (DHS). One of the more familiar of these non-FDA regulations is the Health Insurance Portability and Accountability Act of 1996, better known as HIPAA; an even more restrictive counterpart in Europe is the EU Directive 95/46/EC - The Data Protection Directive. Both require the protection of patient privacy and safeguarding of patient health information (PHI) regardless of whether they are participating in a study.

Computer Systems Used in Clinical Trials: In 1997, the FDA first released its regulations covering the use of electronic signatures and computer systems in clinical trials as Title 21 Code of Federal Regulations, Part 11 Section 11.1 (a), now commonly shorted to 21 CFR Part 11. As computer technology has advanced the regulation has been updated (2003, 2007) and will be updated again as needed. Virtually all software, computer hardware, and electronic systems that generate, transmit, store, or manipulate clinical trials data must comply with this regulation.

1.3 Centralized Monitoring

One time-tested method for reducing the number of locations a monitor must visit is to create a central repository of photocopied patient and study records. However, in order to be acceptable for use in verification of study data, each photocopied page should be certified (usually by initialing and dating of each page by the person doing the copying) as a complete and accurate copy of the original. Also, in order to comply with the privacy regulations all identifiable patient information (e.g. name, address, medical record number, and month/day of birth) must be obliterated (redacted, de-identified) and replaced with a study subject identification number. The resulting binder of photocopied records is called a shadow chart and may be, or not be, an accurate compilation of the study records.

Shadow charts maintained in a central location (central monitoring) are only possible for certain dispersed networks of study sites, and still require significant travel time and cost to visit the central locations. Also, the timeliness of the centralized files may range from good to abysmal. In recent years more and more medical clinics and hospitals have been moving from the use of paper to electronic medical records (EMR). EMRs have increased the potential risk of privacy breaches as more individuals are given access to the EMR computer systems for medical as well as research purposes.

As a result, the FDA's final guidance document (August 6, 2013) defined:

> **Required Functionality in an Effective Remote Monitoring Platform**
>
> The functionality required in a comprehensive remote monitoring platform should include the following attributes:
>
> - Compliance with all applicable privacy protection regulations, including HIPAA and EU-DPD
> - Compliance with 21 CFR Part 11
> - Compatibility with commonplace computer and server systems
> - Accessible from any computer with Internet access
> - Ease of use for study site personnel, monitors, and other sponsor personnel
> - Maintain strong document security protection at all times
> - Support for multiple global languages
> - Permanent audit trail
> - Overall cost for use must be less than traditional monitoring systems

1.4 The Winding Road that Led to TCL

In June 2011, ROMaN began talks with several document management software development firms in search of one with the requisite experience, capability, and interest in creating our remote monitoring application. From the beginning, most were surprised by the proposed complexity of functions and security features outlined in the draft technical specifications; some declined to offer proposals based on this alone. Others were intrigued but could not fit the project into their schedules for many months to even years later, while others yet were not interested as their potential profit for making our products was simply too small.

By September 2011, a potential programming firm was located in New Zealand that initially expressed interested and had relevant experience plus a good pedigree - they have produced cutting edge document management software for more than a decade. Our CEO visited the company and within days they produced a very rough proof of concept application that showed the most critical component called the Associated Data File could, in fact, be made. Unfortunately, as negotiations progressed during the following months it became apparent that several other important features could not be made by their team while their projected budget grew beyond our ability to proceed.

In late October 2012, we contacted an expert in an older programming language known as Clarion. This language was first released in 1986 and though a bit antiquated, its most appealing feature is the use of a proprietary database engine that would allow for systemic encryption of the data as well as its use of readily available "templates" (both open source and commercially available) that can be quickly combined to produce much larger packages of functional code that would otherwise require weeks or months of more traditional programming effort. Within a month he produced a more full-featured proof of concept than his predecessors, and again it demonstrated the overall concept, by then code-named LORACIS, was at least possible to achieve. Unfortunately, over several months, it became apparent that Clarion had significant difficulty in providing the needed functionality as the third-party template library used to produce searchable PDF documents was not able to perform as was desired. It was also difficult to interface with other components using .NET and other more modern languages.

In February 2012, we approached Noumena Corporation based on referrals from the author of one component we were in-licensing. They expressed interest and following a verbal agreement, produced a proof of concept application within a month. Unlike the two previous POC applications, his showed it was possible to overcome the more worrisome challenges by using the Tcl programming language. He was able to begin working in earnest by June 2012, and the rest is history.

LORACIS™ entered beta testing at actual clinical research centers during October, and the first production version was locked down by May 2013 in time for our scheduled global launch date of June 24, 2013.

This concludes the recitation of the motivation, challenges, and decision pathways that led The ROMaN Project to use Tcl for creating what is today the only comprehensive remote monitoring platform available to the clinical trials industry. The next part of this paper is devoted to a more technical explanation of how Tcl achieved this goal.

2 Solution

Some languages and development environments have ceilings that limit their usefulness.

The Clarion approach to developing the LORACIS™ application ran into difficulties when there was a need for functionality that didn't exist within the Clarion framework.

In his keynote talk at the 1997 Tcl/Tk Conference Brian Kernighan reported that he found Visual Basic to be a faster tool for developing an application than Tcl/Tk, but he reached a point where the functionality he needed was not available, and the application could not be completed.

He pointed out that Tcl/Tk does not have a ceiling that an application cannot exceed.

Many languages share this facility of having no ceiling - "C" is a classic example. However, many of the limitless languages are also mid-level or low-level languages that carry long development times with them.

2.1 Choosing a development platform

The first step in determining if the application could be created and what the best development language would be was to define the base sets of functionality.

The primary requirements for this application are:

- Authenticate a local user.
- Validate per site and per study subscription licenses.
- Support multiple languages and alphabets.
- Display shrink-wrap-quality GUI.
- Interact with an encrypted database.
- Accept document from scanner.
- Accept document from print queue.
- Accept existing document.
- OCR process a scanned document.
- Redact personal information from PDF document.
- Modify PDF File metadata.
- Encrypt processed document.
- Perform remote authentication.
- Transmit document via SFTP.

The short development cycle forced the decision to a high-level scripting language as the primary language.

The need to interact with external libraries suggested a language with strong support for connecting to C and C++ libraries.

The following features are either natively supported by Tcl, are available in the `Tcllib` libraries or can be easily constructed with a few lines of code:

- Authenticate a local user.
- Validate per site and per study subscription licenses.
- Support international alphabets.
- Display shrink-wrap-quality GUI.
- Interact with an encrypted database.
- Encrypt processed document.

The other requirements could be met by interacting with existing external libraries which were available either as `.NET` components or linkable libraries.

After considering multiple languages, Tcl was the obvious choice:

- Tcl is a good platform for rapid prototyping.
- Tcl has strong support for integrating with external packages. Tcl supports .NET interactions as well as shared library, direct linking to external libraries and executing separate tasks.
- Tcl uses 16-bit Unicode for all strings, which provides strong internationalization support.
- Tk delivers high-quality GUI tools.
- Tcl tools are mature and stable. In particular the database interface with SQLite is very stable.
- Tcllib provides a wide range of industrial strength libraries.

Tcl is a high level language, thus application development is faster in Tcl than it would be in C or Java.

It's estimated that one line of Tcl replaces 10 lines of "C" code. In *The Mythical Man-Month* Fred Brooks claims that a programmer produces 10 lines of code per day, regardless of the language. Using a high-level scripting language instead of a mid-level compiled language reduces the development time by a factor of 10.

Language features are also important. A language that lacks key functionality will delay a project's completion while the programmers work around or correct the deficiencies.

Tcl has long been plagued by the lack of a native Object Oriented support. OO Programming is not the answer to all problems, but it is a good answer for some problems. The lack of native OO support hasn't stopped people from developing applications using `[incr Tcl]`, `SNIT` or other OO extensions, but having the OO support in the core where it's guaranteed to be available is a benefit.

Tcl 8.6 beta was used for the initial development of the ROMaN application. When the first 8.6 release became available that became the base platform. `TclOO` features were used effectively for complex widgets that were developed for this application.

2.2 Assembling the tools

Tcl stands for Tool Control Language, but that doesn't make it a complete toolbox. There is a rich set of development tools available for Tcl applications. Using these can cut development time even further.

Developing the ROMaN application used several off-the-shelf and semi-custom tools including:

- `Tcllib`
- `SQLite-SEE`
- `SWIG`
- `EditTable`
- `tktest`

2.2.1 Tcllib

Tcllib is not part of the standard Tcl distribution, but as `perl` would be less useful without `CPAN`, Tcl is enhanced by downloading Tcllib either from ActiveState or `http://core.tcl.tk/tcllib`.

These Tcllib packages were used in the ROMaN desktop application:

`twapi`	Invoke windows API calls to set focus, raise windows, when invoking Windows native applications
`dde`	To communicate with native windows applications.
`tcom`	Interact with .NET objects
`des md5 sha256 cryptkit`	Encrypting and decrypting data files
`msgcat`	Internationalization

The `Tcllib` code collection is a controlled library. The contributions to `Tcllib` include validation tests and documentation.

2.2.2 SQLite

The SQLite database library was developed by D. Richard Hipp and was described at his invited talk and tutorials at the 2006 Tcl conference. SQLite is an embeddable SQL engine that uses a single file as the database rather than using a client and server. It is ideal for applications that have complex data representation requirements but do not need to control transactions with multiple writers.

SQLite has been distributed with Tcllib and other "Batteries Included" Tcl distributions for over a decade.

A downside to SQLite for this application is that an SQLite database can be opened and read with the `SQLite3` program. The SQLite database will contain a patient's personal information. Access to this information needs to be restricted to only individuals who require access to it.

Richard also provides a non-free variant of SQLite (`SQLite-SEE`) that encrypts the database file. A user needs to know the encryption key in order to access data in this file.

The SEE variant of SQLite solves the problem of restricting access to a patients personal data.

The SEE extension to SQLite supports the same Tcl interface as the usual SQLite extension. This made it easy to use standard SQLite for the early proof-of-concept and then purchase the SEE extension to be linked with the application in the last phases.

2.2.3 SWIG

Tcl does not have native tools for manipulating a PDF file: changing the metadata, performing OCR, or adding watermarks. This functionality is provided by the PDF-X library from Tracker Software:
`http://www.tracker-software.com/`.

This library is provided as linkable C and C++ dynamic link libraries. As distributed they don't interface with Tcl.

Fortunately, Tcl was designed to be interfaced to external libraries. The glue to turn an external library into a Tcl extension is generally under 100 lines of "C" code.

Getting data into and out of libraries that weren't designed around Tcl's "everything is a string" mantra requires some "C" code to translate from Tcl Objects a function's native `float`, `int` or `struct` formats.

This translation code is not difficult or tricky, but it's faster to let a code generator create it, rather they typing it by hand.

The `SWIG` application will examine an include file and generate the "C" glue code to link a library into a Tcl extension. `SWIG` stands for *Simplified Wrapper and Interface Generator*. This package was designed by David Beazley and introduced at the Tcl conference in 1996. It's available from
`http://www.swig.org/`

SWIG generates an Init function that invokes Tcl_CreateObjCommand to create the Tcl commands and also creates commands to translate from Tcl format to native data formats required by the library.

In practice, the library's include file usually needs to be modified, and reduced to just the parts of the API an application needs. The PDF-X library is extensive, and only a half dozen entry points were needed for this application. The need to rework the include file impacted the development time.

The CriTcl package is also useful for creating interfaces to external libraries. For example, CriTcl was used to create the cryptkit encryption extension.

Using CriTcl would have avoided the cost for reworking the include file at a cost of doing a bit more hand-coding and defining interfaces. I find CriTcl to be better than SWIG for relatively simple external APIs, but the complexity of the data structures used by the PDF-X API made SWIG's parsing and code generation more attractive than creating the glue code by hand.

2.2.4 EditTable

A data-centric project requires data entry screens. These are simple and easy to write, but in the early phase of a project when the understanding of what's needed is changing, the time to recreate simple screens can add up.

The EditTable package will generate a data entry screen from an SQL schema. It was described at the 2012 Tcl Conference.

The EditTable package is constructed using the TclOO mega-widget design pattern described by Donal Fellows (Tcl/Tk Proceedings 2009). This pattern emulates a standard Tcl widget, allowing the new editTable object to be created like any other Tk widget.

Syntax: editTable *widgetName mixin dbEngine args*

widgetName	Name of the widget, normal Tk style
mixin	Name of the db engine mixin
dbEngine	Name of the db engine to use
args	Optional arguments for opening the db engine

Creating an editTable connected to an SQLite database named test.db would resemble:

```
set obj [editTable .t1 SQLITE3_support sqlite3 -dbArgs test.db]
```

Once an EditTable object has been created, the getSchema and makeGUI methods will create a GUI that's adequate for for testing and initial data entry.

The getSchema method retrieves schema information from the database or another source. The default behavior is to query the database. This is used internally to build GUIs for tables containing relations.

Syntax: `editObj` *`getSchema tableName`*

`editObj`	A widget created with `editTable` command
`getSchema`	Return the schema for a table
`tableName`	Name of the table to return Schema for

The `makeGUI` method is the workhorse that builds a GUI within the `editTable` frame. It can build a GUI for any table defined within the database. The `editTable` object can rebuild itself to display a different table as necessary. The default GUI includes buttons to perform simple searches, and add, delete or modify a record.

Syntax: `editObj` *`makeGUI schema`*

`editObj`	A widget created with `editTable` command
`makeGUI`	Construct a GUI within the editTable object frame.
`schema`	a Schema - may be return from `getSchema`

The next example shows initializing a sample database and creating a simple GUI for a table.

```
toplevel .tt
set obj [editTable .tt.t1 TDBC_support sqlite3 -dbArgs test2.db]
set db [$obj config db]

$db allrows {
  CREATE TABLE person (
    id integer unique primary key,
    loginid text, -- loginID
    fname text, -- First name
    lname text, -- Last name
    addrRef integer references addr
    );
}

$obj makeGUI [$obj getSchema person]
$obj config -table person
$obj populateBySearch "loginid = 'aaa'"

pack .tt.t1
```

The generated GUI resembles this:

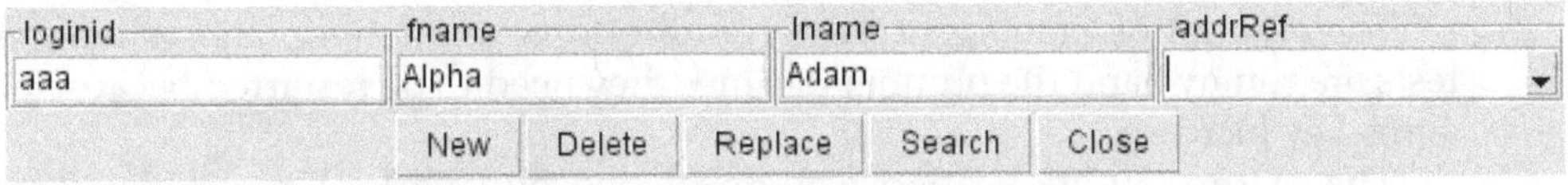

Figure 1: Un-instrumented EditTable GUI

This was suitable for the initial development and constructing bits of functionality. The advantage from a development time perspective is that no time was wasted rebuilding better looking GUIs while the schema was still evolving.

The default GUI generated by `EditTable` was not suitable for end users, but with an instrumented schema it was quite adequate.

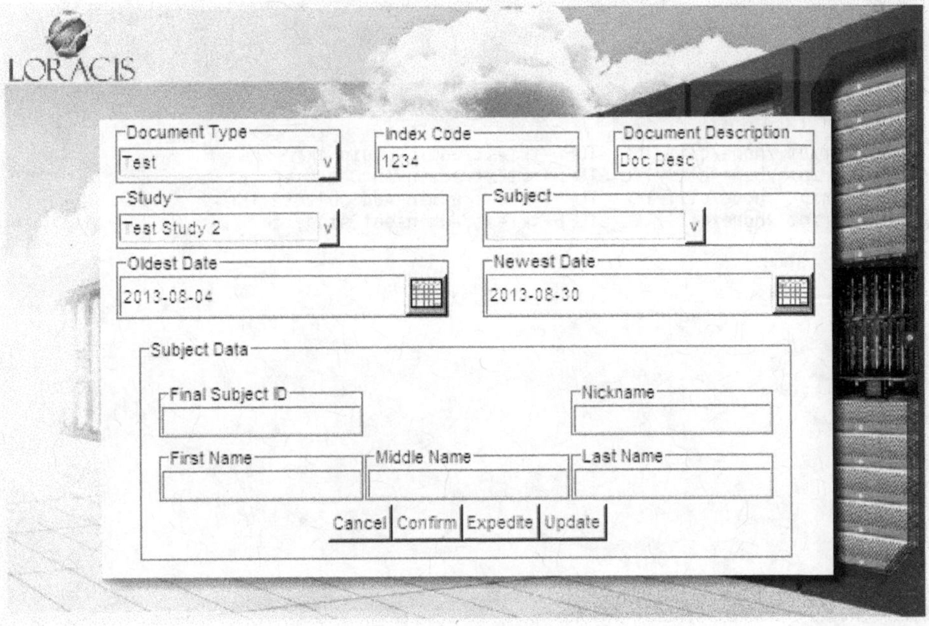

Figure 2: LORACIS™

2.2.5 tktest

Coding projects always proceed faster at the beginning than they do at the end. It can feel like every day completes half of the remaining tasks, and final completion will take forever.

One reason that projects slow as they reach completion is that developing and testing standalone pieces is relatively fast compared to integrating and testing the final application, and then re-testing everything when a low-level bug is discovered.

The amount of time spent in re-running tests gets longer, and when the tests are run by hand the number of times they need to be restarted because of a mis-key increases.

The `TkReplay` application was developed by Charles Crowley, and reported at the 1995 Tcl Conference. Clif Flynt updated and expanded this into the `tktest` package and described in a paper at the 2004 Tcl conference.

In brief, Tk widgets can be configured with a binding to report when an event occurs. These events can then be played back to simulate a user changing focus, typing keys, and clicking buttons.

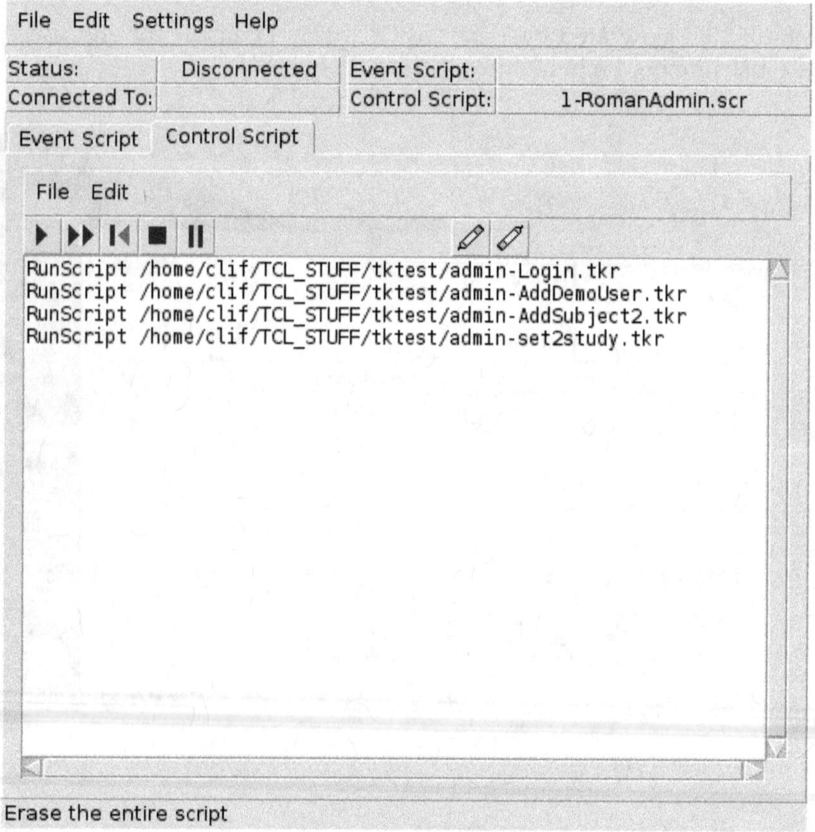

Figure 3: tktest

The `tktest` application was used extensively during the middle and end phases of this project.

During the mid-phase of project, when individual pieces are being integrated and the functionality is being extended it's very common to need to step through several screens and inputs to get to the section of the application where new code is being created and tested.

As that sequence of events gets longer, the probability of mis-typing and needing to restart gets larger and the fatigue factor on the developer grows. Being able to save the initial steps that lead to the new code and replay them both speeds the code/test/debug debug cycle, and enables the programmer to be productive for a longer period of time.

The LORACIS suite of applications is not quite shrink-wrap. The Loracis client and servers must be configured for initial licenses, studies and authentication tokens. The configuration is currently done in separate steps and must be validated before an installation kit is sent to the user.

The final validation of a distribution involves selecting, processing and uploading 16 documents. For obvious reasons, `tktest` is used to validate the distributions before they are sent to a client.

2.3 Conclusion

The extensible nature of Tcl/Tk meant that the complex LORACIS™ application could be written using Tcl/Tk.

The high-level nature of the Tcl/Tk meant that the reduced development cycle was possible using Tcl/Tk.

The available libraries and packages meant that production grade code did not need to be written from scratch, saving even more time.

Code generation and testing packages reduced development time yet again.

In the end, a revolutionary new product was taken from conception to distribution in less than a calendar year and about 6 man months of developer time. This is a fraction of the time and cost that would have been required using other tools. The final product includes about 8,000 lines of new Tcl code and 300 lines of "C" code.

Tcl Beans:

Persistent Storage of TclOO Objects With Minimal Implementation Overhead

William H. Duquette
Jet Propulsion Laboratory, California Institute of Technology
William.H.Duquette@jpl.nasa.gov

Abstract

A Tcl bean is an instance of a TclOO class representing a simulation entity with associated data. The set of all beans can be saved and later restored. Beans can own other beans, and the bean infrastructure supports bean deletion with undo, including cascading deletion, and bean copy and paste. The paper describes the bean implementation, including the current constraints on bean classes, as well as lessons learned while coming to grips with the TclOO framework.

1. Background

The Athena Regional Stability Simulation is a model of political actors and the effects of their actions in a particular region of the world. The region is divided into neighborhoods, in which reside various civilian groups. The actors have a variety of assets, including money, military and police forces, and means of communication, which they use to achieve their political ends. The extent to which they succeed depends on the attitudes of the civilians, which change in response to current events. The set of tactics an actor uses to achieve his goals is called his strategy.

1.1 The Problem

The Athena simulation model contains many different kinds of simulation entity. Most of these entities are implemented as a simple record structure (i.e., a dictionary) coupled with a type-definition ensemble [1]. Athena is a document-centric application, and to ease saving and restoring the scenario data most of the simulation entities are stored at run-time in an SQLite3 database called the *run-time database* (RDB). Each entity type gets a table; each entity gets a row in the table, and each record field gets a column. Entities are extracted from the RDB as required. This pattern has a number of benefits in addition to simplifying the data persistence problem: many of the entities serve as indices in arrays, which are conveniently represented as RDB tables, and many of the algorithms work well as batch operations on tables. Further, the ability to use SQL queries as the basis for algorithms and for data output has been a real win.

Over the last few years, however, we've added an increasing number of entities for which this pattern is at best unnatural. These entities are:

- Polymorphic: any given entity type has many subtypes
- Linked into complex tree structures
- Always processed one at a time, rather than in bulk

The first two points are notoriously inconvenient to deal with in SQL, and the third point means that there's no real advantage to dealing with the inconvenience. Consequently, we've been looking for an alternative architecture for this data.

1.2 The Solution

Polymorphism naturally suggests an object-oriented solution with inheritance, so we began to experiment with a TclOO-based solution. On the face of it, this is both straightforward and appealing: our entity types and subtypes become classes and subclasses, and entities are simply instances of classes. We get inheritance, encapsulation, and efficient execution, and of course objects can be easily linked into complex trees or networks in any of a number of ways.

However, we still had to support persistence. In the past, Athena data has been persistent in one of two ways: either it resides in the RDB to begin with, or it is stored in array variables owned by some singleton. The singleton can produce a checkpoint of its data, a nested dictionary that can be saved in the RDB as a string and can easily be pushed back into its arrays on restore. Complex networks of TclOO objects present a different problem: not only do we need to checkpoint the data contained within the objects, we need to be able to restore the actual network of objects. The requirement to destroy and create a network of small objects when loading a saved scenario is the reason why we have not represented simulation entities as instances of Snit types: the advantages are outweighed by the nuisance factor. But the requirement for polymorphism shifts the equation.

As a result, I defined the notion of a "Tcl bean". A bean is an object that can be easily checkpointed as a string, and easily restored. More than that, the entire collection of beans existing at any given time can be checkpointed and restored as a group. Along the way we were able to support cascading deletion of beans (i.e., deleting a bean automatically deletes all of the beans that it owns as well), cut and copy of beans, and undo of a variety of operations on beans.

The remainder of this paper will describe the bean architecture and implementation.

2. Behavior of an Individual Bean

A bean is essentially a fancy object-oriented record structure. Consider the following:

```
beanclass create address {
    superclass bean

    variable first
    variable last
    variable street
    variable city
    variable state
    variable zip

    constructor {} {
        next
        initialize instance variables...
    }

    methods...
}
```

Beans represent scenario data, which is to say user-editable data. Thus, given an instance of `address` the application can set and get its variables:

```
% set a [address new]
::bean::address1
% $a set first John
John
% $a set last Doe
Doe
% $a get first
John
```

The `set` and `get` methods operate on validly defined scalar instance variables, i.e., any scalar variable that exists in the instance's namespace, and will throw an error if given any other name.

Because beans need to be saved and restored, we need to be able to retrieve a bean's state and restore it again. We assume that a bean's savable state is simply the contents of its scalar instance variables; we can retrieve this state as a dictionary by means of the `getdict` method and restore it using the `setdict` method.

```
% set dict [$a getdict]
id 1 first John last Doe ...
% $a setdict $dict
```

Note that in addition to the variables defined in the class definition, the bean also has an `id`, which is provided by the `bean` superclass. Beans are created and referenced by the user, and so we need an ID by which they can be referred to in the GUI and in user scripts. Thus, every bean has a unique ID, assigned on creation. This ID can be queried, but cannot be reset.

The bean's `set` method is the usual way to modify the value of a bean's instance variable, whether from outside or in the bean's own method bodies: it prevents the value of the `id` variable from being changed, and it can notify the application that some bean has changed (and hence, that there are unsaved changes). The `setdict` method uses the `set` method internally, and subclasses can override it to provide additional behavior.

3. Saving and Restoring Beans

The basic assumption made by the `bean` class is that the application has at most one scenario open at a time, that all beans are part of the scenario data, and that therefore all beans need to be saved and restored *en masse*. We use the `bean` class object itself as the manager for the set of existing beans. Thus, we can make a "checkpoint" of all beans as follows:

```
set checkpoint [bean checkpoint]
```

The checkpoint is a nested dictionary with the following structure:

```
    idCounter -> counter
    beans -> beanID -> serializedBean
```

A serialized bean is a list

```
    class object beandict
```

Thus, in the example above, if the single address record for John Doe is the only existing bean, the checkpoint would look like this:

```
    idCounter 1
    beans     {
        1 {address ::bean::address1 { id 1 first John ...}}
    }
```

The checkpoint string can then be saved to disk in any desired way, and restored as follows:

```
bean restore $checkpoint
```

The `bean restore` command ruthlessly destroys any existing beans, and uses the data in the checkpoint to recreate the saved beans. Note that the recreated beans not only have the same state, they have the same object names as before. The importance of this is discussed below in section 5.

In order to act on all existing beans, the `bean` class object needs to know what beans exist. Consequently, the class object keeps a mapping from bean IDs to object names. This mapping is maintained by the `bean register` and `bean unregister` commands, which are called from the bean class's constructor and destructor respectively. It is also the `bean register` command's job to assign bean IDs.

4. Bean Trees

Beans can own other beans in complex tree structures. In Athena, there is a kind of simulation entity called an *actor*. An actor is a decision maker in the simulation. Each actor has a *strategy* which describes the actor's behavior. The strategy consists of a prioritized list of *blocks*; each block contains some number of Boolean *conditions* and some number of *tactics*. When the block's conditions are all met, the block's tactics will be executed. The strategy, blocks, conditions, and tactics are all implemented as bean subclasses; and there are many different kinds of condition and tactic.

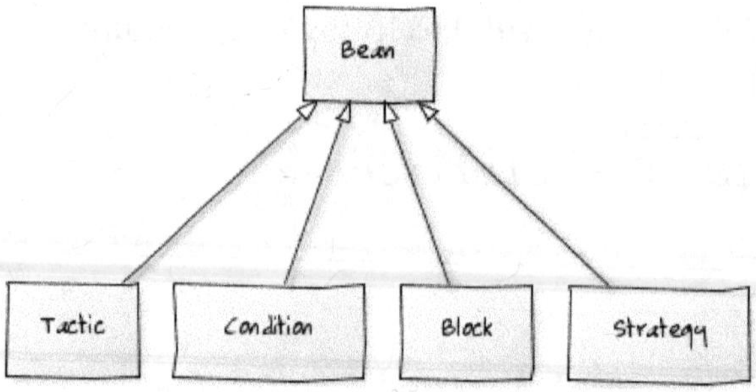

We say that the strategy *owns* some number of blocks, and each block owns some number of conditions and tactics:

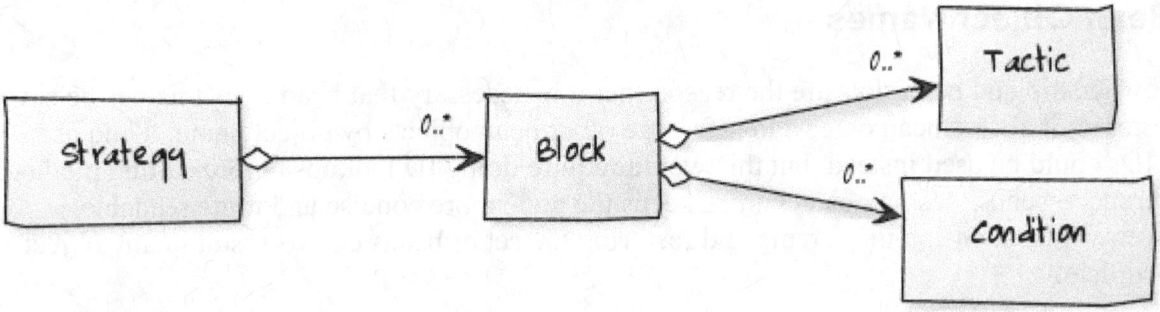

The relationships between the objects in a strategy are part of the scenario data, and need to be saved with the beans. Moreover, if an object is destroyed, the dependent objects (i.e., the tactics and conditions in a block) need to be destroyed with it. We would like these things to happen with minimal effort on the part of the application programmer; therefore we define the notion of a *bean slot*, an instance variable whose value is a list of zero or more names of bean objects that are owned by the object.

Thus, the block class is defined (in part) as follows:

```
beanclass create block {
    superclass bean

    beanslot conditions
    beanslot tactics
    ...
}
```

The `beanslot` command is simply a proc in the `oo::define` namespace. It verifies that the class for which it is called is truly a bean class, declares an instance variable with the given name to contain bean references, and then registers the slot name with the `bean` class object. In this way the `bean` class object's methods have enough information to walk the ownership tree.

Note that not all references to other beans need go in bean slots. For example, each instance of the `block` class keeps a reference to its owning `strategy`. Since the block does not own the strategy to which it belongs, the reference can be stored in an ordinary instance variable.

Thus, when destroying a bean it is straightforward to destroy the beans it owns, and the beans they own, and so on. There is no need for a bean subclass to write any specific destructor code to enable this behavior; the `bean` class's destructor handles it automatically.

5. Bean Object Names

Bean ownership and bean slots are the reason that it is necessary that bean object names be saved and restored: it allows bean objects to reference other bean objects by object name. Unique block IDs could be used instead, but this would require doing ID lookups before calling methods on referenced beans. Using object names keeps the code more concise and more readable. However, we must ensure that saving and restoring the set of beans cannot result in any object name collisions.

Beans can be assigned a unique name automatically by the bean class's `new` method. By default, TclOO objects created using the `new` method are given names like `::oo::Obj12`. Beans can be created at one time, saved, and restored at another into a program with a different execution history. As a result, automatically named beans have to have names that won't conflict with non-bean TclOO object names.

This is why bean classes are created using the `beanclass` metaclass. It redefines the new method to create names that look like "`::bean::`*`<class><id>`*", e.g., `::bean::address1`. Since only bean objects have names in the `::bean` namespace, and since all previously existing beans are deleted on `bean restore`, there is no chance of a name collision involving automatically named beans.

The application can also choose to create beans with specific names using the bean class's `create` method. This is sometimes appropriate for top-level beans like strategies. Strategies are owned by actors (which are *not* beans); each actor has a short, well-known name and a single strategy, so strategy beans can be given names like "`::strategy::`*`<actor>`*", e.g., `::strategy::JOE`. It is up to the application to make sure that explicitly named beans will cause no name collisions on `bean restore`.

6. Deleting and Undeleting Beans

Because beans are scenario objects, users can delete them as they edit the scenario. It is common for beans to own or contain other beans, and these dependent beans must be deleted with their owner; this called a *cascading delete*. And since the user can undo deletions, the Tcl Bean infrastructure has to support that as well.

A bean is deleted by passing its bean ID to the `bean delete` command; bean IDs are used because beans are usually deleted due to user input, and user input usually results in an ID rather than an object name. The command returns a *delete set*: a checkpoint-like string that allows the deletion of the bean and its dependents to be undone (under the usual conditions for a successful undo operation):

```
set delset [bean delete [$bean id]]
...
bean undelete $delset
```

The `bean delete` command starts with the given bean and walks the ownership tree destroying beans. The delete set is accumulated with the help of the `bean unregister` command, which is called during bean destruction, and is returned to the caller. The delete set is simply a dictionary

beanID -> serializedBean

7. Cut, Copy, and Paste

Copy and paste of beans is similar to deletion. When copying a block in a strategy, the user will want to copy the conditions and tactics it contains as well. It differs in that any pasted beans will be new distinct beans.

The ability to copy and paste is still a work in progress; however, copying is logically straightforward. Given a bean ID, the bean copy command walks the ownership tree, copying the class, ID, and state of each bean in the tree. Bean slot variables contain a list of bean object names; in the saved state, each such variable is modified to contain a list of bean IDs instead. The result is called a *copy set*; it can be used to create a new set of beans at any time:

```
set copyset [bean copy [$bean id]]
...
set newbean [bean paste $copyset]
```

The variable newbean now contains the name of a new bean that is the root of the copied tree.

8. Other Operations

The bean infrastructure provides a number of additional operations. The `bean` class object allows the program to get a list of bean IDs, validate bean IDs, retrieve a bean given its ID, and so forth. Specific bean classes provide the same capabilities (via the `beanclass` metaclass) but limit them to beans of the appropriate type.

In addition to the `set` and `setdict` methods, each bean also has `lappend` and `ldelete` methods; thus you can write

```
$bean lappend items $myitem
```

instead of

```
set list [$bean get items]
lappend list $myitem
$bean set items $list
```

Finally, the bean class provides a set of commonly used *order mutator* methods. In Athena parlance, an order mutator is a command that updates a simulation entity given a validated set of parameter values and returns a command that will undo the change. (An *order* is a command that takes a set of parameters entered by the user, validates them, and calls a mutator to do the dirty work.) By convention, mutator methods have names ending with an underscore.

The `addbean_` method adds a bean to a bean slot. The following code adds a new block to a strategy's `blocks` slot, saving the undo script.

```
set undo [$strategy addbean_ blocks [block new]]
```

The `deletebean_` method is similar: it deletes a bean with a given ID from a bean slot. The following code deletes a block from a strategy, returning an undo script.

```
set undo [$strategy deletebean_ blocks [$block id]]
```

The `update_` method handles most other changes to a single bean. It takes two arguments: a list of bean variable names, and a dictionary of parameter names and values. It updates the value of each of the listed bean variables, only if the provided dictionary has a matching entry whose value is not the empty string. (An empty string indicates that the user didn't edit that variable.) Again, it returns an undo script.

9. Bean Constraints

It's been said that architecture is the set of constraints you choose to live with because they make your problem simpler. These are the specific constraints and assumptions made by the Tcl Beans infrastructure.

- Every bean has a unique ID
- A bean's savable state is contained in its scalar instance variables.
- Beans are saved and restored *en masse*.
- Bean object names are restored along with the bean data.

- Beans can own other beans; the ownership graph is a forest of trees. Owned beans are stored in bean slot variables.
- A bean's constructor can be called with no arguments to create a bean in the default state. (This is required by the restore/undelete logic.) A bean's constructor may have any number of optional arguments.
- Every bean class must be created using the `beanclass` metaclass, and must be a subclass (direct or indirect) of `bean`.

Naturally, some of these constraints might be relaxed over time. For example, it would be straightforward to allow array-valued bean variables to be part of the bean's savable state, or to provide for multiple simultaneous sets of beans that can be saved and restored individually. But these were the constraints we thought we could easily live within given our current needs, and so there was no need to complicate things.

10. Bean Implementation

The Tcl Bean implementation consists of three pieces of code: the `beanclass` metaclass, the `bean` class itself, and the `beanslot` `oo::define` command.

All bean classes are created using the `beanclass` metaclass, which provides custom `new`, `get`, `exists`, and `ids` methods for all bean classes. The most important of these is the new method, which ensures that bean names are created in the `::bean` namespace, as described in Section 5. The other three methods simply allow the application to query beans belonging to the class or its subclasses. For example

```
set block [block new]      ;# Returns ::bean::block<id>
set ids [block ids]        ;# Returns all block IDs
block exists [$block id] ;# Returns 1
block get [$block id]      ;# Returns $block
```

If it weren't for the naming requirement, `beanclass` probably wouldn't exist.

Every bean class must be created using the `beanclass` metaclass, and must be a subclass (direct or indirect) of `bean`. It would be helpful if `beanclass` could ensure the latter requirement automatically, but I've not figured out how to do that in a graceful way.

11. TclOO Is Not Snit

Tcl Beans is my first attempt to implement production code using TclOO, and as a long-time Snit [2] user I ran into some surprises and annoyances. While some of them might in theory be fixed in future versions of TclOO, others are simply consequences of TclOO's advanced capabilities and have to be lived with and worked around. I record them here as a starting point for some kind of Snit compatibility layer or other utility library.

I'm aware that Tcllib already includes the beginnings of a TclOO convenience library, `oo::util` [3]; however, I'm not using it. I want to understand TclOO reasonably deeply at the scripting level before I start depending on external convenience libraries.

11.1 Variable Declarations

In Snit, you can declare an instance variable and assign it an initial value in the body of the type definition. In TclOO you can't; instance variables can be declared in the class definition, but can only be initialized in the constructor or in some other method body. This is particularly annoying when adding variables to an object using `oo::objdefine`: there is no way to initialize them from within the object's private (i.e., unexported) code. You have to use a publicly accessible (i.e., exported) method.

11.2 Linkage Between Types and Instances

In Snit, an instance and its type are closely linked. In particular, type variables are visible without declaration in instance code. In TclOO, instances are only weakly linked to the class used to create them; an instance's class can be changed at any time. Hence, variables belonging to the class object are not usually visible in instance methods.

This may an unavoidable consequence of TclOO's power and flexibility. However, it would be useful to be able to declare class variable once in the `oo::define` script and access it without declaration within instance methods, even at the cost of not being able to subsequently give instances a different class.

11.3 Code Layout

TclOO leads to harder-to-read code modules than Snit, in my view. I care very much about code readability, and designed Snit to maximize it—given my particular (or perhaps peculiar) sense of code aesthetics. It's not surprising that another person's system doesn't give me quite what I want, and the following observations might be a sore point only for me.

In my code, a Snit type with instances usually looks something like this template:

```
snit::type mytype {
    # Lookup tables
    # Other type variables
    # Type constructor (executes initialization code on load)
    # Type methods
    # Instance variables
    # Option definitions
    # Constructor/destructor
    # Instance methods
}
```

It's a logical sequence, and the entire type is clearly one thing. When you get to the closing "}" you know you've seen all of it.

TclOO supports a class definition syntax with a Snit-like definition body; and this works well unless you want to define methods on the class object itself. Then you need to use something like this to get the

```
oo::class create myclass

oo::objdefine myclass {
    # class variables
    # class methods
    method init {} { # Initializes class variables }
}
myclass init

oo::define myclass {
    # instance variables
    # constructor
    # instance methods
}
```

It should be possible to add commands to the `oo::define` namespace that would allow the class variables and methods to be included in one body with the instance definitions; I believe the `classmethod` command in `oo::util` works this way. I'm not clear on just what the side-effects are, though, or what constraints it places on the finished class.

11.4 Metaclasses Are Not Inherited

This is a purely TclOO-related surprise, as there's no Snit equivalent.

Tcl Beans defines the `beanclass` metaclass so as to customize the `new` method to generate a name in a particular namespace, and then uses it define the `bean` class. It would seem that subclasses of `bean` would inherit this behavior automatically, but they don't. Every subclass of `bean` has to be explicitly created using the `beanclass` metaclass. This feels wrong to me, though I freely admit that I don't understand it well enough to have an opinion.

12. Future Work

Tcl Beans have been implemented as a part of an experimental redesign of Athena 5's strategy execution engine. This redesign is not yet complete. Thus, the following work remains:

- Complete the re-implementation of the strategy engine. This will likely result in additional features and tweaks to the bean infrastructure.
- Complete the infrastructure to support copy and paste, and use it in the GUI.
- Review the bean code in light of further experience with TclOO, and see if it can be streamlined or improved.

13. Conclusions

As currently implemented, Tcl Beans make it simple to use TclOO objects to contain user data in a document-centric application provided that only one document can be open at one time. Bean classes are trivial to implement, and all bean instances can be saved and restored as a set. The infrastructure supports many other useful patterns, including cascading deletes, undo of user changes, and copy and paste. These features are subject to a handle of constraints, some of which it might be possible to relax in future versions.

14. References

[1] Duquette, William H., "Type-Definition Objects", 12th Annual Tcl/Tk Conference, http://trs-new.jpl.nasa.gov/dspace/bitstream/2014/37573/1/05-2409.pdf.

[2] Duquette, William, Snit Object Framework, found in Tcllib, http://tcllib.sourceforge.net/doc/snit.html.

[3] Kupries, Andreas, and Fellows, Donal, TclOO Utility Package `oo::util`, found in Tcllib, http://core.tcl.tk/tcllib/doc/trunk/embedded/www/tcllib/files/modules/ooutil/ooutil.html

15. Acknowledgements

This research was carried out at the Jet Propulsion Laboratory, California Institute of Technology, under a contract with the National Aeronautics and Space Administration, during the development of the Athena Stability & Recovery Operations Simulation (Athena) for the TRADOC G2 Intelligence Support Activity (TRISA) at Fort Leavenworth, Kansas.

www.ingramcontent.com/pod-product-compliance
Lightning Source LLC
LaVergne TN
LVHW060448061126
851857LV00016B/1762